Telegraph & Argus

Stories of the Century

Contributors

Telegraph & Argus
Stories of the Century

Written by Jim Appleby and Jim Greenhalf
with additional material by Mike Priestley

Bradford-born **Jim Appleby** lives in Bingley and has been a journalist with the T&A for 33 years. He writes a popular weekly nostalgia page for the T&A called Past Times and in 1995 compiled a successful T&A publication called Bygone Bradford.
He is a poet, actor and playwright having performed in the Edinburgh Fringe and is a former member of Group Theater Bradford and Bradford University Drama Group.

Jim Greenhalf was born in London but has spent most of his adult life in Bradford. He has been a journalist at the T&A for 22 years, as a columnist and covering news, City Hall, features and reviews. He was named UK Press Gazette Columnist of the Year in 1990 and Whitbread Feature Writer of the Year in 1991.
Outside journalism he is a prolific author of poems, essays and stories. His books include Salt & Silver: A Story of Hope and The Dog's Not Laughing - Poems 1968-98.

Mike Priestley was born and bred in Bradford and has been a journalist for the T&A for 30 years. He has won a string of awards: Yorkshire Journalist of the Year and was named Columnist of the Year in the Yorkshire Press Awards three times.
He writes three popular columns in the T&A: North of Watford, Who's Counting and Walking With Priestley. The T & A has published three books and three supplements based on Mike's Walks in the Dales.

Designed by
Doug Akroyd, John Walton and David Harrison

Research by
Alan Magson
with additional research by T&A library staff Frances Wood, Odele Ayres and Duane Smith.
Thanks also for the assistance of Brian Craven, Jonathan Smith, Tony Williams and Stephanie Reynolds

First published in Great Britain by
The Breedon Books Publishing Company Limited
Breedon House, 44 Friar Gate, Derby, DE1 1DA.
1999

ISBN 1 85983 185 0

Printed and bound by Butler & Tanner Ltd., Selwood
Printing Works, Caxton Road, Frome, Somerset.

Colour separations and jacket printing by Green Shires
Group Ltd, Leicester.

Plenty of books have been written, over the years, about Bradford and the surrounding district. None of them, we believe, has been like this one. Never before has anyone produced a detailed record of the news events which shaped the city and its associated towns and villages throughout the most momentous century in history.

This is Bradford as seen through the eyes of Telegraph & Argus reporters and photographers who were privileged to occupy a ringside seat as the century unfolded. Here we retell a hundred of their stories. Some of them, like the nightmare reign of the Yorkshire Ripper, or triumphs and an appalling tragedy at Valley Parade, are events unique to Bradford. Others show how Bradford responded to events in the wider world: how the people coped with wartime or reacted to news of the death of Queen Victoria.

Newspapers do not just report the major events, though. They are there, too, for the lighter moments. Those are well-represented in this collection, reflecting the diversity of life in Bradford. Why a Lord Mayor wore Union Jack socks, what a civic dignitary said to the Queen Mother as she toured the sewage works, the reception that Bradford gave to The Beatles.....these are stories which over the years have offered readers a welcome distraction from more serious issues.

This book tells the story of Bradford in the 20th century. But it is also the story of the role in its affairs played by the Telegraph & Argus - a newspaper which has been around, in one form or another, since 1868 and has been throughout that time the prime provider of news and information for the people of Bradford and district.

We are rather proud of this special book. We see it as a reminder of what a special place Bradford has been, and indeed remains despite the many changes that have taken place here. We hope you enjoy it and cherish it as a souvenir of the old century to carry with you into the new Millennium.

Perry Austin-Clarke,
Editor, Telegraph & Argus
September 1, 1999

Contents

Contents

1900 Massive floods brought fear of killer disease

Typhoid in the air

The 1900s were only a few months old - and the Twentieth Century hadn't actually begun - when the elements turned against Bradford

Condemned by its geography to suffer every time the weather became savage, Bradford was always susceptible to heavy rain. In its bowl of hills, with only one flat way out, to the north, and with only the narrow beck to cope with flooding, the three-year-old city was not yet equipped with the sort of drains that could cope with a downpour - particular-

Wednesday, July 13, 1900

ly the sort of downpour which was brewing up during the morning of Thursday, July 14, 1900.

Like the great storm of 1968 - which also happened in July - the first inkling of trouble came from up the Aire Valley. There was a cloudburst over Rombalds Moor and the village of Morton was badly damaged when Morton Beck burst its banks, sending torrents of water on a destructive rampage down to the River Aire.

At Oxenhope, farmer William Smith was 'struck speechless' in his house by lightning. He was luckier than the four cows at Wilsden which were killed in their field. More animals died at Allerton.

Humans, too, were among the casualties - 21 in all, in Leeds, Dewsbury, Keighley, Ripponden, Wakefield and Otley.

It wasn't all doom.

In Shipley trout, swept from their usual streams, were stranded on the pavements and enterprising passers-by picked up a free meal.

Bradford did not lose a life to the storm, despite 'almost continuous' lightning and thunder which was 'a constant roar'. Every cellar in the city centre was flooded, it seemed, and a foot of water stood for a long time before dispersing, and businesses were left counting the cost. Walls collapsed and the sewage works

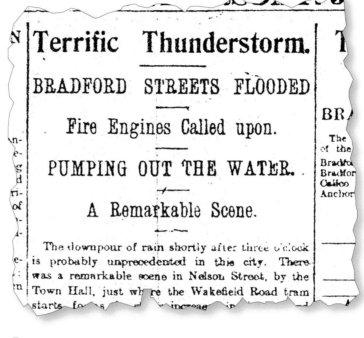

Terrific Thunderstorm.

BRADFORD STREETS FLOODED

Fire Engines Called upon.

PUMPING OUT THE WATER.

A Remarkable Scene.

The downpour of rain shortly after three o'clock is probably unprecedented in this city. There was a remarkable scene in Nelson Street, by the Town Hall, just where the Wakefield Road tram starts f...

NEAR DISASTER: *How the floods and their consequences were reported in the Bradford Daily Telegraph*

It seemed that every cellar in the district flooded...

at Frizinghall overflowed. This was a hint of dangers to come; but the Bradford Daily Telegraph, not wanting to cause a panic, treated the subject cautiously:

'By half-past four o'clock there was a total subsidence of the dirty flood in the streets, but most of the cellarage accommodation in the centre of the city was yet under water, and the fire engine was still pumping from the basement of Messrs Watson's premises. Where the flood was heaviest it has left behind it a slime, evil-smelling mud, and the hygienic question occured to a 'Telegraph' reporter when he ran against Dr Evans, Medical-Officer for Bradford, in Market Street.

"'There seems to be a typhoid smell in

the air?" suggested our representative. 'The doctor shook a thin stream of rain from the brim of his hat. "No wonder," he replied, "with all that filth from the beck".

"'Do you think the residuum of sewage left in the streets will affect the health of the city?", queried our reporter, rolling back the clinging wet collar of his mackintosh.

"'I'll be very much surprised if we do not hear of the after-effects in the course of a month," was the answer.

"'Typhoid?"

"'Typhoid," was the laconic rejoinder. And the doctor went on his way with the resigned air of a man who has to battle with an inevitable fate.'

Typhoid, sometimes known as enteric fever, is not usually fatal in itself in a healthy community, but not even the most starry-eyed optimist would have called Bradford's population in the last year of the Victorian age 'healthy'.

It must have been a very nervy Doctor Evans who surveyed his domain for the next few weeks.

Luckily the feared epidemic didn't happen.

Long live the King!

Queen Victoria's death was common knowledge in Bradford within half an hour of its occurring.

Her predecessor, King William IV, would probably have been in his grave for some days before the further outposts of his kingdom knew of his passing.

It was the Bradford Daily Telegraph which broke the news here - a title which would have been meaningless to the subjects of Good King Billy.

The telegraph (which means 'distant writing') was just being perfected when the 18-year-old Victoria came to the throne in 1837. Samuel Morse was putting the finishing touches to his words-by-wire system, which depended not so much on the technology (most of which already existed) as on the ingenious dots-and-dashes code he invented to convey messages.

Friday, January 22, 1901

At the same time a Frenchman called Louis Daguerre was experimenting with the effects of light on chemical-coated copper plate. The result was the Daguerrotype, a light-generated image. Today we call it a photograph.

Printing had been around for a few hundred years but news was slow in arriving - the speed of a galloping horse has

been, for much of human history, the limiting factor in the spread of information.

Suddenly the building blocks of the information age were to hand.

The big drawback for would-be newspaper tycoons was that fewer than one in ten of Victoria's new subjects could actually read. It took the 1870 Education Act, brainchild of Bradford MP W E Forster, to bring literacy to the masses.

By the time the Queen died on January 22, 1901, the news was at the Bradford

Continued on Page 3

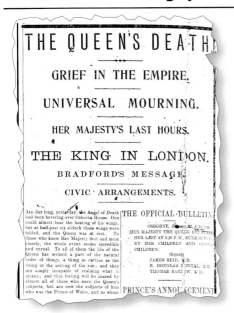

THE QUEEN'S DEATH

GRIEF IN THE EMPIRE.

UNIVERSAL MOURNING.

HER MAJESTY'S LAST HOURS.

THE KING IN LONDON.

BRADFORD'S MESSAGE.

CIVIC ARRANGEMENTS.

END OF AN ERA: *The Queen with her son, who became King Edward VII on her death, her grandson, later King George V, and great grandson later Edward VIII*

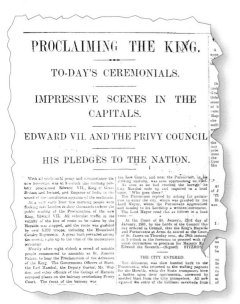

PROCLAIMING THE KING.

TO-DAY'S CEREMONIALS.

IMPRESSIVE SCENES IN THE CAPITALS.

EDWARD VII. AND THE PRIVY COUNCIL

HIS PLEDGES TO THE NATION.

Continued from Page 2

Daily Telegraph within minutes by 'a private telephonic message' (in other words somebody rang us).

She had ascended the throne as the daughter of the Duke of Kent - the hard-up brother of the late King William - at the age of 18, a slip of a girl, with slightly bulbous eyes and a strong sense of duty. Nor did she lack a sense of her own importance. One of her first acts was to tell her mother, Princess Victoria of Saxe-Coburg that she no longer exercised any authority. She told her mother's secretary, Sir John Conroy, to clear off out of London and stay away. Then she booted out her uncle, Leopold of Belgium.When she first met her Privy Counsellors they handed her documents naming her Alexandrina Victoria.The

New technology brought news of her death quickly

Alexandrina bit, she announced, Would Have to Go. And it did. By the time of her death she was an Empress, presiding (as far as her political leaders would let her) over an empire with land on six of the seven continents. One third of the humans living on the planet were nominally her subjects. The Bradford Daily Telegraph devoted two out of its four pages to the melancholy news. 'To say that Bradford was unprepared for the intelligence would scarcely be true, but at the same time it created profound depression,' said the paper. 'The cry of the newsboy "Death of the Queen" had a magic effect. All thought of amusement at such an hour was banished from the hearts and minds of the people. Bradford had put mourning first.'

T&A

Ready to go to blazes

GIFT:
Mr E J Smith, chairman of the Fire Brigade Committee, was handed the golden key used for the opening ceremony as a keepsake of the occasion. On it is a miniature fire engine painted in enamel, and emerging from the sides are two heads representing the horses that pulled the fire engines

There is an apocryphal tale of two Bradford woolmen who met in Market Street in the 1960s, at a time when many of the city's textile warehouses and mills were burning down in a rash of fires which some blamed on

Tuesday, October 28, 1902

'insurance jobs' - cutting losses at a time of failing fortunes.

'I were sorry to hear about your fire' said the first woolman.

'Shurrup, you daft b———, that's tonight!' hissed the second.

Fire has been friend and foe to humans throughout history; but

when it struck in the wrong place it could destroy lives and prosperity.

For many years towns and cities had private fire brigades. Householders and businesses would pay a premium and, if fire struck, the insurance company sent out its own engine and firemen. A metal badge on the wall carried the company insignia, and woe betide the victim who was insured with the wrong company if there was more than one fire to tackle.

The municipal fire brigade was slow to evolve, but by 1902, when Bradford was at its most prosperous and confident, it

Applause as Lord Mayor acclaimed the 'best' station in the kingdom

was decided that the local firefighters deserved a new headquarters.

Being Bradford, it had to be a showpiece and, on Tuesday, October 28, 1902, when the new station at Nelson Street opened, there was applause and satisfaction when the Lord Mayor, Mr W C Lupton, described it as the best and most advanced in the United Kingdom.

The £16,000 building, part of which still stands, was designed in a simple renaissance style around a courtyard, with a 100-yard long drill hall at the back and a recreation room for the crews, with gymnastic equipment and a billiards table.

It had been three years in the building and the opening was impressive, with a drill display, a life-saving display and a

BRADFORD'S NEW FIRE STATION.

THE OPENING CEREMONY.

Bradford's new Fire Station in Nelson Street was opened on Tuesday by the Mayor (Mr. C. Lupton). The premises and the general equipment embody all the latest improvements in fire extinguishing department, a fact which—and it is freely admitted—enables our city to boast of now being in possession of one of the most modern and up-to-date fire stations in the United Kingdom.

Continued on Page 5

Continued from Page 4

parade to show off the smartness of the brigade.

Members of the Fire Brigade Committee each received a gold medal, fashioned at Fattorinis, to mark the occasion, and after the ceremony the assembled dignitaries departed for the Town Hall for lunch with the Mayor.

The committee chairman, Mr E J Smith, did not leave empty-handed, either. He received the golden key used at the ceremony - 'one of the most artistic that has been given at a public function for a considerable period.

On the front is a miniature fire engine painted on enamel, and above the Bradford Arms and Crest in correct heraldic colours, and issuing from the sides, are life-like heads of "typical" fire horses.

On the back was a picture of the new station which, apart from housing firemen and engines, had plenty of stables - the horse was to be the motive power at the time and for a few years to come.

T&A

MEMENTO: *The medal given to committee members*

1903 *Buffalo Bill brought a world of adventure to city*

A wild welcome!

REAL-LIFE HERO: *Buffalo Bill, former Pony Express rider and Civil War soldier as well as buffalo hunter, had been on the road for 18 years when he visited Bradford, recreating incidents from his life, right*

For Bradford the year 1903 was memorable for two events: the founding of Bradford City Football Club, and the arrival of world-famous Buffalo Bill's Wild West Show.

Ninety-six years ago, before TV, radio, records and CDs, people had to go out to find ways of entertaining or diverting themselves. Sports of all sorts, religious gatherings, concerts, political meetings, parades, circuses, the cinema, theatre and vaudeville - people flocked to them all for colour, excitement and social intercourse. Buffalo Bill's Wild West Show didn't really need to advertise its coming in the sober broadsheet columns of the Bradford Weekly Telegraph in October, 1903. The fame of the thing preceded it like a blast of warm air.

Sitting Bull himself, the mighty Sioux chief who had presided over Custer's Last

October 5 and 6, 1903

Stand at Little Bighorn in June, 1876, had spent a season with the show in 1885 before his eventual murder at the age of 59 in December, 1890. Geronimo, the fierce Apache chieftain, also toured with William F Cody's ever-increasing troupe of men and horses.

Cody, better known as Buffalo Bill, was a legendary figure from the Atlantic to the Pacific. An authentic Pony Express rider, Civil War soldier, buffalo hunter, Army scout, Indian fighter and now showman, his Wild West Show had been on the roads of America and Europe for the best part of 18 years.

The visit to West Yorkshire in wet and windy October, 1903, was the third time Buffalo Bill had been to Britain. The show had been eagerly reported in 1887 (Queen Victoria's Golden Jubilee) and 1892, hence the build-up of curiosity and expectation in

Continued on Page 7

REMINISCENCES OF COL. CODY.

HIS SINGLE-HANDED FIGHT WITH YELLOW HAND.

There were nearly 14,000 people at Monday afternoon's performance of the Wild West Show, and despite the rough night there was another large attendance in the evening. We have previously touched upon some of the principal ... in the spectacle presented by Colonel

THE WILD WEST IN BRADFORD.

BUFFALO BILL'S GREAT SHOW.

Buffalo Bill's Wild West Show paid a visit to Bradford at the comencement of the week and was visited by large crowds of people. At the opening performance on Monday everything was carried out with fire, colour, and dash. The spectator was carried along at a fine pace, and there was something exciting going on all over the vast arena all the time.

TALKING POINT: *The Bradford Weekly Telegraph reports the Wild West Show's colourful performances, which took a battering from the wild Yorkshire weather. Right: One of the posters produced for the 1893 World's Fair in Chicago. Below: Cody flanked by Pawnee and Sioux performers*

Continued from Page 6

Bradford. Nigh on 28,000 people watched the two shows put on at Thornbury on Monday, October 5. Gale force winds and driving rain threatened the security of the vast canvas tent covering the 11-acre seated arena: the organisers had to reinforce the pegging.

Nearly 800 costumed performers and 500 horses re-enacted cowboy and 'injun' chases and battles. Cody, who had personal experience of this sort of combat in the war of 1876, created virtually single-handed a formula which Hollywood and schoolboys the world over would soon copy.

The centre-piece of this part of the show was the appearance of the Deadwood Stagecoach. Cody had purchased his first from the Cheyenne and Black Hills Stage Company in 1883 at a cost of 1,800 dollars. Having the stagecoach hurtle round the arena pursued by whooping war-bonneted and painted indians on horseback never failed to excite and thrill European audiences.

Demonstrations of sharp-shooting followed, though not by the legendary Annie Oakley. Her real name was Phoebe Anne Moses. She adopted her stage name in 1884, the year before she teamed up with Buffalo Bill's Wild West Show. She retired from the show in 1901, but continued to show off her marksmanship up until 1923. She died peacefully in November, 1926. Annie Oakley's successor was Johnny Baker, and it was he who plugged nickels and whatever else that rainy Monday in

It took three trains to transport his large entourage

Thornbury. The crowd were also treated to displays of horsemanship by exotic Cossack and Arab riders. The show concluded with Buffalo Bill himself, resplendent in fringed buckskins and silver spurs, a real-life hero whose bravery had been acknowledged in 1872 with the award of the Congressional Medal of Honour.

We tend to be sceptical about heroes of the Wild West. Buffalo Bill, however, appears to have been a good man as well as a courageous one. Annie Oakley said of him: "He was the kindest hearted, broadest minded, simplest, most loyal man I ever knew… He was courtesy itself,

and more like a patron than an employer. "His relations with everyone he came into contact with were the most cordial and trusting of any man I ever saw."

The shows scheduled for the Tuesday had to be cancelled because of the weather. More than an inch of rain pelted the ground straw deeper into the thickening mud; and turbulent winds blew down a house, crushing part of the arena's wooden seating.

There was no spare time for another. Buffalo Bill's vast entourage, which took three trains to move, was due in Keighley, with further shows at Halifax, Wakefield, Doncaster, and Sheffield ahead.

Buffalo Bill took part in his last show in America in November, 1916. He died on January 10, the following year, aged 70. News of his death flashed round the world, displacing war news about the stalemate on the Western Front. He was buried on Lookout Mountain in Denver, Colorado.

In the summer of 1999 the Buffalo Bill and the Wild West Show re-appeared in Yorkshire, in the form of a fascinating three-month exhibition at the Royal Armouries, Leeds.

T&A

1904

A time for the city to let its hair down

An exhibition fit for a Prince

BUILT TO IMPRESS: *The gleaming white concert hall constructed specially for the Exhibition in Lister Park and pulled down at the end of the year. It was opened by the then Prince of Wales (above)*

Things could only get better for Bradford in 1904 - not that they were that bad to start with. The British Empire was at its zenith, with the little local difficulties with the Boers in South Africa more or less resolved, and the future for trade looked rosy. It was, Bradford decided, time to celebrate.

If, during the celebrations, there was the chance of making a few contacts or a few bob, so much the better. Trade was what the city's prosperity was based on and a shop window wouldn't be a bad idea at all. So the Bradford Exhibition was born.

At the centre of the beanfeast was the opening, on Wednesday, May 4, of the new city art gallery at the Cartwright Memorial Hall. It had been the gift of Lord Masham, formerly Samuel Cunliffe Lister, creator of the massive Manningham Mills, who named it after the developer of the power loom and the woolcombing machine.

Wednesday, May 4, 1904

What was needed was a big name to do the opening, and the Prince of Wales was the obvious choice. He was next in line to the throne, a dutiful if somewhat dull man who seemed to embrace the family values of thrift and domesticity. What's more, while he was here he could unveil the statue, at the bottom of Morley Street, of his late grandma, Queen Victoria, who had died three years earlier.

To pull the whole thing together, there would be a great exhibition in Lister Park, home of the new gallery, for the interest, education and edification of the public. It would last from May to October and would, by the standards of the day, be pretty spectacular - within the budget.

There was an industrial hall actually bigger than the Cartwright Hall, and a con-

cert hall about the same size - but impressive as they looked, gleaming white in the park, they were temporary buildings which would vanish when their purpose was served. It kept the cost down.

A new bridge appeared over the park lake, and alongside it was a water chute for those with more robust souls or baser tastes.

Long before Channel 4, the exhibition boasted a Crystal Maze - nowadays we'd call it a hall of mirrors.

The outside world was not ignored. Russia and Japan, who had been at one another's throats for some time, had recently fought a naval action at Port Arthur, where the Russian fleet was anchored.

With the exhibition barely a couple of weeks old, the Russian Baltic Fleet, which had staggered around the world to take revenge on Japan, was destroyed by Admiral Togo's warships in the Straits of Tsushima - a historic battle

Continued on Page 9

PRIDE OF PLACE: *The temporary bridge (top) and water chute (left) were other attractions of the Bradford Exhibition in 1904. The statue of Queen Victoria in Morley Street (above) was unveiled by the Prince during his visit*

Continued from Page 8

which provided the plot for countless replays on Lister Park lake between miniature battleships.

There was a gravity railway 'which never fails to amuse and commands attention by the screams of its votaries' - in other words, a white-knuckle ride. Gas lights, the new-fangled electric ligh and Chinese lanterns turned the park into fairyland, said the organisers, and there was a weekly fireworks display, too.

A 'village' of about 100 people were brought from Somalia in the Horn of Africa. They had been touring Europe, demonstrating wrestling, spear-throwing and other 'picturesque, native arts'. They braved the weather, established a rapport with the locals, and even threatened mayhem if they weren't paid what they reckoned they were owed at the end. During the visit, the first Yorkshire-born Somali child made her appearance.

And Bradford flocked to the great show. In the first week, 78,651 paid the entrance fee. By the end nearly two and a half million had passed through the gates.

Part of the profit of £18,000 was allocated to help start a permanent collection at the Cartwright Hall. Probably more people had visited the St Louis World's Fair in the USA, which was on at the same time, but few would have experienced quite the same pride of place that the Bradford Exhibition engendered.

T&A

Death of an acting great

Sir Henry Irving is widely regarded as having been one of the greatest actor-managers in British theatrical history. His name became forever linked with Bradford on the evening of October 13, 1905, when he died after a performance at the Theatre Royal. It was a Friday.

It was a tragic, premature end to a farewell tour which had begun the previous week in Sheffield, from where the company had moved to the Bradford theatre in Manningham Lane.

The week had begun well. On the Wednesday Sir Henry attended a civic lunch

Friday, October 13, 1905

in his honour at the Town Hall and was presented with an illuminated address by the Mayor, Alderman William Priestley. In his speech of thanks Sir Henry referred to himself as "one, the sands of whose life are running out fast".

That evening he took the part of Louis XI in the play of that name, and seemed very tired at the end of the performance. He appeared to be back on form, though, the following evening for his celebrated production of The Bells.

The Friday night production was Tennyson's play Becket, with Irving in the title role. The final words of the play, following an attack on

Continued on Page 11

SIR HENRY IRVING: *A special edition of the Bradford Weekly Telegraph carried reports of his death. Here the great man is playing Hamlet*

FINAL BOW: *The Theatre Royal, Manningham Lane, which saw Sir Henry's last performance. The bearded figure, centre, is reputedly his business manager, Bram Stoker, author of Dracula*

Town Hall bell tolled as flags flew at half mast

Continued from Page 10

the Archbishop by soldiers, are: "Into thy hands, O Lord! Into thy hands!"

In the audience was a young Bradford man, Sam Smith, who years later recalled for the Telegraph & Argus the events which followed.

"He then lay flat on the floor and the soldiers fled. The curtain slowly came down and when it went up again Irving was still lying there. Then the curtain came down and went up, and he got to his feet. It was only then that the applause started."

Sir Henry's business manager was Bram Stoker, better known as the author of Dracula. He left Sir Henry sitting in his dressing room and went off to his lodgings. However, he had hardly settled in before he was summoned to

the Midland Hotel to be told by a doctor that Sir Henry was dead.

The great actor had left the theatre shortly after Stoker and travelled by cab down Cheapside to the Midland Hotel.

A Mrs Simpson had been at the theatre on that bitterly cold night and was walking down Cheapside with her friends when Sir Henry's hansom pulled up and out stepped - or rather stumbled - their idol. "He looked so tired, muffled up in a heavy overcoat," she recalled. "There was another man with him, but Irving walked slowly, unassisted, up the hotel steps. We had no idea how ill he must have been until we read the Special on Saturday morning."

From her newspaper, Mrs Simpson had learned that only seconds after she had thrilled at the sight of her hero in the flesh, Sir Henry had collapsed in the foyer. He was helped to a chair but fell from it and died

almost immediately, a few minutes before midnight.

The following evening, just past 9 o'clock, his body was conveyed to the Great Northern Station (later the Exchange Station) through streets lined with silent, respectful crowds, with flags flying at half mast and the Town Hall bell tolling solemnly.

For many years afterwards, until its demolition in 1989, the Theatre Royal was reputed to be haunted by Sir Henry Irving whose final scene that night in Becket was, according to one member of the audience, "almost a rehearsal for his own death so soon to follow."

One final mystery remains. Sir Henry died in the closing minutes of October 13, yet a three-column report of the death appeared on the back page of the Bradford Weekly Telegraph dated.....October 13.

This was not thanks to a premonition by the newspaper's staff. Although the Bradford Weekly Telegraph carried the Friday date, it was not actually on the streets until the Saturday - which gave the staff time to include the story of Sir Henry's death for a special edition.

SIR HENRY IRVING DEAD.

SUDDEN COLLAPSE AT THE MIDLAND HOTEL.

PATHETIC END OF A GREAT CAREER.

PROPHETIC LAST WORDS ON THE STAGE.

"Into Thy Hands, O Lord."

LIFE OF OUR PREMIER ACTOR.

1906   *The day Charlie Chaplin came to Bradford*

The silent genius

Go up Great Horton Road and on the right hand side, just past the Alhambra Studio Theatre, there's a car park. It wasn't always that. Ninety-three years ago this was the site of the Empire Theatre - later a cinema and later still part of the Alexandra Hotel until the building's total demolition in 1993 - one of the city's many imposing theatrical venues.

In 1906 it was a grand edifice, lamplit without and lavish within, the sort of place that stuck in the mind of anyone arriving in Bradford with the usual preconception of what a Northern industrial city must look like.

The Empire certainly made an impact

Monday, May 14, 1906

on Charlie Chaplin. In May, 1906 the 17-year-old Chaplin appeared at the Empire in a show called Casey's Court. He made two more appearances at the Empire, in 1909 and again in August, 1910, with Fred Karno's Circus, a vaudeville troupe putting on sketches and revues.

In those four years Chaplin's natural talent and versatility had made him a star. His last role at the Empire, as Jimmy the Fearless, was his biggest to date. After that he went to Hollywood to make movies.

Half a century passed during which Chaplin's cinematic creation, the little tramp in the battered bowler, outsize pants and broken boots, twirling the cane that was an extension of his personality, became the best-known icon of the 20th Century.

Then one Saturday early in March, 1956, a little man in a dark three-piece suit and overcoat arrived at Bradford's Exchange Station (now the County Court opposite the T&A) and had a look around, before asking a police constable where he could get a "quiet meal".

He was directed to the Victoria Hotel, outside the station. Inside the Grill he removed his hat, revealing a head of silvery hair. A passing journalist, attending the annual dinner-dance of the Bradford branch of the National Union of Journalists upstairs, quickly realised that the little man was indeed Charlie Chaplin: comic actor, movie director, script-writer and film-score writer - the

greatest comedian who ever lived, according to Buster Keaton.

Within minutes Chaplin was chatting amiably with journalists and their guests, having accepted an invitation to join them for dinner.

"I am very happy and a little overwhelmed by your wonderful reception. I thought I'd come to Bradford, and stopped at Leeds on my way to see if I could recapture the feeling of some of the old days when I was touring.

"There's an old adage that Bradford was the comedian's grave, but now I feel as if I had been resurrected! I came through the streets and nobody recognised me, and that was very nice," he said.

He'd come to Bradford to look for the Empire Theatre and instead found the remains of a disused cinema. Stage and screen embraced Chaplin's past and present.

But before he left to catch the 9.37pm back to London, he pulled a large five-pound note from his wallet, sketched a cartoon of the tramp, and signed it. The fiver was later auctioned to raise money for the Bradford Lions Club fund for crippled children.

Charlie Chaplin, awarded an Oscar in 1972 and knighted in 1975, died on Christmas Day 1977.

T&A

1907

Salvation Army leader finds 'receptive audience'

General's rousing welcome

BRADFORD WEEKLY TELEG

GENERAL BOOTH'S TOUR.

Visits to Skipton, Bingley, and Shipley.

An Appreciation by Lord Ribblesdale.

ENTHUSIASTIC WELCOMES.

I t has often been said that the British Labour Party owes as much to Methodism as it does to Karl Marx. Certainly its Bradford birthplace based much of its radicalism on Nonconformist Christianity.

So it was hardly surprising that the city should turn out in force to greet the 78-year-old William Booth, founder of the Salvation Army, when he visited on Wednesday, July 24, 1907.

The General was touring the West Riding and made his first call at Skipton, where he was greeted by a large crowd

Wednesday, July 24, 1907

before addressing a gathering in the Town Hall, presided over by Lord Ribblesdale. What Booth said there went unrecorded.

His convoy of four of the new-fangled motor-cars then travelled on to Bingley, where he spent just a quarter of an hour, receiving an illuminated address from the chairman of the Bingley Urban District Council, Samuel Rushforth. The address expressed the town's 'hearty appreciation of your life-long and devoted work to the spread of the teaching of Jesus Christ, and for the improvement of the submerged portion of the people in all parts of the world'. The General's party then left for Shipley, and at Saltaire Booth started the real barnstorming. At the Victoria Hall in Saltaire, built by a man who was no stranger to evangelism and social uplift,

he found a receptive audience.

The Salvation Army, he said, was not some spasmodic thing - it was a revival which continued the year round. People had asked what would become of the Army when the General was dead. Well, said Booth, he wasn't dead yet and had no immediate plans to die (he lived another five years).

Meanwhile he had seen 7,500 army societies spring up around the world, and seen its message published in 32 languages.

He now hoped, before his death, to establish a university of humanity in London and New York to 'seek to remove those damnable things from which the greater part of humanity suffered'.

He left to rousing cheers and the gift of a gold scarf pin from a man who said: 'Here's to the good the General has done and here's to the good the Army has done me'.

Then it was on to Bradford, where he arrived just after 6pm to be greeted by a large crowd in Town Hall Square and the City Council, meeting in special session.

The Mayor, Councillor John Godwin (who was a couple of months later to become the first Lord Mayor) spoke glowingly of the man who 'for a long time has laboured ungrudgingly for the poor. Today his great work is acknowledged on every hand and his tour throughout the world bears testimony to the love and confidence in which he is held'.

Booth, replying, said the world was feeling that something besides punishment was needed to deal with those who were a discredit to the community and an eyesore and heartsore for those who wished to see men, women and children housed, fed and cared for.

It was a message that went down well…

T&A

1908 *Crowds flocked in their thousands to new skate arena*

Roller hall packed them in

Radio was a new-fangled device for signalling ships at sea. It was certainly not a means of home entertainment. Television was an idea which simply could not be conceived, given the technology of the times.

Bradford's entertainment, in the reign of Edward VII, embraced the music hall, the theatre, the infant cinema and the pub. And none of these offered a guarantee of meeting members of the opposite sex.

Certainly they did not offer the chance of social ice-breaking afforded by colliding with somebody at a combined speed of about 20 miles an hour while teetering along with a

Friday, November 20, 1908

set of wheels fixed to your feet.

It's no wonder, then, that the Rolarena, which opened its doors on to Manningham Lane for the first time on Friday, November 20, 1908, was an instant hit.

Roller skating had been popular in Bradford for almost 30 years, with three rinks in the city at one time. It went into a bit of a decline in the 1880s, but the Rolarena changed all that.

It was purpose built from wood - not an uncommon material at the time. It was also express-built - the foundations went down on October 8, 1908, and six weeks later it was open for business.

It could accommodate 2,000 skaters at a time and had a floor of maple, 30,000 square feet of it. That's about half a football pitch, allowing each skater about one and a half square yards to manoeuvre - provided they were all on the floor at once.

Of course it wasn't what happened on the

floor which mattered for many patrons. Skating provided a chance for showing off - as it still does today - to the opposite sex.

There were those who took it more seriously. The Rolarena produced first-rate figure skaters and dancers, as well as speed skaters - the Bradford Roller Speed Club had 50 members. On Saturday nights it had its own band. Because it also provided a big open area, it staged flower shows, budgie shows and boxing bouts. Freddie Mills, world light heavyweight champion, fought there.

But the name of the game was really speed and noise - the Rolarena provided as much fun as you could have without loudspeakers. Careering round the rink with the music blaring was the nearest thing to a disco our

Rolarena was the place to flirt with the opposite sex

OPEN DOORS: *How the opening of the Rolarena was reported in the Bradford Daily Telegraph*

great grandfathers could know.

The Rolarena led the way for three other rinks, all of which opened in 1909 - the Coliseum in Toller Lane, the Hippodrome in Barkerend Road and the Towers Hall in Manchester Road.

The Coliseum later became a circus and menagerie and later still a cinema. Silver screens also replaced maple floors at the Hippodrome (which became the Roxy) and the Towers.

The Rolarena lasted until 1955 before disaster struck.

Once again it was quick. The rink, six weeks in the building, took just 40 minutes to be destroyed in a fire. Its wooden construction caused it to disappear in a blaze so spectacular that people rushed from far and near to watch it. It was a fittingly showy end to what had been one of Bradford's premier night spots.

T&A

1909 Funds for new Bradford hospital were hard to come by

BRI's difficult birth

It was a massively ambitious scheme but, at the time, Bradford was 'a great and wealthy community' according to the Weekly Telegraph.

So £100,000 for a new Royal Infirmary was a stiff target, but not an impossible one when the Lord Mayor, Sir James Hill, launched the appeal on August 20, 1909.

The old infirmary in Westgate had served its purpose. It was a stately building but getting old - the oldest parts dated from 1843 - and as the 20th Century got into its stride, it was in the wrong place.

One of the last straws was when a secretary

Friday, August 20, 1909

put a piece of white paper near a window. Within minutes it was covered in smuts. Since many of the patients were suffering from respiratory problems, it was clear that it was time for a move to somewhere where the air was cleaner.

All this was happening fully 40 years before a national health service came into being. If Bradford wanted a new infirmary, it would have to pay for it.

There was a lively debate between Socialists, Tories and Liberals, with the former favouring a municipal enterprise and the latter pair favouring 'voluntaryism' - public subscription from the great and wealthy. Within a day, there had been offers of £5,000 each from the Lord Mayor, and from businessmen Jacob Moser and from Joseph Craven - so the appeal was 15 per cent of the way there.

'It may take a few years to raise the amount' said the Telegraph, and it wasn't wrong.

With the new hospital firmly in sight, the First World War broke out, and all bets were off for the duration.

Progress had been slow in 1914 and it was then that the municipalists and the voluntaryists reached a compromise. The Corporation would buy the old building and its land for £100,000 if subscribers would provide the money for the new buildings.

The slump of 1921-22 held things back, but the site had been in hand since 1909 - at Field House, between Duckworth Lane and Smith Lane. And in 1920 work began - though by now the city had a hospital, St Luke's - converted from the old Poor Law Institution in Little Horton Lane. It was the first municipal one in Britain.

At the BRI the first building to begin was on the nurses' hostel. The cost had risen to £250,000, but there had been promises of more money from benefactors.

By 1927 the cost had become half a million but the first block of wards was under way. In 1929 radiotherapy equipment was bought and a second block of wards was under construction.

Then, in 1930, the first block opened. The Duke of York, later to become George VI, opened the home for paying patients which still bears his name.

By 1934 the money was all in hand and it was all systems go.

On June 8, 1936, the last patients left the old Westgate building to move into the newly-opened hospital.

12 years - and another world war - later, it was to become a showpiece for the new National Health Service.

T&A

1910 *Churchill attacked after rallying* *speech in Bradford*

Lords and ladies join battle

The country was divided as almost never before when it went to the polls just before Christmas in 1910.
The Liberals, in power since 1905, had run into extreme opposition from the largely Tory House of Lords over reforming legislation including the introduction of old age pensions.
Herbert Asquith, the Morley-born Prime Minister, went to the country to look for some sort of mandate to deal with the Lords.
Among the Liberals' armoury was the 36-year-old Home Secretary, Winston Churchill, who was despatched to Bradford a couple of weeks before the election to address a meeting organised by the League of Young Liberals, on Saturday, November 26.
Young Winston had been elected to Parliament in 1900 as a Conservative, but 'crossed the floor' in 1904 and sat on the Liberal benches for 18 years. He was one of the finest orators the party had, and in Bradford was greeted with cheers from a St George's Hall which had been packed to the seams half an hour before the meeting was due to begin.The meeting was treated to some rousing stuff. We were, said Churchill, in the middle of a memorable constitutional

struggle. History was being made there and then.
The Lords, he said, had wrecked the main work of the Government - temperance, education and the People's Budget [which was to lead to pensions].
There was no concealment as to what the Lords intended, he said. It was to control the country whether the Tories were in power or not.

Friday, December 2, 1910

It was good rousing stuff, but throughout the speech there were the sounds of dissent.
For all the fine words about the people, half of the population were disqualified from voting because of their sex.
The women's suffrage movement was at its height and few politicians would speak uninterrupted or unchallenged through the 1910 election campaign.

It was not just verbal hostility which Churchill faced, though, during his Bradford visit. On his way back to London, he was ambling down the train to the dining car when he was attacked by a man with a dog whip.
The man rushed at the Home Secretary, brandishing the whip, and shouted: 'Winston Churchill, take that, you cur!'.
There was nothing to take, however, because the attempted blow across the face was stopped by Churchill's bodyguard, Detective Sergeant Sandercock.
Sandercock was in action again, at King's Cross, when three women tried to get at Churchill, who escaped, smiling.
The dog whip merchant appeared in court in London the following Monday, and gave his name as Hugh Franklin, his age as 21, his address as Pembridge Gardens, Notting Hill, and his organisation as the Men's

Continued on Page 17

2.—THE BRADFORD WEEK...

Mr. Churchill in Bradford.

"DEAD BLANK WALL" OF THE LORDS.

Bradford Liberals made their demonstration against the House of Lords on Saturday. It was in every way effective. A huge meeting in St. George's Hall, high enthusiasm, a great fighting speech by Mr. Winston Churchill—these were the features of Bradford's answer to the Peers.

Although the meeting was not arranged to begin until 3.30 the hall was filled by three o'clock, and later it was packed to the doors. The interval of waiting was filled by the singing of rousing Liberal songs, of which "God Save the People" was the favourite.

Everybody was in the highest spirits, and demonstration was of good augury for triumph of the Liberal candidates in the to-morrow.

The meeting was organised by Bradford League of Young Liberal naturally a great many "Old Liberal present—in fact the demonstration rep the united Liberalism of the distric "gallery" was very lively during liminaries, and a favourite query we downhearted?" followed by a "No."

Mr. Percy Illingworth, M.P., th of the Bradford and Shipley bran National League of Young Libera

to the democracy... ritain.
He had spoken one hour and nine minutes.

SUFFRAGETTE INTERRUPTER INJURED

One of the interrupters at St. George's Hall on Saturday, Mr. Alfred Hawkins, a commercial traveller, aged 53, of 2, Gaul Street, Leicester, was taken to the Royal Infirmary suffering from an awkward fracture of the left ...cap sustained during his ejection from the Hall. Mr. Hawkins was visited by a number of sympathisers, male and female, on Sunday.

ATTACK ON MR. CHURCHILL.

DOG WHIP INCIDENT IN A TRAIN.

Winston Churchill appears to be a special the suffragists as he travels about the ...e speeches.
...asant experience was while ...o London after addressing ...rge's Hall, Bradford, on ...e was passing through ...the restaurant car, and ...o a third-class carriage ...ly-built man who had ...ing the door. ...ushed at the Home ...ston Churchill, take ...o strike the Home ...ntercepted by Det.- ...s sitting on the ...after struggling ...the sergeant and ...and Yard officers ...Churchill. ...s Hugh Frank- ...otting Hill, W. ...ent a night and ...Music Hall, in ...oyd George's ...three women ...Secretary, but ...s.

...COUNT.
...r for Messrs. ...elling to Lon- ...the attempted ...a passenger by ...ion on Saturday ...urchill travelled ...e train was pass- ...walked through ...the restaur-

Continued from Page 16

Political Union for Women's Enfranchisement.

He was remanded for a week, and bail was refused, to the anger of a number of supporters present, including Christobel Pankhurst, daughter of Emmeline Pankhurst, founder of the Women's Social and Political Union.

The great debate on votes for women was not resolved until after the First World War, an event which also put other Liberal concerns like Home Rule for Ireland on ice.

Also on ice, for a while, was Asquith's administration.

The election, which was supposed to answer the question: 'Who rules Britain?', came up with a fascinating answer: the one and only dead heat in British Parliamentary history. Liberals and Tories had 272 seats each.

Asquith stayed in power with the reluctant backing of 42 Labour MPs and 84 Irish Nationalists. The Peers versus People battle still had a way to run.

Churchill, meanwhile, wasn't clear of controversy. He was almost mobbed in Lincoln while trying to make a polling day speech, in defiance of convention and the gentlemanly rules which governed the politics of the time.

T&A

SPEECH:
Winston Churchill used his fine oratory in Bradford's St George's Hall, but was heckled by supporters of the Women's Suffragette Movement, far left

1911

Bradford City won the FA Cup Final

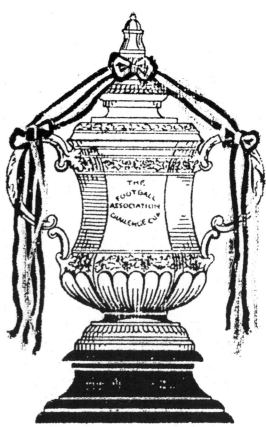

Glorious 1911

Cup glory that will live forever

O n May 22, 1999, Newcastle United suffered their second consecutive FA Cup Final defeat. But in April, 1911 the First Division side reached their second final in two seasons confident of victory.

In 1910 the North Easterners had defeated Barnsley 2-0 in the final held at Goodison Park (Wembley had not been built). Newcastle had also won the

Wednesday April 26, 1911

First Division Championship three times between 1904 and 1909, and could field a team packed with seven or eight Internationals.

City, by comparison, were in only their eighth season as a professional club. One of their best players, the England International Dickie Bond, was suspended.

Newcastle were confident for another reason too: earlier in the season they had thrashed City 6-1 at St James' Park. During their Cup run, however, City reached top form and became very

difficult to beat - perhaps because eight of them were Scotsmen.

The run had seen the team beat New Brompton (now Gillingham) away 1-0;

Continued on Page 19

CUP SUCCESS OF BRADFORD CITY.

of the Final.

MELLORS.
CAMPBELL.
TAYLOR.
ROBINSON.
TORRANCE.
McDONALD.

Heroes of the Fin

7. P. LOGAN.
8. J. H. SPEIRS.
9. F. O'ROURKE.
10. A. DEVINE.
11. F. THOMPSON.

FRONT PAGE NEWS: *How the Bradford Weekly Telegraph depicted the glorious victory*

Continued from Page 18

Southern League Norwich City 2-1 at Valley Parade; Grimbsy Town 1-0 at Valley Parade; Burnley 1-0 at Valley Parade; and Blackburn Rovers 3-0 in the semi-final at Bramall Lane.

The Final took place before a crowd of 70,000 at Crystal Palace on Saturday, April 22. The 0-0 result came after one of the dullest finals on record, according to the Bradford Weekly Telegraph correspondent, 'Adjutant'. Of the two sides, he thought Newcastle had played the better football and was particularly impressed by their inside-left, one Alex Higgins.

Ninety years ago professional football was a different game with different rules. Take the players' kit, for example. Boots had hard toes and covered the ankles. Studs were nailed into the soles. City's claret and amber shirts, laced at the collar, and United's black and white ones, were unadorned by sponsors' names or logos, just the club badge.

Penalty area semi-circles didn't exist (until 1937). Players could be ruled off-side from a throw-in. Three defenders had to be between an attacker and the goal when the ball was kicked to remain on-side. Goalkeepers were not obliged to stand on the goal-line for penalty kicks. Goal kicks could be taken direct or the ball passed to a colleague and then punted upfield from his return pass.

LINE-UP: *The Bradford City squad of the 1910-11 season that brought home the FA Cup for the only time in the club's history*

A football was made of an inflatable inner-tube, and a casing of sewn leather rectangles. A lace tightly collared the ball which on wet days soaked up water and increased in weight. Referees wore a black jacket and a white shirt open at the collar, as did the linesmen.

The replay took place at Manchester United's Old Trafford on Wednesday, April 26, in spite of the fact that City were due to play Middlesbrough in a

First Division game at Valley Parade on the Thursday.

City's team was as follows:- in goal, Mark Mellors: right back, Robert Campbell: left back, David Taylor: right half, George Robinson: centre half, Bob Torrance: left half, Jimmy McDonald: outside right, Peter Logan: inside right, Jimmy Speirs: centre forward, Frank O'Rourke: inside left, Archibald Devine: outside left Frank Thompson.

Continued on Page 20

Continued from Page 19

The game was fast, robust and full of incident and to some of those paid to watch and pass judgement it was the epitome of good old-fashioned British virtues.

'Adjutant' in his post-match despatch wrote imperiously: "Is clever footwork, deft dodging, pretty passing, and all that sort of thing any more football than a strong, robust, dashing, go-ahead style?

"Sir George Robertson (MP for Central Bradford), in his interesting telegram to the 'Telegraph' hit off the situation exactly. He said 'The forwards and half backs played with the brilliance and impetuosity of the old-fashioned amateur cup teams, while the full backs and goal were as steady and deadly as the guards at Waterloo.'

"I particularly like the first part of the sentence. There was no finer football ever played than that of the 'old-fash-

There was no finer football ever played than that of old-fashioned amateur teams

ioned amateur cup teams,' and the older critics are never tired of telling us so. But that style has gone out of fashion."

The only goal of the game was knocked in by Jimmy Speirs, a 12-stone Scottish striker who scored 33 league and cup goals in 96 games for City during three seasons at Valley Parade. He was later transferred to Leeds City for £900, but abandoned his career to join the Army and fight in the 1914-18 War. He gained the rank of Sergeant and was awarded the Military Medal - a very high honour. He was killed on August 20, 1917, and was buried in Belgium.

Thousands packed the city centre waiting to welcome home the team. City's train arrived at Exchange Station at 9pm.

"She came in grandly with, it seemed, a special majesty, with deliberate dignity, yet swiftly too when one saw how the

How we reported the news

At 3.43, or thereabouts, on Wednesday afternoon, the head of a certain person came into contact with an inflated leather sphere, which in accordance with the laws of impact, rebounded, falling within a certain netted space near Manchester.

It sounds simple enough, thus badly put, and yet the incident was so pregnant with importance, so almost incredibly great in its consequence, that only those who were in the centre of the city of Bradford in the evening can form any idea of what it really meant.

But that, happily, is but saying that

Telegraph & Argus
From the Bradford Weekly Telegraph

everybody will understand, for everybody was in the centre of the city of Bradford. That 'everybody' indeed, was the prime consequence to which we refer.

Was there ever such a crowd in Bradford? Fifty thousand? A hundred thousand? Who shall say? How shall one attempt to begin to think of describing it? Town Hall Square, teeming with humanity; Market Street one mass from end to end; Bridge Street worse than impassable - irresistible. It was an unparalleled popular demonstration, overwhelmingly, unforgettably terrific.

carriage windows flashed by," rhapsodised 'Adjutant'. "It seemed she would never pull up in time. She was slowing down now though, and there, at last, on the saloon table one caught the glitter of the Cup."

A good deal has been written about the trophy and its Bradford origins. Contrary to rumour it was not made in Bradford but in Birmingham. However, it was designed here by William Norman who

Continued on Page 21

GOAL!: *Jimmy Speirs heads home the goal that gave Bradford City their 1-0 victory over Newcastle United, below, at the replayed FA Cup Final in front of a packed Old Trafford ground in Manchester*

Continued from Page 20

worked for the internationally famous Bradford firm of gold and silversmiths Fattorini & Sons.

His design was chosen from 250 entries in February, 1911. The Football Association wanted a new trophy for their prestigious knock-out competition which had gained tremendously in appeal since beginning in 1872.

Norman's sterling silver trophy, the third FA Cup in 39 years, was manufactured at Fattorini's Barr Street works in Birmingham, where William Norman later went to work. It cost 50 guineas (£52.50). Norman's trophy was replaced in the 1990s.

Bradford City made history in 1911 by being the first club to win the original trophy.

T&A

1912 *Yorkshire musician led deck orchestra as liner sank*

TITANIC SUNK.
WORST DISASTER IN HISTORY.
Feared Loss of 1,500 Lives
866 Rescued.
PITIFUL SCENES AT SHIPPING OFFICES.
Anguished Relatives Clamour for News.
BOATS AND WRECKAGE
WHAT THE CARPATHIA FOUND

TRAGIC: *The 'unsinkable' Titanic which went down with the loss of more than 1,500 lives, including Dewsbury musician Wallace Hartley*

A swansong on the Titanic

Wallace Hartley was getting fed up with a life on the ocean wave. The Dewsbury musician - his family lived at West Park Street and worshipped at St Mark's Church nearby - had crossed the Atlantic 80 times on the liners Mauretania and Lusitania.

He was a professional violinist, and as a young man had travelled all over Britain with opera companies before adding another string to his bow by hitting the high seas. But by 1912, his 34th year, what he really wanted to do was get married and settle down.

It took the persuasive charm of Bruce Ismay, managing director of the White Star Line, to change Wallace Hartley's mind. Ismay doubtless told him that the trans-Atlantic maiden voyage of the luxury liner Titanic would go down in history, for the 852-ft vessel of 46,328 tons was the biggest, most opulent ship afloat.

Among the 1,308 passengers would be some of the richest people on earth (11 millionaires had each paid £870 for First Class accommodation for the five-day crossing from Southampton to New York). It would be something to tell his children, that he had been asked personally to lead the orchestra on the first trip of the greatest ship in the history of the world.

Titanic steamed into the chill waters of the North Atlantic. The sea was flat, the weather cold. On Sunday night at 9.40, April 14, a warning of pack ice and icebergs was received on the ship's new Marconi radio equipment. The news was never relayed to the bridge. Phillips, the radio operator, was too busy telegraphing messages to New York. Twenty miles to Titanic's starboard the

6,000-ton cargo and passenger ship Californian radioed another ice warning at 11pm to the big vessel lit up like a hotel; there was no response so the Californian's radio operator went to bed.

Within the next hour Titanic collided with a huge brownish iceberg which punctured the hull ten feet above the ship's keel.

Within ten minutes 14 feet of freezing sea-water had poured into the forepeak, holds one and two, the baggage and mail hold,

Sunday, April 14, 1912

and numbers five and six boiler rooms.

Thomas Andrews jnr, managing director of Harland & Wolff and the ship's designer, quickly worked out that within a couple of hours the rate of water penetration would drag the ship under by the bow.

No one had given serious thought to the possibility that the ship might founder. The ship only had a total of 20 life-saving craft, enough for 1,178 if each was filled to capac-

ity. There were 2,206 passengers and crew on that maiden voyage. Only 703 of them were to survive.

Distress rockets were fired and the new SOS call tapped out repeatedly. Only the Carpathia, 58 miles away, responded. At 1.30am Phillips sent his last message, and then the power failed. At 2.20am, on April 15, Titanic finally sank.

Legend has it that Wallace Hartley and his orchestra played Nearer My God To Thee at the last, before perishing with the ship. Some believe that instead of the hymn the musicians played Ragtime to try to keep up the spirits of those still aboard.

What's certain is that as the ship's list got steeper no one aboard could stand upright let alone play an instrument.

Titanic plunged nearly 16 times its own length before hitting the seabed in two places, strewing out debris over a wide area. Any human body that went down with the ship would have been crushed by the enormous pressure long before the wreckage settled at 13,200 feet.

T&A

1913 Adventurer gave Bradford its first sight of the aeroplane

A magnificent flying machine

HAMEL'S AEROPLANE

FIRST FLIGHT INTO BRADFORD

THE EXHIBITIONS AT CLOCK HOUSE

Though the aeroplane may now be described as a familiar and almost commonplace matter of our day, it was not until yesterday that the first aeroplane flew into Bradford. It was the Bleriot monoplane flown by Mr. Gustav Hamel, the well-known aviator, who brought his machine over from Harrogate in readiness for the exhibition flights at the Clock House estate today.

Leaving Harrogate at five-and-twenty minutes to four Mr. Hamel made a rapid flight under favourable conditions to the Clock House, which he reached in just over twenty minutes, the distance being about twenty miles.

As those who are familiar with the Clock House grounds will imagine the descent to the ground was a matter of no little difficulty. The field there is surrounded by buildings, and, though large, it contains obstructing trees. Mr. Hamel, however, came down very clever...

It wasn't like Bradford to be so slow in keeping up with the times. It was almost ten years after the Wright Brothers' flight at Kittyhawk that the city saw its first aeroplane.

The problem for aviator Gustav Hamel was that flat ground was at a bit of a premium in Bradford - aircraft being new-fangled things, with a tendency to frighten livestock, were looked at with some suspicion by landowners.

However, Hamel finally arranged to make some exhibition flights at the Clock House estate, near Lister Park, during the Bradford holiday week of 1913.

Two trees had to be cut down to give him some landing and take-off space and, at teatime on Friday, August 1, 1913, after a 20-minute flight from Harrogate, he touched down without mishap 'but' - reported the Bradford Daily Telegraph - 'with an abruption that seemed hardly to his taste, and at first some doubt was expressed as to

Friday, August 1, 1913

whether further flight would be advisable'. He in fact stopped just five yards from a wall at the end of the field.

The youthful Hamel was not going to deny the holiday crowds their excitement, however, and a packed Lister Park the next day saw the flight - a solo one, as Hamel's Bleriot monoplane could not handle the Clock House slope and a passenger.

'It's quite out of the question to take anybody up from here' he said. 'It'll be quite bad enough getting myself up.'

The ground was bad enough, and the surroundings were worse - trees, houses and hills had made him wonder where he was going to land if anything went wrong.

It was a fine and sunny day and the crowd marvelled at the 'gadfly buzzing' of the plane, reported the Telegraph.

Some of the players in the bandstand devel-

TAKE-OFF: *Gustav Hamel causes a sensation with his Bleriot monoplane in Bradford's Clock House Estate on an August holiday afternoon*

oped temporary squints while trying to watch both the plane and the conductor.

The plane itself would be familiar by name. In 1909 Louis Bleriot had flown his own design across the English Channel - the first man to do so.

Suddenly Britain was no longer a series of islands which could be defended by a navy alone. The military use of aircraft had not escaped the more far-sighted and even some senior military officers had been

stirred into something resembling thought.

One year and two days after Hamel's flight over Bradford, war was declared. And it was over the trenches of Flanders that the aeroplane developed from a rickety means of reconnaissance into a weapon which would come to dominate modern warfare.

But in that last year of innocence and sunlight, Bradford just tipped back its collective head and marvelled. **T&A**

1914

Seconds out with the brave lad from Bingley

In the ring with a Euro-star

CHALLENGE:
George Mitchell, who reckoned he could stay on his feet against boxing champ Georges Carpentier

Boxing, say its supporters, is a combination of art and science. Sometimes the art and the science are matched against one another, as when a slugger comes up against a stylist.

But when young George Mitchell, from Bingley, met the European heavyweight champion Georges Carpentier, it was a case of heart versus science.

Carpentier was French and all elegance. He wore an orchid in his buttonhole and was popular with

Easter Tuesday, 1914

women because he had managed to retain both his title and his looks.

In December he fought British hopeful Bombardier Billy Wells and won in 73 seconds. Wells was put on his back by a flurry of blows and didn't get up.

The news of the defeat shook Britain's sporting public, among them the 22-year-old George Mitchell, of Upwood, Bingley. He and his brother Tom were gifted amateur boxers. Their dad Thomas was no softy, either, having given a burglar a leathering even in middle age. He had given the intruder the choice of being handed over to the law or fighting one of the family, and the miscreant thought

DAY, APRIL 15, 1914

PLUCKY BRADFORDIAN.

MR. MITCHELL'S FIGHT.

KNOCKED DOWN FOUR TIMES.

"I DID MY BEST."

CARPENTIER'S APPRECIATION.

Mitchell senior was the best option. He was wrong.

George Mitchell, hearing of Wells's defeat, said he reckoned he could have stood up to Carpentier for longer than 73 seconds.

Word of this reached a family friend, a textile man with business connections in France. Was George serious? He asked. George was serious. So Carpentier was challenged.

He had little choice but to accept. If he had turned down the fight his reputation would have been tarnished. He asked for two things - a fee of 3,500 francs to cover his expenses, and that the fight should take place in secret.

Five Bradford businessmen put up the

Continued on Page 25

FROM LEISURE...TO KILLING FIELDS: *George Mitchell following the pursuits of the country, before his big-city battle with European heavyweight champion Georges Carpentier. Right, as an officer in the Black Watch. He was killed by a grenade in 1915*

Continued from Page 24

money, and a location was found in the Latin quarter of Paris.

Then George Mitchell received a cable: 'Have fixed up fight with Carpentier. Reply with 'yes' or 'no'. There was no question as to what the reply would be.

It was all very clandestine. Mitchell was smuggled into France by night with just two friends who were to act as his seconds.

Even his family were in the dark, until Percy Illingworth MP sent a telegram to the Mitchell home wishing the lad luck.

The lad had departed, and his father looked at the telegram in some bafflement. Then he got another telegram, this time from his son, explaining that he was taking on Carpentier simply to show he could last longer than 73 seconds. Which he did.

On the night of the fight - Easter Tuesday - some of the cream of Paris society,

Some of the cream of Paris society turned up

women as well as men, turned out to see the contest. Carpentier entered the ring in silk shorts, and the preliminaries were quickly settled.

As the bell went for round one, the Frenchman advanced across the ring with his arm out, confusing the young Yorkshireman.

'I thought he was going to shake hands but he shot out his left to my body almost before I realised the fight was on' recalled Mitchell later.

The first blow was followed by a punch to

the chin, but Mitchell stood his ground, though it was clear to the crowd that he was outclassed.

Many of them had their eyes on their watches as much as on the fight, and when the 73-second mark was passed there were shouts to the referee to stop the bout. Mitchell had been on the canvas four times but had got back up four times.

But after 95 seconds his corner, deciding there was a difference between being game and having your marbles scrambled, threw in the towel.

The champion and the challenger shared a bottle of champagne after the fight, with young Mitchell seeming more concerned about facing the wrath of his father than facing the champion.

George Mitchell returned to France one more time, and never returned.

As Lieutenant Mitchell of the Black Watch, he was killed by a grenade in 1915.

T&A

1915
Wrangle over 'blackout' was only hint of conflict horrors

READY FOR ACTION: *Part of the Bradford Pals Battalion gathered before being sent to France - and the horrors of The Somme*

I f you were at home, living your everyday life, there wasn't much evidence, for a lot of the time, that the world was in conflict.

The First World War started with much cheering, waving of straw boaters and singing. Then, as a war of mobility bogged down into a stalemate in the trenches, it was quite possible for civilians to forget there was a war on.

There were no daily reminders in the early days, like ration books, sandbags outside public buildings, or nightly blackouts, which

Friday, April 15, 1915

were to characterise the home front in the Second World War.

But with hostilities a few months old, civilians began to feel the impact a little more. One of the early regulations involved lighting restrictions. Air raids on the scale of the Blitz were unimagined, but Germany had Zeppelin airships capable of carrying bombs, so it seemed sensible to keep things darker at night.

The public was told to buy green blinds and keep them pulled at night. Unfortunately, Britain being a bureaucracy, this led to some snotty comments on April 25, 1915, when the repeal of these regulations meant that Bradford, which had its own police force, remained dark while all the surrounding areas, which were covered by different bobbies, could have their lights blazing out of the windows again.

'This', said the Bradford Daily Telegraph, with a hint of resignation, 'is how it will work out.

Dark days of war

BRADFORD ISOLATED.

THE CENTRE OF DARKNESS.

Restrictions Withdrawn in Surrounding Districts

A CURIOUS SITUATION.

By the repeal of the military lighting restriction order in most parts of the West Riding police area, there will arise the curious anomaly of Bradford being in almost complete darkness at night and all the adjoining districts having the inestimable privilege of full lighting facilities.

'On the Shipley side of the Frizinghall penny tramway stage, lights can blaze away at full pressure, whilst on the Bradford side darkness must still prevail.

'In the borough of Keighley and in the Keighley Petty Sessional Division, and in Shipley, Cleckheaton, Clayton and other West Riding townships, the shopkeepers may illuminate their windows, but the Brad-ford tradesman will have to be content with all the display he can get in the daytime.

'The order shows an extraordinary lack of uniformity and what is in the official mind we cannot attempt to explain…'

A couple of days earlier, on St George's Day, the Lord Mayor, George H Robinson, had inspected the growing band of Bradford Pals, who had volunteered for the army as bunches of mates, and who were to go to France. It had been a festive occasion at Bradford Northern's ground at Birch Lane, and had included quite a lot of the fun of the fair, as well as a rugby match and military music.

Just over a year later, on July 1, 1916, was the event which brought home to Bradford what was really happening in the war.

On that day, the first of the Battle of the Somme, the Bradford Pals - and tens of thousands more like them from around Britain - were to be mown down as they advanced slowly and steadily across no-man's land in a piece if military 'planning' which could almost count as mass murder on the part of the British generals.

The daily-growing, ever-growing list of casualties, which infested the pages of the Bradford Daily Telegraph like some deadly plague, was a heart-numbing reminder of what the 'war to end all wars' had become.

T&A

1916

39 killed as Low Moor munitions factory is wrecked in blast

Bradford Daily Telegraph (reproduced front page with multiple headline columns including:)

Send your "Want" Ads. to the "Telegraph." Our Columns do the rest.

Bradford Daily Telegraph

WEDNESDAY, AUGUST 23, 1916.

BRITISH PRESS ON.

FURTHER SOMME GAINS.

FIERCE BATTLE ON THE STOKHOD.

THE FIGHTING IN THE BALKANS.

GERMAN BATTLESHIP TORPEDOED.

DETAILS OF YORKSHIRE EXPLOSION.

BRITISH PRESSURE.

THE OPERATIONS AGAINST THIEPVAL.

MORE GROUND GAINED.

BALKAN FIGHTING.

GREEKS RE.IST BULGAR ADVANCE.

BRITISH DESTROY RAILWAY BRIDGE.

MUNITION DISASTER.

HOW EXPLOSIONS BEGAN.

WORKS PRACTICALLY DEMOLISHED.

FIREMEN KILLED BY BURSTING ENGINE.

ROLLING STOCK DESTROYED BY FIRE

GERMAN BATTLESHIP

TORPEDOED IN NORTH SEA.

BELIEVED TO BE SUNK.

BRITISH SUBMARINE'S ATTACK.

KING OF RUMANIA

RETURNS TO BUCHAREST.

BUKOVINA BATTLE.

RUSSIAN SUCCESS.

NEWS CLAMPDOWN: *The front page of the Bradford Daily Telegraph with the story of the massive munitions factory blast in Low Moor, Bradford, tucked away among other items of news as the scale of the disaster was 'disguised' for the war effort*

Silence that followed the killer blast...

The reporting of war and civil disasters has changed completely in the years since the fatal explosion at the munitions factory in Low Moor on August 21, 1916.

Although everyone in Bradford got to know by word of mouth about the 99 casualties, 39 of them fatal, the rest of the world was

Monday, August 21, 1916

deliberately kept in ignorance because Britain was at war and the Low Moor explosion was deemed war-sensitive information by the Ministry of Munitions.

The day after, the Bradford Daily Telegraph, a largely un-illustrated broadsheet of six pages with classified ads on the front page

Continued on Page 28

Factory workers fled, hair bleached and faces stained

Continued from Page 27
and, news on the back, merely reported that an explosion had taken place at a 'Yorkshire' munitions factory and put the death toll at 20.

Two days later the news only merited half a column, and that was largely confined to the short Parliamentary exchange in the House of Commons.

That Friday's Bradford Weekly Telegraph simply summarised the non-information that had appeared in its sister paper. Neither newspaper contained the slightest bit of local reaction to the inferno, nor photographs of the six firemen and one police constable among the dead.

The First World War was in its middle and bloodiest phase. The only photographs in the papers were head-and-shoulders snaps of dead or wounded soldiers, casualties of the Somme 'advance' that July.

Even today mystery surrounds the cause of the explosion that summer Monday at 3.16pm. It has been attributed to a fire, though how that could have occurred in such an establishment is not known.

There was a hell of an explosion at Low Moor Chemical Works, that much is certain. Highly combustible substances used in the manufacture of military explosives

went up, raining chunks of debris on the roofs of houses in the vicinity. Gasholder No I was punctured and deflated like a balloon.

Factory workers fled from the scene, their hair bleached and their faces stained yellow by the picric acid with which they worked.

Bradford, commonly thought of as a mainly textile town, had been making ammunition and armaments "of a truly pulverising quality" for years, due to vast local deposits of coal and iron ore. In 1868, for example, there were 56 collieries in Bradford and Bingley. The same year the West Riding produced nearly 790,000 tons of iron ore, nearly 600,000 tons of which came from Low Moor.

Bradford's significance in the war effort may explain the reticence of Dr Addison,

Continued on Page 29

BLAST: *The gas cylinders after the fatal explosion which rocked Low Moor, and right, the memorial in Scholemoor Cemetery to the firemen who died in the aftermath of the disaster*

Continued from Page 28

head of the Ministry of Munitions. The last thing he wanted was to hand the Central European powers a propaganda coup.

One of Bradford's worst disasters was without question the worst-reported. For example, little is known about how exactly those six firemen died. It was said that they died after a boiler on one of the fire engines had exploded.

Only in February, 1985, was the public told another explanation. Former fireman John Rose was celebrating his 100th birthday and the T&A went along to mark the event. Mr Rose, it turned out, had been a fireman in 1916 and had told his son Leslie that a big wall had collapsed on a fire engine from Odsal. The men inside didn't have a chance.

Further revelations came from fireman Martin Ruscoe, then based at Fairweather Green. Mr Ruscoe, who had researched the disaster, dismissed the exploding fire engine boiler theory.

"That couldn't have been correct because it would have had to have been a horse drawn appliance - and they were out of service by that time," he told the T&A.

Apart from the six firemen and the policeman, 32 people died and another 60 were injured. Precious little is known about them, presumably because of secrecy when Europe was at war eighty-three years ago.

T&A

1917 *German medic led way in beating the killer disease Anthrax*

'Bradford disease' meets its match

HONOUR: *Frederick Eurich who came to Bradford and conquered the Bradford Disease*

Anthrax was a scourge which threatened all those who handled wool and other animal hair and hides.

Because this was a central part of the city's trade and industry, the killer became known as the Bradford Disease.

And a killer it was - a woolsorter could come home from work feeling ill, and be dead within hours.

On July 12, 1917, there was an inquest on wool warehouseman Bernard Stuttard, who had died after handling acknowledged 'dangerous' wools like Scotch skin wool, Persian grey, white East India and white goat hair.

Stuttard had seemingly had nothing worse than a sore throat when he turned up at the Royal Infirmary on a Thursday.

By Sunday his glands were swollen and he was semi-conscious.

At this point he was examined by a man who was to become a great man in Bradford's history.

Frederick William Eurich was born in Chemnitz in Germany in 1869 and came to Bradford as a small boy with his parents.

Chemnitz, later renamed Karl-Marx-Stadt by the East German Communist regime, had been a major textile centre in Saxony since the 1350s, and the Eurichs were among a host of Germans who came to Bradford, recognising a place which was on the up,

Friday, July 12, 1917

and compatible with their line of business. The young Frederick, brought up in a home where art and culture were the norm, chose medicine for his future and took his degree at Edinburgh, specialising in mental illness.

He started work as a physician in Bradford in 1896, struggled for a while, then got a position with the Eye and Ear hospital and at Bradford Royal Infirmary.

About this time, the Bradford and District Trade and Labour Council was pushing for a pathological and bacteriological laboratory in the city.

Eurich was appointed and started work at £100 a year in a small room in the Technical College. From there he began the work which led to the conquest of Anthrax.

Its elimination had baffled the industry for 35 years. Eurich masterminded the break-

Continued on Page 31

KILLER: *Bradford wool workers were susceptible to anthrax from their contact with fleeces. Right, the death of warehouseman Bernard Stuttard led to its eradication*

FATAL ANTHRAX.

BRADFORD WAREHOUSEMAN'S DEATH.

CORONER AND THE COURT PROCEDURE.

REPLY TO A RESOLUTION.

At the Bradford Coroner's Court, to-day (before Mr J. G. Hutchinson) an inquiry was held into the circumstances attending the death of Bernard Stuttard (48), wool warehouseman, of 28, Elizabeth Street.

Mrs. Stuttard stated that her husband had worked for Messrs. John Cure and Co., Ltd., about fifteen months. He was taken ill at his work on Thursday morning last, and died on Monday morning last.

John Turner, a foreman, employed by John Cure and Co., stated that shortly after ten o'clock on Thursday morning last Stuttard came to the office. He was trembling and complained of generally feeling out of sorts. He was allowed to go home and a doctor was sent to see him. The deceased had been engaged on dangerous wools such as grey Scotch skin wool, grey Persian, alpaca, white goat hair, white East India, white skin, etc.

The Coroner intimated that the Factory Inspector had assured him that this wool was dealt with according to Home Office regulations, and separate accommodation was provided for meals, washing, etc.

Witness further stated that Stuttard was a very clean man, and always took care in cleaning his hands, etc., before partaking of his meals.

John Tyman, a warehouseman, who had worked with the deceased, said they had been engaged for the past month on Persian wool. Their duty was to sort out the blood-stained and hand them over to be destroyed. They received a bonus according to the amount of blood stains found.

Dr. Hutchinson, lady house physician at the Royal Infirmary, said that when the deceased came to the institution on Thursday last, he complained of a burning sensation in the throat. On the Sunday the glands of the neck were swollen and he was semi-conscious. He died during the following morning.

In answer to Mr. Trenholme, who appeared for the relatives, Dr. Hutchinson said they did not come definitely to the conclusion that it was a case of anthrax until the post-mortem.

Dr. Eurich gave corroborative evidence, and said that when first he examined Stuttard he found nothing but a sore throat. Though they could not definitely conclude that the deceased suffered from anthrax on the Sunday prior to death, they (witness and Dr. Hutchinson) decided to take precautions against anthrax. At the post-mortem examination witness was able to cultivate anthrax bacteria very sparingly from the blood covering the brain and the lungs. The cause of death was anthrax, the seat of inoculation being the throat.

In answer to the Coroner, Dr. Eurich said he had had considerable experience with anthrax patients. At times it was beneficial to give inoculations of anti-toxine serum. A great amount of time and research had been given to the question.

The Coroner said that having to deal with a case of anthrax gave him an opportunity of drawing attention publicly to a letter he received yesterday from the secretary of the British Union for the Abolition of Vivisection, in which it was stated that she was instructed to ...

Continued from Page 30

through after some years of experiment in which he often put himself at risk of anthrax by culturing the bacteria in the lab.

All dangerous wools were to be directed to one port – Liverpool – while rigorous precautions would be instated at the various mills.

Eurich realised anthrax was caused in humans by contact with blood from an infected animal. He refused to take on trust the word of suppliers who said their wool was blood-free. Eurich became adept at spotting the minutest speck.

Formaldehyde was to be used as disinfectant. This, and careful inspection of fibres, was to mark the beginning of the successful battle against anthrax.

The unfortunate Bernard Stuttard had his own place in history – his case came in the middle of the worst year for anthrax cases Bradford ever had. From then on, the disease would be on the retreat. Antibiotics, which were to come along a few years later, would

Dr Eurich saved the lives of thousands of wool workers

cure when prevention and immunisation had failed.

Eurich, a modest, kindly and considerate man, retired in 1937. In recognition of the fact that he had saved thousands of lives, he was awarded the Gold Medal of the Textile Institute – a rare honour for someone outside the industry.

And 25 years after his death, in 1954, Bradford Civic Society presented an oak seat to Bradford Technical College as a memorial.

T&A

1918

Explosion of joy as the Great War drew to a close

END OF THE HORROR: *Soldiers are able to relax near the front as the end of the terrible conflict drew near. Right: The sober reporting in the Bradford Telegraph of the news the whole world had been waiting to hear*

THE TRIUMPH OF RIGHT.

CEASE FIRE!

Germany Submits

ARMISTICE SIGNED.

END OF HOSTILITIES.

KAISER A FUGITIVE.

Seeks Refuge in Holland.

HINDENBURG'S FLIGHT.

ARMISTICE TERMS.

EVACUATION OF BELGIUM.

ALSACE-LORRAINE AND RHINELAND.

ALLIES TO OCCUPY RHINELAND.

GREAT REJOICINGS.

SCENES IN LONDON.

NEWS IN BRADFORD.

STIRRING SCENES IN THE CITY

BUSINESS SUSPENDED

RECRUITING SUSPENDED

Thank God, the war is over

A fter 52 months and some 20 million casualties the Great War ended on the 11th hour of the 11th day of the 11th month of 1918. The eerie silence that descended on the shell-shocked battle-fronts in Europe contrasted with civilian explosions of joy and thanks.

The Bradford Daily Telegraph soberly focused its attention on the bigger picture - the terms of the peace, what was going to happen to Germany's Kaiser.

Monday, November 11, 1918

The same pattern followed on the 12th and 13th. But on the 14th most of the front page was taken up with a huge advertisement from the Bradford Dyers' Association Ltd offering back jobs to textile workers in the forces. Those too crippled or maimed for work were offered awards from a specially-

Continued on Page 33

OUT COMES THE BUNTING:

Workers at the cloth warehouse and spinning mills of Salts Mill decorate their workplace with bunting after news of The Armistice came through

Continued from Page 32

created fund worth £180,000. The Bradford Daily Telegraph saluted the venture in that day's editorial.

Today, after such a war, newspapers would give themselves over almost entirely to reports and pictures, commemorating the historic event and reflecting on what had led up to it. The day after the Gulf War ended, for example, the T&A published an eight-page supplement.

But 81 years ago The Bradford Daily Telegraph, price 1 penny, only had six broadsheet pages and these were crammed tight with adverts, stories, and snippets. 'Triumph of Right' ran across all six columns on the back page, the main news page in those days. News of the Armistice, however, was carried below a modest two-column headline. As though conscious of the inadequacy

News of the Armistice was greeted with joy

of its main news coverage, the paper published a four-page extra. Again, however, this tabloid-sized special concentrated entirely on the war at large. Neither the main paper nor the special edition had any photographs either from the Western Front or here in Bradford. The only war photographs the paper carried were of Bradford soldiers, killed or wounded in action: and there were plenty of those.

From 1916 onwards the number of

these photographs increased in volume. After the first day of the Somme in July, 1917, during which the British Army suffered 60,000 casualties, 20,000 of them fatal, whole broadsheet pages were surrendered to the cigarette card photographs of these men.

In all, the armed forces of Britain and her Empire lost about one million men. Of these up to 5,000 came from Bradford and the surrounding district; and of these the majority served with the 16th and 18th battalions of the Prince of Wales' Own West Yorkshire Regiment - the Bradford Pals - so gravely decimated during that penultimate summer of the war.

Bradfordians had to wait until The

Continued on Page 35

LOCAL HEROES IN THE WORLD'S GREAT CONFLICT.

[558th SERIES.]

ROLL OF HONOUR: *Columns of faces stared out of the pages of the Bradford Weekly Telegraph listing those who had given their lives in the service of their country in a four-year campaign that resulted in the deaths of millions of soldiers across Europe*

Continued from Page 33

Bradford Weekly Telegraph was published on November 15 to see how the peace was celebrated.

The front page carried a cartoon from Punch, showing a distraught Kaiser contemplating his ruin. 'The Sands Run Out' was the caption. On page three there were numerous un-illustrated reports.

On the Monday evening, after council business, the newly-elected Lord Mayor, Alderman Joseph Hayhurst, accompanied by his wife the Lady Mayoress, and representatives from the Labour, Liberal and Conservative parties had mounted a spot-lit rostrum outside City Hall and given speeches of thanks for the peace. Two rockets were fired after each speech. A band then played 'Pack Up Your Troubles'.

Before the Monday evening show at Manningham Lane's Theatre Royal the manager, Mr W Havers, addressed the audience who cheered and sang the National Anthem. On behalf of all assembled he dispatched a telegram of congratulations to Sir Douglas Haig, commander-in-chief of the British Army.

The Bradford branch of the YMCA, then based in Forster Square (completely different then to what it looks like today) organised an open-air celebration in which massed choirs led by the Central Hall Brass Band sang popular hymns. Messages from prominent people were flashed up on a screen fixed to the side of the YMCA building.

"Now that we have won the peace in this war, let us see to it that a League of Nations makes it secure for all the world," read the one from J M Hogge MP.

The paper reported services of thanksgiving at both Bradford Cathedral and the Methodist-based Eastbrook Hall. The latter service was packed. Handel's Hallelujah Chorus was sung. The Rev W Bradfield said the next job God had given the Allies to do was to feed the German people; the conscience of the world was not going to allow them to starve.

Page 8 of The Bradford Weekly Telegraph included a sombre reminder of the cost of war: 104 head-shots of Bradford soldiers killed or wounded in action.

But there were other soldiers' photographs too, not included in the role of honour. These belonged to men like Private Harry MacDonald of Keighley, Private Arthur Wild, Private Herbert

JOY: *Workers at Mitchell Bros (Bradford) Ltd in Manchester Road break out the bunting after news of peace, left*

Crimmins, and Private Louis Harris of Leeds.

They were all shot at dawn for alleged cowardice in the face of the enemy. Louis Harris, who had been rejected by

the Army on medical grounds two years before he was called up (such was the slaughter on the Western Front) was shot in October, 1918, a month before the Armistice; the last British soldier in the 1914-18 War to be executed by firing squad.

More than 300 British soldiers were executed. Most of them were battle-front veterans. Private Harris, for example, served for two years before he succumbed to shell shock. Harry MacDonald had fought in the Boer War. He had volunteered for service in 1914 and had seen action at Gallipoli.

Wild and Crimmins, both Bradford Pals (they served in the 18th Battalion), had volunteered for the Army. They were non-combat troops who carried food and drink to the Front. On the eve of Haig's proposed advance on the Somme the two had gone drinking after their day's duty and had missed that evening's parade. They panicked but after three days' absence returned to the Army.

They were shot at dawn on September 5, 1916. The firing squad vented their feelings by placing flowers on their graves.

Men such as Wild, Crimmins, MacDonald, and Harris were forgotten during the post-war thanksgiving services in November, 1918.

The Hallelujah Chorus was sung at packed church services

T&A

1919 *Women showed their true worth in in wartime roles*

Clippies step down.. for now

PASSING OF THE TRAM GIRLS.

AN APPRECIATION.

PLUCKY WAR WORKERS.

This is the last day on which the women conductresses on the Bradford Corporation tramways are to carry out their duties. To-morrow they will all be replaced by men. "Good-bye, lady conductress!"

To-day was the leave-taking of the dainty conductresses who in war-time emergency "punched our tickets" on the Bradford tramways.

"How sorry we shall be to see the last of you we cannot fully express. You have been a war-time wonder. Munition girls, land girls, W.A.A.C.'s and W.R.E.W.s and all the great host of patriotic girls who slipped into the breach when the boys went away, all have had their pæans of praise, but you seemed to be in danger of passing without recognition and unhonoured.

"It must not be.

"You achieved the impossible. At least, everybody told us when you went on the cars that it was 'no woman's job,' and that you would be under the doctor most of the time.

"Were you? Experience showed that in the severest of weathers you stuck to your post with heroic fortitude.

U rban women started to do 'men's work' for the first time during the First World War - and the men weren't always happy.

Trades unions often protested at 'dilution' of skilled labour in factories, but there was a shortage of males and so they had to put up with it.

Many thought the genie would be put back in the lamp when the war was over - but for many women the whiff of freedom and independence was too alluring, and things were never to be the same again.

That wasn't too obvious, how-ever, on April

Tuesday, April 8, 1919

8, 1919, when Bradford's tram conductresses stepped from the platform for what seemed to be the last time.

The Bradford Daily Telegraph recorded the event in a way which would make the blood of modern women boil: 'Today was the leave-taking of the dainty conductresses who in war-time emergency "punched our tickets" on the Bradford tramways.

'How sorry we shall be to see the last of you we cannot fully express. You have been a war-time wonder. Munition girls, land girls, WAACs … and all the great host of patriotic girls who slipped into the breach when the

boys went away, all have had their paeans of praise, but you seemed to be in danger of passing without recognition and unhonoured.

'It must not be.

'You achieved the impossible. At least, everybody told us when you went on the cars that it was "no woman's job" and that you would be under the doctor most of the time.

'Were you? Experience showed that in the severest of weathers you stuck to your post with a heroic fortitude…

'In the words of your Australian soldier admirer you were "the most dinkum, dainty ornament" he had seen…"It required no little courage, as you often did, to turn out week after week in the cold small hours of the morning and begin your daily toil when most people were still snug in bed. But you stuck it - manfully! - and you don't seem to be the worse for it!

'The shop girls and office girls of Bradford may well envy your rosy cheeks, glowing with the bloom of a healthy, open-air life'… Yes, and toes glowing with the bloom of healthy chilblains as well, no doubt…'

Sadly the world's economy took a downturn almost immediately the war was over and jobs became hard to get, for men as well as for women.

The Roaring Twenties of the jazz age soon gave way to the Hungry Thirties of the Depression.

It was to take another world war to get women out of the home again - and this time there was to be no going back…

T&A

1920 The 'Factory King' is given a new Bradford home

Tribute to a champion of child workers

SUFFER THE CHILDREN: *The statue of Richard Oastler, now in North Parade, commemorating the 19th century benefactor who worked tirelessly for the rights of children forced to work in Britain's factories during the industrial revolution*

The statue of Richard Oastler, the great factory reformer in the Nineteenth Century most of whose pioneering work was done in Bradford, can be seen in North Parade, not far from the Manor Row and Manningham Lane junction.

This is the third site of John Birnie Philip's fine sculpture. Cast from three tons of bronze and costing £1,500, the three-figured piece was originally located in Forster Square: it was unveiled on Saturday, May 15, 1869, eight years after Oastler's death at the age of 72.

In October, 1920, the statue was dismantled and removed to a new site in Rawson Square where, according to the Bradford Daily Telegraph, it was hoisted into place on Thursday, November 11, and remained there until 1968 when it was removed for a

Thursday, November 11, 1920

third time to its present place.

Most records declare that the statue was re-located in October, 1920: they are incorrect. The actual date is significant because on that November Thursday, when workmen hauled Oastler on to his pedestal in Rawson Square, the body of the Unknown Solider was being lowered to rest inside Westminster Abbey. Just as the Unknown Soldier represents all Allied troops killed in battle, Richard Oastler battled for more than 20 years to represent the unknowns of the 19th Century factory system.

Born in Leeds in 1789, the year of the French Revolution, this fiercely single-minded man

Continued on Page 38

Continued from Page 37

spared neither himself nor his diminishing band of friends in his battle to persuade Parliament to lower factory hours for children.

He was 41 when he was given a graphic description of working conditions for children in the new textile factories springing up in the West Riding. The hours were long, the wages low, the treatment often brutal. He described the new worsted mills of his day as "Magazines of British infantile slavery".

Children were expected to work 12 to 14 hours a day in stiflingly hot rooms. If they were unfortunate enough to fall asleep they risked a beating or being dowsed with cold water by the crueller charge-hands. Oastler's blood boiled.

He was not a man to be trifled with and set his obstinate mind against this social evil. He campaigned up and down the land, addressing meetings in all weathers, lobby-

Oastler set his obstinate mind against this social evil

ing the great and the good - including the Duke of Wellington. He wanted a reduction in working hours to a maximum of ten.

He got it in 1847 when Parliament passed the Ten Hours Act specifying that no child or woman factory worker should labour for more than ten hours per day. This difficult but good man became known as The Factory King.

His pen was fiery and prolific - he wrote more than 100 pamphlets on a wide range of subjects. Even four years in a debtors' jail didn't stop his writing. Every week he wrote the next edition of Fleet Papers, published by two Londoners.

Oastler's enemies called him a fool and a madman.

He died in Harrogate on August 22, 1861.

Thousands of factory workers attended the interment at Kirkstall, and services were held in both Huddersfield and Bradford. Committees were set up to collect funds for a public memorial, and Bradford was honoured to be chosen as the place where it would be.

Alas, Bradford has the habit of shunting the statues of its public benefactors about to suit the needs of motor traffic. The statue of Sir Titus Salt was moved from outside the town hall to the front of Cartwright Hall in Lister

PRIDE OF PLACE: *The Oastler statue is moved to its second home in Rawson Square, above and right, where it stayed until 1968, finally forming the centrepiece of a pedestrianised area in North Parade at the top of the city, below*

Park, and then to the darkest and dankest corner of the park where it has lingered ever since.

Similarly, The Factory King's statue was considered a traffic nuisance and was moved to Rawson Square and then to its present site on North Parade. Between 1988 and 1990 the area was tidied up and turned into a little piazza. But few people pass that way, and even fewer know of the achievements of the man on the pedestal.

T&A

1921 Bradford got the first machine outside London

X-ray hospital vision

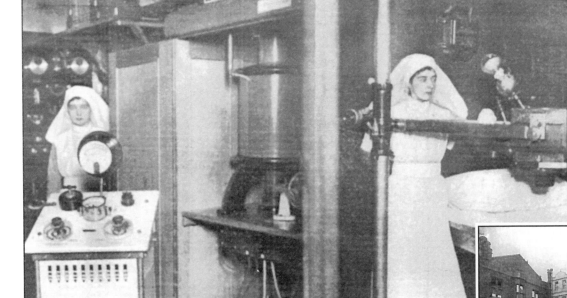

X-RAY CURE: *Nurses at Bradford Royal Infirmary get to know the huge new £1,000 X-ray machine which it was hoped would help cure cancer*

Bradford has never been slow to put its collective hand in its pocket when help was needed - even when there hasn't been much in the pocket.

So when the board of management of the Bradford Royal Infirmary heard about a new X-ray machine for the treatment of cancer in 1921, they went ahead and bought one - confident that the city would make sure that the apparatus was paid for in a short time.

The Bradford Daily Telegraph of August 8, 1921, was enthusiastic: 'This is a department of scientific investigation and research in which great strides are being made; in fact the advances already recorded are such that it is claimed there are now hopes for sufferers which could not have been entertained a few years ago.'

The new 230,000 volt machine, said the Telegraph, 'is the result of gradual evolution and improvement of X-ray plant to enable it to give out rays of very high voltage … which are capable of penetrating to a depth of six inches or more below the skin surface without running any risk of damaging the skin itself.

'By this means it is possible to treat many cases of malignant disease, such as can-

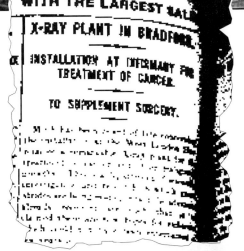

WITH THE LARGEST
X-RAY PLANT IN BRADFORD
INSTALLATION AT INFIRMARY FOR
TREATMENT OF CANCER
TO SUPPLEMENT SURGERY.

**Monday,
August 8, 1921**

cer of the stomach, even when the patients are in such a condition that a surgical operation would be impossible.

'With the apparatus now installed at Bradford very valuable work has been done in treating malignant growths of a more superficial character.

'It is not intended that the new apparatus shall supplant surgery in suitable cases,

but rather that it shall supplement it, and perhaps bring hope and relief to the many sad cases which are beyond the surgeon's skill.

'Excellent results obtained on the Continent and in America are vouched for by undoubted authorities and several of the London specialists speak most highly of the treatment. Not only is the apparatus capable of doing the heavy class of work involved in the treatment of desperate cases, but it is also suitable for the efficient treatment of the lightest class of work, such as surface skin conditions.'

The machine was the first to be installed anywhere outside London - the sort of thing which was always a matter of pride to Bradford.

'In this respect [it] will no doubt be warmly appreciated by the public, to whom the call of suffering humanity always makes a strong appeal' said the Telegraph.

The Infirmary's existing X-ray equipment had been largely paid for by public generosity. The new plant was to cost £1,000 - 'and the board feels that in this latest venture it will have behind it the practical sympathy and support of the citizens of Bradford.' It did.

T&A

1922

Day the canal became redundant after 150 years

A SORRY SIGHT: *The derelict Spinkwell Lock (above) before it was removed in the mid-1990s. LEFT: Bradford Canal basin in its heyday back in the early 19th century*

Goodbye to Bradford's 'River Stink'

There was nothing in the way of fuss when the Bradford Canal was officially closed in mid-July, 1922. The city was glad to see the back of the waterway which had been known for decades as "River Stink".

The final journey of a barge along it, before the canal was allowed to dry out and be filled in piecemeal, was marked by the Bradford Daily Telegraph only with a photograph and caption.

An active life of almost 150 years was

**Saturday,
July 15, 1922**

over, and the general view was "good riddance!"

The idea of the Bradford Canal had been hatched in 1770 after the Leeds-Liverpool Canal Company was formed with two prominent Bradford business men - John Hustler and Abraham Balme - representing the Yorkshire committee in discussions with their Lancashire rivals.

Continued on Page 41

MEMORIES: *The Leeds-Liverpool canal at Dockfield, Shipley, with the start of the spur which was the Bradford Canal on the left*

Continued from Page 40

The two of them were understandably keen to have a link with Bradford. In 1771 Parliament granted an application "for making a navigable cut or canal from Bradford to join the Leeds and Liverpool Canal at Windhill".

By 1774 the Leeds-Liverpool canal, being built in stages like the Aire Valley road more than 200 years later, had progressed eastwards as far as Thackley and the Bradford link had been cut along the valley bottom, from Dockfield at Windhill to the end of Kirkgate. It immediately halved the cost of transporting goods in and out of the city centre.

As the Leeds-Liverpool Canal marched further to the east, Bradford soon had a direct link with the North Sea through Leeds and Hull as well as with the Irish Sea through Liverpool. But it was very much a mixed blessing.

Water for the canal had to be drawn from Bradford Beck, which before the

Water for the canal had to be drawn from the polluted beck

Industrial Revolution was a pleasant trout stream. But as industry grew, and the population with it, so did pollution. The grease which was scoured out of the wool was flushed back into the Beck. Refuse was dumped in it, too. It became little more than an open sewer, t'Mucky Beck of popular memory.

By 1860 the water in the canal basin - which was, of course, water from the Beck but no longer flowing - had become so stagnant and foul that little lads used to tie tapers to the end of poles and for laughs would set light to the gases rising off it.

The canal went out of action in 1867 but was soon opened up again by a new company, which not only built a

new canal basin but also new warehouses and a pumping station to take rather fresher water from the Leeds-Liverpool Canal rather than the beck.

The amount of traffic using the canal had declined dramatically following the arrival of the railways. However, it continued to be used until July 15, 1922, when a Bradford Daily Telegraph photographer was on hand to record the last journey of the barge Beta from Bradford to Shipley. Gradually it faded from sight and from memory, although a reminder of it came in 1960 when workmen excavating Forster Square found the old wooden foundations of the wharf at the canal basin. They also exposed the canal bed which was found to contain thousands of oyster shells from an oyster bar once used by the canal workers.

The canal lingers on in the names of Wharf Street and Canal Road. There is a bridge which once crossed it at the bottom of Livingstone Road, Bolton Woods. And until very recently there was the solitary, surviving, weed-entangled Spinkwell Lock, close to the junction of Canal Road and King's Road. It was dismantled to make way for new car showrooms and the stones and timbers from it are piled up on a piece of land on the Boar's Well nature park nearby. All that remains of the Bradford Canal is the canal basin at Dockfield, Shipley, which was once the point at which it joined the Leeds-Liverpool canal.

T&A

1923
Park Avenue filled to capacity to see the Yorkshire greats

LOCK-OUT: *Stewards struggle to close the gates at Park Avenue for the Roses match against the old enemy in August, 1923*

OLDEST DAILY PAPER

BATTLE OF THE ROSES: AMAZING SCENES.

GATES CLOSED BEFORE THE START.

AMBULANCE REQUIRED FOR MAN WHO CLIMBED THE WALL.

BRILLIANT BATTING BY HOLMES

(By Our Own Reporter.)

PARK AVENUE, Monday. — a perfect summer's morning.
the Battle of the Roses in a favourable
Several contributory factors responsible for
the scenes at Park Avenue this morn-

been scored. One run later, namely at
Leyland was out to a weak stroke, b ing caught
at short leg by E. Tyldesley, and the home
interval arrived with Yorkshire 152 for 3.

Further Encroachments on the Playing Area.

Special took advantage of the

The stuff of true legends

FEARSOME: *Bad-wicket specialist Edgar Oldroyd and 'temperamental' fast bowler George Macaulay, above, and right, the legendary Wilfred Rhodes*

There was only one place to be on August Bank Holiday Monday in 1923 - Park Avenue cricket ground in Bradford, where Yorkshire were facing the old enemy, Lancashire. The day was hot and sunny, the match was nicely poised - if you were a Yorkshireman - and by three quarters of an hour before play began the ground was full Thousands were locked out, even after ground staff had toured the seated spectators asking them to 'shove up a bit' to let another one

Yorkshire were on one of their charges towards the county championship

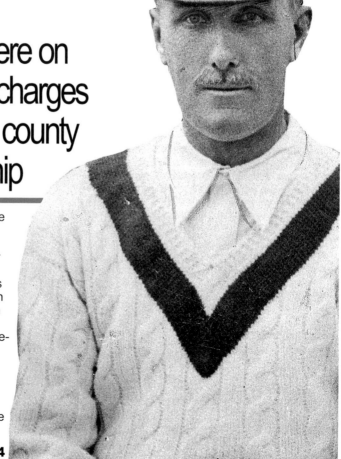

Monday, August 27, 1923

or two sit down. 26,000 were reckoned to be crammed into the ground that day.

The happiest, said the Bradford Daily Telegraph, were those who had to sit on the grass. At least they could move their legs. After the lunch interval, during which spectators had spilled on to the hallowed soil of the pitch, a mounted policeman, at the suggestion of Yorkshire skipper Rockley Wilson, was used to

usher them back behind the boundary ropes - a tactic which had worked just the year before at the first ever Wembley Cup Final.

Roses matches had always roused greater interest than any other (sometimes even more than Test matches).

But the 1923 game was special.

Apart from the glorious weather, there was the prospect of a victory because Yorkshire were on one of their most formidable rolls. The County

Continued on Page 44

Continued from Page 43

Championship was well within reach - in fact nothing short of an outbreak of bubonic plague was going to stop them winning it. Lancashire were not a bad side - they had the Tyldesley brothers playing, and England wicket-keeper George Duckworth. But Yorkshire had a side which could - and did - trouble Test teams. Not surprising, since eight of the team at Park Avenue were, or were to become, Test players themselves.

The list is, in fact, part of the Who's Who of great White Rose cricketers:

● Percy Holmes and Herbert Sutcliffe, one of the greatest opening pairs any county ever had;

● Edgar Oldroyd, probably the best bad-wicket batsman never to play for England, and the man who, at Pudsey St Lawrence, helped guide the young Len Hutton;

● Maurice Leyland, a stylish but powerful left-hander of whom Hutton once recalled, with awe, 'his forearms were thicker than my thighs!';

● then came the stuff of legend - Wilfred Rhodes, the greatest all-rounder of his or any other time, who had opened the batting for England and took more wickets than any other player in the history of the game;

● Roy Kilner, left-arm bowler, was also handy with the bat and popular outside the county (when he died tragically young while coaching in India, 100,000 were said to have lined the streets of Wombwell for his funeral);

● Emmott Robinson, the essence of Yorkshireness, handy batsman and a seam bowler who cherished the shine on the ball like a lover;

● George Macaulay, hot-tempered fast bowler who could change to quickish off-spin and be just as destructive;

● Abe Waddington, mercurial fast bowler with what we'd now call 'an attitude';

● Arthur Dolphin, wicket-keeper who could bat a bit but in this season rarely needed to - Yorkshire usually declared;

● and Rockley Wilson, captain and spinner whose bowling had sometimes changed the course of a game.

Wilson probably had the easiest job of any county captain. Indeed up to a couple of years before, before the retirement of the other great all-rounder, George Herbert Hirst, the title of captain had been almost an honorary one.

The skipper would toss the coin and then retire to the outfield, leaving the important decisions to his senior professionals - Rhodes, Hirst and Robinson.

Along with Schofield Haigh, and before the arrival of Emmott Robinson, Rhodes and Hirst made up The Triumvirate - a title for the rule of three which came from Ancient Rome, but which was appropriate for Yorkshire in their great days.

Any number of players

LEGEND: *Herbert Sutcliffe is surrounded by eager autograph hunters who worshipped at the feet of the Yorkshire greats of the 1920s' championship sides*

There was never any question that Yorkshire meant business

have been credited with the description of the terseness of the Roses game: 'We say good morning on t' first day then after that we just say 'ow's that?'.

But there was never any question that Yorkshire meant business when they went on the field. It was a hard school but it bred greatness.

Herbert Sutcliffe, elegant and with unflappable dignity, the man who put the silk shirt on the professional cricketer, was to see his opening partner Percy Holmes, a victim of lumbago, replaced by a young lad from Pudsey called Leonard Hutton. And Wilfred Rhodes, in his 50s and approaching the end of a career which would never be surpassed, was asked to cast an eye over some of the slow left arm hopefuls aspiring to his crown.

The lad who finally got the nod was called Hedley Verity, and the Rhodes verdict was simply: 'He'll do'. And he did.

Thus was the torch handed on.

It's hard to understand or appreciate, at a time when television provides a diet of top-rated sport almost round the clock, what Yorkshire's cricket meant to its inhabitants for the first half of this century.

Len Hutton once said: 'You get the impression in some of the counties, particularly in the south, that they don't much care about who's winning. But here, it's very, very important that Yorkshire are winning'.

For the record, Yorkshire beat Lancashire by eight wickets over that Bank Holiday weekend. Before the middle of August they had again won the County Championship - and there were still five more games to play. They had lost only a single game. They had won the championship the year before and were to win it again in 1924 and 1925.

LINE-UP: *A 1950s reunion of Herbert Sutcliffe, Abe Waddington with his wife, Maurice Leyland and Brian Sellars*

T&A

1924

Dozens in miracle escape as building caves in on workers

Four killed in mill collapse

WRECKAGE: *The collapsed Zetland Mill building which killed two wool workers and two builders, and how the Bradford Daily Telegraph reported the disaster*

T he cracks in the ceiling at Zetland Mill had been spotted a couple of days earlier, and builders had been called in to do something about them. But they were too late. As they manipulated beams and supports, a terrible, rending crash shook the three-storey mill. The top floor collapsed, crashing onto the second floor, and smashing that into the ground floor.

At half past nine on the morning of Thursday, January 10, 1924, the staff, mostly women spinners and twisters employed by G H Leather Ltd at the mill in Wharf Street, on the Wapping side of Canal Road in Bradford, were minding their

Thursday, January 10, 1924

machines and conversing by lip-reading. Many had their minds on the weekend ahead. Christmas was still a cosy memory. Some were as young as 14.

Then, seemingly with no warning, Zetland Mill collapsed, even while the builders were trying to shore it up.

Four people - a woman and three men - died. Two of the men were the builders' workers, in the basement, which took the full force of three collapsing floors full of machinery.

The woman who died was a widow, Mary

Anne Edmondson, whose body was the first to be recovered, almost five hours after the disaster. Her five children all worked for Leather's.

Two of the dead men were from Ellis Balmforth's, the builders.

Meanwhile rescuers tore the skin from their arms, hands and faces pulling at the wreckage to locate survivors.

Police and firemen joined millworkers. They in turn were joined by Salvation Army officers, priests - many of the employees were Catholic - and the Reverend W Cunliffe, vicar of nearby St Chrystostom's, who knelt bareheaded in prayer on the debris.

What tore at the hearts of the rescuers was the knowledge that there were people trapped inside who were badly injured, maybe dying, who could not be reached quickly and in safety. The wreckage had settled uneasily - a shout may have caused it to collapse further.

By four o'clock, six and a half hours after the collapse, up to a dozen were still feared trapped, while warper Isabella Devine, from

Queensbury, had been reported dead. She turned out to be badly injured, but survived.

Other survivors had stories to tell of miraculous escapes - one warehouseman saw the ceiling sagging towards him and made it to the exit just in time.

Errand boy Tom Grady had just been sent out into the yard on a 'message' from the combing room. A few seconds later and he would have been under tons of rubble and steel.

Considering the nature of the accident, and the fact that up to fifty people were in the mill at the time, the casualties were mercifully light - four dead and 21 injured.

T&A

1925 *Bradford put on a great show to outdo York's offerings*

We showed them!

REST: *Show goers take a breather from the huge number of attractions at the Thornbury showground to take advantage of the excellent refreshment fare on offer, lovingly described by a T&A reporter*

The third and last day of the Yorkshire Show ended at Thornbury on a note of satisfaction. Nearly 60,000 people had attended, and overall receipts in excess of £8,600 were expected.

Although total attendance was 22,000 down on the last show hosted by Bradford in 1914, the difference was compensated for by the increase in receipts from £5,393 to the eventual figure of £10,295.

Above all, however, the numbers attending the Bradford show was more than 20,000 greater than had gone to the show at York in 1924. And that was what seemed to count beyond any other consideration, presumably because York was the historic home of the Yorkshire Show.

As the Bradford Daily Telegraph of July 22, the first day of the show, explained to its readers: "It is interesting to recall at this juncture that the Yorkshire Agricultural Society was founded on October 10, 1837, under the chairmanship of Earl Spencer. The expressed object of the society was to

Friday, July 24, 1925

further the industry and science of Agri-culture. The first show was held at York in the following year."

So, anything York could do Bradford had to do better.

The railway companies assisted by offering single fares for return journeys to anyone living within a 50-mile radius of the show. A daily excursion was run from Goole.

The Telegraph was highly conscious of this competitive spirit throughout the three days of the show, constantly comparing the quantity of visitors, the number of entries, the receipts, even the volume of private cars parked, with the York show.

"There are no fewer than 4,128 entries, against 3,464 at York last year, and 2,038 in Bradford in 1914," the paper

announced, and then went on to specify the total for each category of animal, fowl, and vegetable even down to allotment holders' produce (635) and something called implements (261).

The show was held on 55 acres of land off Thornbury's Woodhall Lane; another ten acres was set aside for parking, the arrangements for which were managed along the lines of the so-called Ascot System. This entailed parking vehicles in a herringbone pattern, which was supposed to maximise numbers and minimise inconvenience.

On the first day 9,000 "gainly-dressed folk" paid five shillings admission (25p) and made their tour of inspection. Among them, "swarthy farmers and their ruddy-cheeked daughters were as much interested in the seemingly endless variety of attractions as the more fashionably dressed town-dweller's wife and daughters, though

Continued on Page 47

HAND-OUT: *Surplus milk from the Great Yorkshire Show is commandeered for distribution to the poor in Thornbury by Central Hall Mission Sisters.*

Continued from Page 46

the typical country folk were in the ascendancy today," declared the Telegraph's anonymous reporter.

A rain storm during the morning briefly clouded the day. Another downpour overnight merely freshened up the air for day two. More visitors were expected, partly because admission had been reduced to three shillings (15p).

More than 30,000 spent the Thursday admiring the animals on show and the various other diversions, such as the Italian sunken garden. The Telegraph kept up its barrage of comparative statistics, striking a melancholy note when they let the side down.

"Yesterday there was a falling off, however, of the number of motorcars parked. The official park garaged only 420, as compared with about 500 on the previous day, while there were twenty-one motor-bicycles, about the same number as on Wednesday."

Disappointment turned rapidly into incredulous jubilation, however, when the Telegraph's reporter chanced to bump into Mr Fred Redhead, the obliging managing director of Messers. Spinks, Ltd., the caterers, who offered the consolation of food, mountainous quantities of it.

You can almost see the reporter shaking back his shirt cuffs and licking his lips before compiling with relish:- "360 7lb sand-wich loaves were used for the 8,000 sandwiches,

which required 1,200lbs of ham; 5,000 tea-cakes were sold, 600 fancy cakes, 170 gallons of milk were used, and 189lbs of tea…Two thousand bottles of mineral waters were sold, while the number of bottles of ale ran into many thousands."

But not all the milk was kindly used. When the farm animals had been assembled prior to the opening of the show the Telegraph discovered that quantities of milk from freshly-milked cows were being poured away.

The waste so enraged the Reverend Sam Rowley that he went along to Thornbury and "commandeered" the milk for the poor of his Bradford parish.

The Telegraph published a photograph showing the Central Hall Mission Sisters distributing free Yorkshire Show milk to people in terraced houses.

"For luncheons the figures were almost as astonishing," the reporter went on, his excitement mounting with the approach of the main courses. "600lbs of beef, 21 carcasses of lamb, 500 chickens, 350 ducks, 1,500 dinner buns, 5cwt of cheese, a ton of

potatoes…1,100lbs of slab cake, 15 gallons of cream, 450lbs of jam, and 150lbs of marmalade."

Could the people of York boast such a collective appetite? The question, though never asked, was implicit in the gargantuan amount of detail.

And so the third day dawned, with admission down to two shillings (10p). Half Thursday's crowd turned up to take advantage of it, however; nevertheless, the Telegraph reported that the overall attendance of 58,130 was still greater than the average for the five previous shows.

All the timber used for the stands, the fences, and other erections was taken down and sold off at auction the following month. Even the set of offices put up at the entrance was offered for sale.

In July, 1934, the show returned to Thornbury. Attendance was only 52,894. The poor figures were attributed firstly to excessive heat, and then rain, thunder and lightning on the third day.

T&A

1926
New Zealand tour party lifted the gloom of harsh times

Relief from the Great Depression

HARSH: *Textile workers at Tong Park, Baildon, who were on short-time working, cut up logs for fuel. Right, a new daily newspaper is created for Bradford as the year ends*

TO-MORROW.

AMALGAMATION OF THE BRADFORD TELEGRAPH and ARGUS.

FROM TO-MORROW, 16th December, the Bradford Daily Telegraph and the Yorkshire Evening Argus will be amalgamated and produced under the title of the Bradford Telegraph and Argus. The best features of both papers will be retained and developed.

The arrival of New Zealand to pit themselves against Bradford Northern came at a time when the nation's mineworkers were still in conflict with Stanley Baldwin's Government. The General Strike had come and gone, but the miners were still angry and the Bradford Daily Telegraph's back page (the

Wednesday, October 20, 1926

main news page in those days) was still leading on the story.

It was also the year that John Logie Baird gave the first demonstration of a television image to the Royal Institution of Great Britain, in London - four years after the BBC began regular broadcasts by means of the wireless.

And it was the year when today's Telegraph & Argus was born, created out of an amalgamation of the Bradford Daily Telegraph and the Yorkshire Evening Argus on Thursday, December 16.

Seventy-three years ago Northern played their games at Birch Lane, just across the road from Odsal. Up to 5,000 spectators turned out in dull weather for the afternoon match (floodlights didn't arrive for another 21 years), which was kicked-off by Bradford's Lord Mayor, Alderman J Stringer.

"Northern got plenty of possession from the scrums, but their backs could make little headway chiefly on account of dropped passes," reported the later edition of the Telegraph.

At half-time Northern were trailing 18 points to five. At the end of the second period, which took place too late for the paper, the New Zealanders trotted in winners by 33 points to 17.

That Saturday's Yorkshire Sports was disposed to be rather dismissive about the

Kiwis' play:- "Against representative opposition their opportunities are bound to be limited because of the probability of being beaten in the pack as, in fact, they were by Bradford Northern."

Between October and early January 1927, the Kiwis had three matches against a representative side from Great Britain. The New Zealanders lost the first 28-20, the second 21-11, and the third 32-17.

Today, of course, the New Zealanders are a rugby super power - second only to the Australians in League, and at least on a par with the World Champions of Union, South Africa.

T&A

1927 Half a million crowd at Giggleswick experience total eclipse

Awesome spectacle of nature

MAGICAL: *The total eclipse of the sun viewed in all its glory from Giggleswick, where top astronomer Sir Frank Dyson set up camp, right*

PHOTOGRAPHING THE ECLIPSE AT GIGGLESWICK.

It was, said the Astronomer Royal, a race between the sun and the clouds; and the sun won - just.

The total solar eclipse of Wednesday, June 29, 1927, was a spectacle Yorkshire was determined not to miss, since the last one had been 203 years before. The last one in Yorkshire had been before the Norman Conquest, fully 900 years before.

This time it would be all our own. The Astronomer Royal, Sir Frank Dyson, was setting up his observation base at Giggleswick and that, decided thousands of people, was where the action was going to be.

Almost half a million people were estimated to have travelled to the north to watch the

Wednesday, June 29, 1927

moon pass across the face of the sun - the greatest natural spectacle. Giggleswick rubbed its hands, but not without a few worries - lots of people meant lots of trade, but also a fair bit of disruption.

The other worry, which nibbled at the travellers, was the weather. If it was cloudy, the whole thing would be a washout. The most they could expect would be a brief period of darkness just after six in the morning - not uncommon in the industrial West Riding. The Telegraph & Argus of the night before

announced happily that the sun was shining over Giggleswick; but the weather had been unsettled for days and there was cloud about.

All through the night the sightseers kept arriving. Among them was former Prime Minister Ramsay MacDonald, complete with binoculars which he obligingly brandished for photographers.

School parties, scouts, guides and students from all over the north spent the first hours of dawn trudging up the road from Settle. Other visitors admired Giggleswick School, next to which Sir Frank had set up his equipment, guarded by the school's Officer Training Corps.

As the great event approached, and sunrise arrived at 4.47, there were leaden hearts to match the leaden sky - but just after five the first rays of the sun showed above the cloudbanks.

Spectators with protective glass 'ooooh-ed' when they saw that the moon was already crossing the disc of the sun. As it rose, more and more of the surface disappeared.

Suddenly the sun was clear of the clouds. There was going to be a show. Birds stopped singing. The air grew colder. The watchers stopped talking. Many of them felt a vague, unspecified fear which must have crossed the human mind throughout its history.

No matter that this was the scientific age - here was the source of all life on earth … disappearing. A coppery light shone on the earth as totality approached. The scientists were counting off the seconds.

When it arrived there was an awe-struck silence. As the sun disappeared completely behind the moon the corona, the sun's atmosphere of blazing gas, burst into view. A pink solar prominence, maybe half a million miles long, soared above the surface. In the all-too-brief moments of totality, it was seen to change its shape.

It was the outstanding moment for the Giggleswick watchers. They were the lucky ones. Elsewhere on the track of totality, just 30 miles across, cloud had defeated sightseers. In Bradford the eclipse, which would have been over 99 per cent total, offered nothing more than an eerie darkness in the morning. For the Giggleswick travellers, it was an experience of a lifetime.

T&A

1928

Bradford picked up on a craze sweeping into the country

STILL POPULAR: *Speedway drew big crowds in the 1970s at meetings like this one at Odsal Stadium*

The latest craze sped into view...

The 1920s was the decade of The Latest Thing. It didn't much matter where it came from (though America was tops) - as long as it was absolutely the latest it didn't even much matter what the thing was. The public wanted it. The newest dances, the freshest films, the most gimmicky records - we gobbled them up.

About the only thing we didn't go a bundle on from the USA was Prohibition, a doomed experiment which lasted not quite 14 years and sparked a wave of

Thursday, June 21, 1928

lawlessness which put organised crime firmly on the map - and on the cinema screen.

On June 1, 1928, the Telegraph and Argus announced the latest thing - this

Continued on Page 51

RACE TRACK: *The grey-hound track at Dudley Hill, where a 'dirt track racing' circuit was to be built.*

‘RAPH AND ARGUS, FRIDAY, 1 JUNE, 1928.

A BRADFORD BROOKLANDS?

DIRT TRACK RACING TO BE HELD AT GREENFIELD: THE NEW SCHEME.

Motor-cycling dirt track racing—the new and popular sport from Australia—is likely to be held in Bradford. A conference towards coming to an arrangement for the use of the greyhound racing track at Greenfield, Dudley Hill, was held this morning between the Bradford and District Motor Club and the Greyhound (Greenfield), Ltd., (writes "Rob").

The conference lasted for some time, but was adjourned till Monday, when further ails of the scheme, including that of

cindered track, 16 yards wide, which will be of greater extent than many other tracks, and it will afford space for light cars participating. One end of the track will be slightly banked, giving one style of cornering. The other end will be flat and will give an entirely different mode of cornering—that is, skidding from broadside turns.

The greyhound track, which was opened on 8 October, 1927, is an excellently ... having eight ... ered

WOME

MRS. C
TF

SU

"I thi
trained, co
well as a
of the w
now is dire
training shi
sentative to

Continued from Page 50

time from Australia. Greenfield greyhound stadium at Dudley Hill was proposed as the arena for the new sport of motorcycle dirt track racing, an exciting spectacle with a fair proportion of thrills and spills as riders roared round a shale track on brakeless, gear-less bikes. A Bradford Brooklands?', wondered the T&A, Brooklands being the banked race-track where marques like Bentley, Bugatti and Auto-Union competed. Probably not.

The Bradford track was a lot smaller. It was planned to put the dirt track inside the line of the dog track which was about 150 yards by 75 - a bit longer than the average football pitch, and about as wide.

The promoters hoped to have the track up and running in a few weeks, and were pleased with the existing facilities. But they were adamant that there would be one major difference between watching the dogs and watching the motorbikes - the latter would have no betting involved at all.

The T&A motoring correspondent, 'Rob', reported: 'If wagering is discovered at any meeting the events will be suspended until the offenders are ejected or otherwise dealt with.' The idea was to have one end of

'Dirt track racing' stayed in the city, off and on, for nigh on 70 years

the track banked for fast cornering, and the other end left flat, for sliding round the bend in broadside turns.

'Dirt track racing' was not the catchiest of names, certainly not for the decade of The Latest Thing.

So it was little surprise when it became universally known as speedway, which tripped off the tongue much easier. It was to be a part of the Bradford sporting scene on and off for nearly 70 years, having its last fling at Odsal Stadium in the late 1990s.

In the end it seemed to be running out of steam, and the fans were no longer turning up in large numbers. But it was still one of the longest-lasting Latest Things from the 1920s.

T&A

1929 JB Priestley produces an instant best seller

A novel approach

The publication of a major new novel by the 35-year-old Bradford-born writer J.B. Priestley in the midsummer of 1929 was an eagerly-awaited event. The Bradford Daily Telegraph had been anticipating it since the end of the winter.

The newspaper's "Topics" column of March 6 had reported that the new novel "is to be of exceptional length." It added: "The average novel of today is of about 80,000 words, but the well-known Bradford author is to break away from this convention, and he will employ some 250,000 words in the telling of his story. This will be a return to the practice of the great nineteenth century novelists."

The columnist concluded: "Anyone who is acquainted with Mr Priestley's previous books will anticipate that though the new one may be long, it will never be tedious."

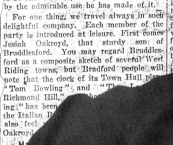

AUGUST, 1929.

ADVENTURES OF 'GOOD COMPANIONS.'

MR. J. B. PRIESTLEY'S NEW NOVEL.

DELIGHTFUL COMPANY.

In his new book, "The Good Companions" (Heinemann, 10s. 6d. net), Mr. J. B. Priestley trumpets defiance to the cult of the tabloid novel. Here we have a tale which takes 640 large and well-filled pages for the telling.

Mr. Priestley has apparently said to himself, "This England is an enthralling country. It is dotted all over with fascinating towns and villages, each crowded with folk who say and do odd, pathetic, jolly, brave, or whimsical things. Let us ramble around and talk to as many of them as possible, and not hurry about it."

Obviously when one sets out on such an adventure one's observations are not compressed into any ridiculous little pocket volume. The author requires ample space. Mr. Priestley has taken it, and, let it be said at once, has justified his liberty by the admirable use he has made of it.

For one thing, we travel always in such delightful company. Each member of the party is introduced at leisure. First comes Jesiah Oakroyd, that sturdy son of Bruddlesford. You may regard Bruddlesford as a composite sketch of several West Riding towns, but Bradford people will note that the clock of its Town Hall plays "Tom Bowling" and "The [...] Richmond Hill," [...] ing," has been [...] the Italian R[...] also feel [...] Oakroyd [...]

Tuesday, August 6, 1929

When The Good Companions was published, the Bradford Daily Telegraph's reviewer certainly wasn't disappointed. In fact, like millions of readers since, he was enthralled by the story of Jess Oakroyd and his adventures after leaving the mill town of Bruddersford to explore the wider world and eventually join the Dinky Doos concert party.

Continued on Page 53

J.B. PRIESTLEY O.M.
1894 - 1984
novelist, playwright
and essayist
was born here
13 September 1894

Continued from Page 52

"The reader is inevitably reminded of another writer who loved public houses and wayside encounters with anybody and everybody - Dickens, of course," he enthused. "Mr Priestley has the same gusto, the same zestful appreciation of their comic qualities. He invests his worst characters in a glamour which obscures their baser characteristics, and presents them mainly as figures of fun."

The Good Companions was a huge success immediately. An initial print run of 7,000 - considered to be quite a risk by the publishers - was repeated 25 times over within two years. Bradford Public Library acquired 120 copies for its bor-

His novel was 'like a cool shower on an arid land'

rowers but there were still long waiting lists as the novel broke all library records.

The Bradford Daily Telegraph commented: "This may be attributed to the fact that it struck a new line in literature. People had got tired of 'sex' books and 'problem' books, and The Good Companions came like a cool, refreshing shower on an arid land."

There was nothing but praise from every quarter for this masterpiece from the writer who was born in Mannheim Road, Bradford, on September 13, 1894, the son of a teacher at Belle Vue Boys' School - which the young Priestley was later to attend and, indeed, become its most famous pupil.

He left school in 1910 to become a junior clerk with wool merchants Helm and Co in the Swan Arcade in Market Street. His heart was no more in the wool trade than it was in formal education, though. He spent as much time as he could mingling with local journalists and artists, or visiting theatres and music halls. He also began to write.

After 1914-18 war service he returned to Bradford for a while and began to write articles for the Yorkshire Observer (then a morning daily) on walking trips in the

FAMOUS SON: *J. B. Priestley in the 1930s, far left, and above, the house where he was born in Bradford. Left, at last a statue in recognition of his achievement is lowered into place in Bradford*

Yorkshire Dales. But soon after his marriage to his first wife, Pat Tempest, Priestley moved to London and never again lived in Bradford - though he visited the place frequently, and its influence continued to show itself in his work for many years.

Indeed, it was Bradford which inspired what is probably his best-known short piece of work - his 1939-45 wartime morale-boosting broadcast about a perpetually-steaming meat pie in the window of Robert's pie shop.

He was also instrumental in the founding of the Bradford Civic Theatre, where many of his plays were performed and which now honours him under its new name of The Priestley Centre for the Arts.

The author had a love-hate relationship with his home city, which often took offence at the things he said and did. But nevertheless in 1973, 11 years before his death in Warwickshire at the age of 89, he was made an Honorary Freeman of the City of Bradford, which finally deigned to acknowledge him as its son.

T&A

1930

Bradford needed to clean up its sales pitches

OPEN MARKET: *John Street market in 1954, with glass-roofed stalls and all the merchandise on open display*

A bit of order to market!

There had been a market in Bradford since 1251, thanks to Henry III. It was a bit late in coming, since Alfred the Great had established the first ones in England 380 years before.

Still, once it had arrived it was embraced enthusiastically, not only for the chance to buy and sell farm and craft goods, but also for the bit of excitement to be had from seeing strangers from such strange and outlandish places as Keighley or even Halifax.

What took the markets of Bradford out of the mediaeval

Friday, February 28, 1930

and into the modern world was the growth which came with the Industrial Revolution. Suddenly there were too many mouths for the local producers to feed. Although Bradford had much farmland within its boundaries, it wasn't enough to provide food for the whole population.

In the last century the markets grew, but they were sprawling and tatty in the main and less than healthy.

By the middle of the 19th century Bradford, proud of its

Continued on Page 55

COVERED: *Rawson Market, with the ubiquitous Albert Hanson's stores part of the 'furniture' of the landmark marketplace*

Continued from Page 52

municipal status, decided to clean up its various acts. In 1865 the Town Council voted in favour of making 'an application to Parliament for an Act enabling Miss Elizabeth Rawson, the Lady of the Manor, to grant, and the Corporation to accept, a lease for 999 years of the property in and about the Market Place, Kirkgate, and the Fair Ground, Darley Street, with all the appurtenances, belonging to Miss Rawson, and all the manorial and other rights and privileges to which she was entitled for life, as Lady of the Manor of Bradford, in connection with the holding of markets and fairs within the borough; or with respect to the inspectorship of or jurisdiction over weights and measures; to authorise the alteration or removal of the said markets and fairs to more suitable localities; to enable the council to take upon lease or appropriate other premises for a Cattle Market and Fair Ground, and to erect or provide suitable buildings and appliance for such markets; to prohibit the holding of any cattle market or fair in the streets, or other public or private places within the said borough, except upon the land so appropriated'… and so on, and so on.

In short, Bradford wanted clean markets on its own terms and without a lot of bull ordure littering the streets.

One of the first results was the opening, in

Now, a trip 'into town' became a memorable event

1872, of Kirkgate Market, an imposing building between Kirkgate, Darley Street and Godwin Street, selling everything from hats to books to pots, pans and bedding. It was demolished in 1974 in one of the acts of civic vandalism for which Bradford was to become notorious. Swan Arcade and the Mechanics' Institute were other casualties.

Between the opening of Kirkgate and its completion came Rawson Market, for meat and vegetables. This stood across Godwin Street from the other market.

It was on February 28, 1930, that the picture became complete. The Corporation bought a disused burial ground from the trustees of the Kirkgate Wesleyan Methodist Chapel for £3,750. On this was built the James Street market.

Now it was possible to furnish a house from top to bottom and put food on the table from stalls all within a short walk of each other. What the new set-up didn't provide, of

course, was excitement and spectacle. This needed a short walk across John Street where, in 1930, the open market became a reality, on the site of the Coppy Quarry Estate. This incorporated a new idea - glass-roofed stalls to keep off the weather but let the customers see what they were buying.

Not that this was ever a problem at John Street. You could see what you were buying because the stallholder would wave the merchandise around, juggle with it - enthralling if it was a 32-piece dinner service - and practically bash you over the head with it.

This, along with a plate of peas and mint sauce and a glass of pop, made a trip 'into town' on Saturday a memorable event.

The modern John Street, with its roof, its hygiene and its regulated calm, is a fine market - but it hasn't a tenth of the atmosphere of the old, open one. It reflected, on a small scale, what had made Bradford - doing the business, not being too flash, making a bob or two and making sure you kept hold of it.

It was epitomised by the pet stall which sold homing pigeons. It sold the same ones, it was rumoured, week after week because, being homing pigeons, once released, they flew straight home - to the stallholder's loft, where they went back into the basket and back to the market.

T&A

1931

Turning the city's waste into clear profit

The great clean-up

Construction of sewage works a wonderful engineering feat

It was John Wesley, a frequent and influential visitor to these parts, who said that cleanliness was next to Godliness. If he was right, then Bradford, in the 1860s, was the devil's backyard.

Plague, cholera, smallpox and typhus were frequent visitors and a government official, visiting the place in 1843, described it as 'the most filthy town I visited'.

Up to 1862, when the first sewage works was built, human waste and

Saturday, May 11, 1931

refuse was dumped into narrow cobbled streets and oozed its way to what is now Forster Square and into what was then the Bradford Canal.

Mill and other muck went straight into numerous becks and streams which turned black, smelt vile, and spread disease.

In 1868, six years after the first sewage works, a private citizen sued Bradford Corporation for polluting the River Aire. But nobody knew what to do.

Then, in 1874, work began on a sewage purification plant at Frizinghall. It worked, but wasn't able to keep up with the rush. 20,000,000 gallons of effluent a day was too much for a 38-acre processing site.

Something, clearly, was needed on a grander scale.

It was found in 1906. After long negotiation, the Corporation bought the Esholt estate of 1,900 acres and began to learn a new science and art - that of sewage and sanitation - to deal with what was acknowledged as some of the most difficult waste in the world at that

FROM THE DEPTHS:
The T&A picture of members of the Bradford Corporation Sewerage Committee emerging on a narrow gauge train after making the three-mile journey through the newly-constructed tunnel from Frizinghall to Esholt, left

time. There was also a major piece of civil engineering required - a tunnel to link Frizinghall with Esholt. Work on the boring started in 1913 but was interrupted by the First World War. It resumed afterwards but was a slow process.

Then, at three o'clock on a May morning in 1923, a charge of gelignite punched a hole through a six-foot barrier of rock and the tunnellers from Esholt shook

hands with those who had started from Frizinghall. They had met up with an error of only an inch or so over a distance of about three miles.

While the tunnel was being lined with two million bricks, work started on turning Esholt into a two and a half million pound waste enterprise. Tanks, pits, a

Continued on Page 57

A MAGNIFICENT ACHIEVEMENT:
Workmen constructing filter beds at Esholt in the Fifties

Continued from Page 56

presshouse, a grease house, soap and solvent plants, acid plants, filter beds, syphon systems and bridges were created and 27 miles of railway track laid to link them.

For Esholt was not just about disposing of waste. It was about proving the greatest Yorkshire adage about muck and brass.

Washing wool produced lanolin, a must for cosmetics and soap. Human waste could be turned into fertiliser. Industrial waste could be turned into oils, greases, waxes, paint and other useful little sidelines.

The selling operation began in 1903. By 1947, when Esholt had been in operation for a dozen years or so, £3,250,000 worth of sales had been reached.

No wonder then that a proud civic father, conducting the then Queen, now the Queen Mother, around the enterprise, is said to have happily told her: 'You know, ma'am, that lipstick you're wearing probably started life here'. Esholt's job specification was simple: to take Bradford's waste and turn it into pure water, a smell, and a profit. It succeeded so well after its official opening in 1931 that it became an unlikely attraction for civic delegations from around the world.

T&A

1932 Boom time for the dog tracks as race fever hit town

City goes to the dogs!

TOP DOGS: *The best racers in the country came to Bradford's new dog track*

Since time immemorial people have liked a bet - preferably on how fast an animal can run.

Since dogs and cats are the oldest associates of the human race, and since cats don't like exertion, it's a fair bet that the earliest wagers would be on dogs racing. The Egyptians probably did it.

In 1927 greyhound racing arrived in Bradford. Whippets, of course, had been raced for much longer than that. Greyhounds, needing a track, were somehow more glamorous and Greenfield Stadium, which opened in 1927 at Dudley Hill, Bradford, provided at least the illusion of glamour.

Monday, August 15, 1932

But the City Greyhound Track, which opened on August 15, 1932, was more ambitious. It announced itself as The Ascot of the North - and all this for as little as 9d (not quite 4p), with entry to the smartest part of the track for half a crown (12.5p).

The Legrams Lane track may not have had royalty riding down the course in carriages, or women in silly hats - but it did have 'Ascot-style' car parking. We now know it as herring-bone parking, where cars are placed like pieces of a parquet floor, making it easier to drive out and away without too much sawing at the gears. It probably also made it

easier for bookies to use binoculars to spot the number plate of the car they had just won, having already relieved the owner of his shirt, his pension and his wife.

Bradford easily supported the two stadia and they even enjoyed a boom after the Second World War, with the City Stadium's totalisator turnover running at £750,000 a year at one stage.

It even had a moment of fame worldwide when it featured in the film of John Braine's Room at the Top. And the crowds continued to flock in. There were, at one time, 11 meetings a week - day and night racing.

All was fairly rosy until June, 1963, when a fire broke out in the Tote office. It spread to the stand and to other buildings and did £50,000 worth of damage - say half a million at today's prices.

Racing started again, minus the tote. This was badly missed and attendances started falling. The killer blow, though, came from the Government. Up to the 1960s, betting was a furtive and surreptitious business unless you were actually on the racecourse. The writing and passing of betting slips was a criminal offence. The bookie's runner was somewhere between a figure of fun and what the boys' magazines called 'shady'. All this changed with the legalisation, in the 1960s, of betting shops.

On October 30, 1965, the 'Ascot of the North' closed. A month later the stadium, equipment - and even dogs - were flogged off in an auction. Greenfield held on until 1969 before the site was sold to property developers.

T&A

1933

Fears of repeat disaster of 'flu epidemic unfounded

PREVENTION: *Bradford City players keep healthy in Blackpool, and Park Avenue players gargle to keep the germs at bay during their Bradford training*

Nowadays if we get 'flu we tend to be philosophical about it. There's no cure, and it generally goes away within a couple of days or so. It can kill, but by and large it's a nuisance, not a menace. When an outbreak swept Britain in the winter of 1932-33, it was taken very seriously. Apart from affecting industrial output (already badly hit by the slump which was turning into the Depression), it carried memories of 1918-19, when 'flu was the scourge of the world, killing more people than the First World War. As many as 21,600,000 died world-wide. The toll in Britain was nearly a quarter of a million. When the 1933 epidemic was in full swing, Bradford took precautions, and it took them very seriously. On Tuesday, January 10, the footballers of Bradford City were photographed walking on the North Cliffs at Blackpool, preparing for their home Saturday Cup-tie with Aston Villa. Blackpool was a longish way to go for a stroll, but it was seen by the club as healthier than the sulphurous and sooty environs of Valley Parade. Across town, at Park Avenue, Bradford players were pictured indulging in regimented gargling as a precaution against illness.

'Flu is kept at bay

Tuesday, January 10, 1933

Sportsmen weren't the only ones taking care. Lister's Mill was sprayed with disinfectant and employees offered a gargle. And Corporation employees reported themselves as doing not too badly, thank you. Across in Leeds, the Tramways Department reported 200 workers down with 'flu. Bradford had about the seasonal norm for absentees. Naturally the T&A's advertisers were keen to trumpet the health-preserving qualities of their products.
Bovril, said its makers, was a pretty good way of not catching 'flu. 'Large employers

ADS: *'Flu was a great excuse to plug prevention products like Bovril, above, and Stout, left*

of Labour' were advised that tipping hot Bovril down staff at about 11 in the morning was 'a valuable safeguard' against infection. It would also be a valuable safeguard against falling Bovril profits.
Whitaker and Sons, the Halifax brewers,

were more reckless in their claims. Like the Bovril people, the brewery reckoned that a well-nourished body was the best defence against the virus. Standard Stout was a source of such healthy nourishment, a positive battlement against germs.'Take it daily and you won't take 'flu' promised the Whitaker's advert.
At least it would have been more cheering than beef extract at 11 in the morning…
As the epidemic went on, statistics started to come in - happy ones. Although there had been 70 deaths in Bradford in the week up to Friday, January 6, none of them had been directly attributable to influenza. The usual Bradford killers - bronchitis, pneumonia and emphysema - had taken their toll, but 'flu wasn't a factor.
Perhaps beef extract and stout worked after all…

T&A

1934
Bradford's debt to a brilliant composer

Death of a genius

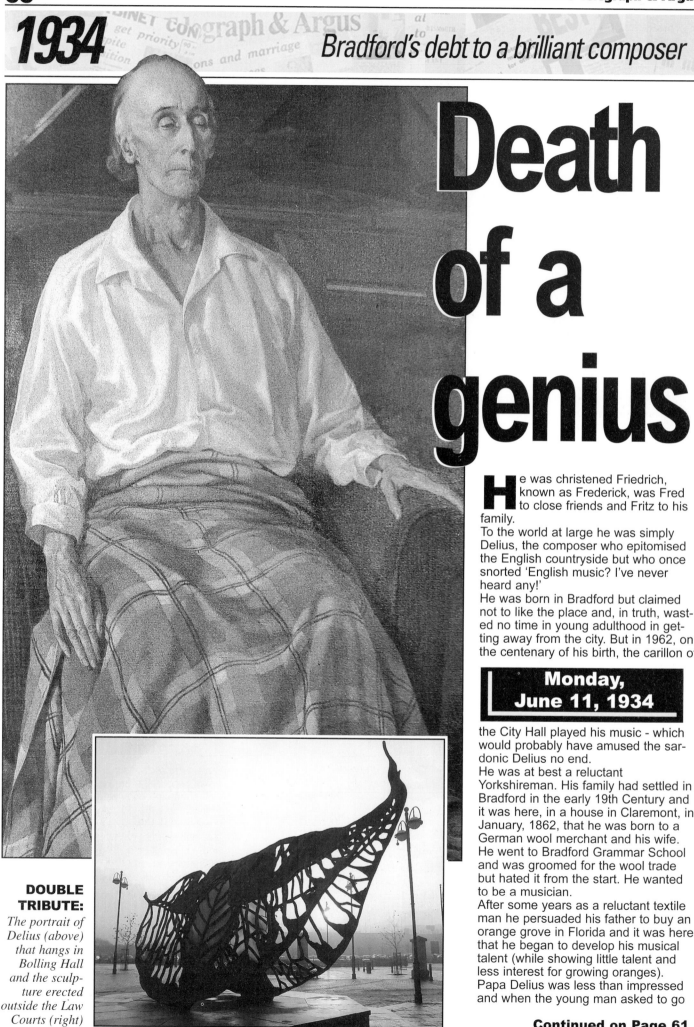

He was christened Friedrich, known as Frederick, was Fred to close friends and Fritz to his family.

To the world at large he was simply Delius, the composer who epitomised the English countryside but who once snorted 'English music? I've never heard any!'

He was born in Bradford but claimed not to like the place and, in truth, wasted no time in young adulthood in getting away from the city. But in 1962, on the centenary of his birth, the carillon of

Monday, June 11, 1934

the City Hall played his music - which would probably have amused the sardonic Delius no end.

He was at best a reluctant Yorkshireman. His family had settled in Bradford in the early 19th Century and it was here, in a house in Claremont, in January, 1862, that he was born to a German wool merchant and his wife.

He went to Bradford Grammar School and was groomed for the wool trade but hated it from the start. He wanted to be a musician.

After some years as a reluctant textile man he persuaded his father to buy an orange grove in Florida and it was here that he began to develop his musical talent (while showing little talent and less interest for growing oranges).

Papa Delius was less than impressed and when the young man asked to go

DOUBLE TRIBUTE: *The portrait of Delius (above) that hangs in Bolling Hall and the sculpture erected outside the Law Courts (right)*

Continued on Page 61

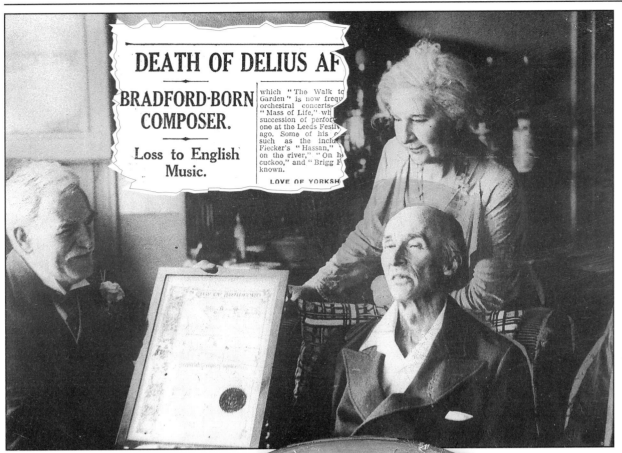

DEATH OF DELIUS AF

BRADFORD-BORN COMPOSER.

Loss to English Music.

which "The Walk to Garden" is now frequ orchestral concerts— "Mass of Life," wh succession of perfor one at the Leeds Festi ago. Some of his c such as the inclu Fiecker's "Hassan," on the river," "On h cuckoo," and "Brigg F known.

LOVE OF YORKSH

HONOUR: *Delius receives the Freedom of the City of Bradford, watched by his wife Jelka, two years before his death. The plaque on the left can be seen on the house in Claremont where he was born*

Continued from Page 60

to Germany, he was flatly refused. But teaching in America gave him some independence and he made it to Leipzig, birthplace of Wagner. He finally settled, with a growing musical reputation, in Paris and began a distinguished career, which was almost ended prematurely by syphilis. The blind and paralysed composer was living in Grez-sur-Loing, unable to feed himself and quite unable to pick up a pen and compose, when a young English music student called Eric Fenby heard of his predicament.

Saddened by what he heard, the young Yorkshireman offered his services to his fellow 'Tyke' and thus began one of the most remarkable artistic collaborations of the century.

Fenby acted as eyes and hands for the

FREDERICK DELIUS
THE COMPOSER
1862 - 1934
WAS BORN HERE

older man, though not without some tears of frustration. Delius, it seems, was tone deaf. He could hear his music in his head but, when he tried to sing it, it came out as a monotone.

He and Fenby finally worked out a system of composing, and works like A

Song of Summer were created. Delius may have turned his back on his native soil, but before trying to put down the opening bars of this, one of his last works, he said to his young assistant: 'Imagine we are sitting in the heather, on the cliffs by the sea'. Fenby, a native of the Yorkshire coast, knew just what he meant.

Although never held in the same regard as Elgar or Vaughan Williams, Delius's music has found its place in the hearts of many.

His major works, like A Mass of Life, require large ensembles and are not often performed.

But his 'miniatures', like On Hearing the First Cuckoo in Spring, or Summer Night on the River, or Brigg Fair - An English Rhapsody, are popular in the concert repertoire.

He died in 1934. It was a bad year for English music - Edward Elgar and Gustav Holst died in the same year. Delius was buried at Grez.

A wreath made of heather from Baildon Moor, a favourite haunt of the young Delius, was sent from the Lord Mayor and Citizens of Bradford.

It was only two years earlier that the freedom of the city had been bestowed on the composer, by this time already a Companion of Honour.

And when his desire to be buried in an English churchyard was fulfilled, it was at Limpsfield in Surrey that he was reinterred, 11 months after the first funeral.

FINAL RESTING PLACE: *Delius's grave in the churchyard at Limpsfield in Surrey*

T&A

1935

Yeadon's first step towards international status

Airport given OK to extend

SPREADING ITS WINGS: *How Yeadon aerodrome looked in 1935 (above) - a far cry from the arrival of Concorde around ten years ago (left)*

Ambitious plans for Yeadon aerodrome were reported by the Yorkshire Observer following a meeting of the Bradford-Leeds Joint Municipal Aerodrome Committee.

The proposals involved adding about 16 acres of common land and 120 acres of farmland to the aerodrome's existing 100-acre site, which accommodated a 1,000-yard runway from east to west.

"Negotiations for the acquiring of this land are proceeding and, if successful,

Tuesday, June 25, 1935

will enable the aerodrome to be developed in a southerly direction," reported the newspaper. "This will bring the boundary of the aerodrome to the boundary of the Horsforth Golf Club. And will provide for a runway in a northerly and southerly direction of 1,000 yards."

The committee also proposed illuminating the aerodrome for night flying. The work would involve installing floodlights, defining the boundaries by orange-coloured lights at 100-yard intervals, and using lights to mark all obstacles, such as hangars, club-house, chimneys

AERODROME PLANS.

Developments at Yeadon.

NIGHT FLYING PROVISION.

Floodlighting And Wireless.

THE ...dford-Lee... Join...

and trees. It would all be controlled from a central switchboard.

Wireless masts were to be installed, and there was also a proposal for building a small hotel where passengers and staff could find meals and sleeping accommodation.

Reported the Yorkshire Observer: "These improvements will obtain for the aerodrome the Air Ministry's highest

classification in their category for aerodromes and will enable it to be used by the largest planes at any time of the day or night."

They were grand designs and took some years to come to fruition. Gradually, the sleepy Yeadon aerodrome has been transformed into the modern, successful, Leeds-Bradford airport from which services now operate to many parts of the world and which is regularly visited by Concorde. The runway has been extended, and extended again.

But it wasn't until 60 years after that bold plan for night flying that it became a reality for commercial flights.

It was on May 1, 1995, after a long campaign waged by local opponents who were afraid that the noise of planes flying in and out would disturb their sleep, that the regulations were relaxed. No longer was the airport to be silent between the hours of 10pm and 6am. The first night-time flight in, from Las Palmas, arrived at 12.30am. That summer saw an increase of 48 per cent in inclusive holiday passengers passing through Leeds-Bradford.

The success foreseen by the members of the Joint Muncipal Aerodrome Committee all those years earlier had finally arrived.

T&A

1936

Speech to Bradford Diocese led to King's abdication

Bishop of Bradford's Reference to the King's "Need For Grace"

SKIPTON "CHIRRUP."

TRUE ASPECT OF THE CORONATION.

Why the Free Church Should Not Take Part.

Bishop helped in fall from grace

CHOICE: *The King and his wife-to-be, Mrs Wallis Simpson, a relationship which threatened the very fabric of the British monarchy*

On January 20, 1936, King George V died. His reign of 26 years had encompassed the First World War, the General Strike of 1926 and the Great Depression of the early 1930s.

Tuesday, December 1, 1936

The death of the avuncular, bearded King came at a time of growing anxiety and false optimism in Europe.

Continued on Page 64

How we reported the news

Emphasising one point which was material for a proper understanding of the intention of the service, the bishop said: "On this occasion the King holds an avowedly representative position. His personal views and opinions are his own, and as an individual he has the right of us all to be keeper of his own private conscience.

"But in his public capacity at his Coronation, he stands for the English people's idea of kingship. It has for long centuries been, and I hope still is, an essential part of that idea, that the King needs the grace of God for his office. In the Coronation ceremony the nation definitely acknowledges that need. Whatever it may mean, much or little, to the individual who is crowned, to the people as a whole it means their dedication of the English monarchy to the care of God, in whose rule and governance are

Telegraph & Argus
From the T&A of Tuesday, December 1, 1936

the hearts of kings.

"Thus, in the second place," continued the bishop, "not only as important as, but far more important than the King's personal feelings are to his Coronation, is the feeling with which we - the people of England - view it. Our part in the ceremony is to fill it with reality, by the sincerity of our belief in the power of God to over-rule for good our national history, and by the sincerity with which we commend King and nation to his Providence.

"Are we going to be merely spectators or listeners-in as at any other interesting function?" asked Dr Blunt "with a sort of passive curiosity? Or are we in some sense going to consecrate ourselves to the service of God and the welfare of mankind?"

Continued from Page 63

Promised social and agrarian reforms in Spain were to spark off a Right-wing revolt against the Government, which led to civil war. Germany was firmly under the heel of Adolf Hitler's National Socialist Party. Trades unions had been outlawed and opposition parties banned; discriminatory laws against Jews had been passed, and worse was to happen that November when synagogues were burned, shops smashed and looted, and Jews murdered.

But both British and American political conservatives only saw the new autobahns, the work programmes, the revival of Germany from economic and political chaos.

In Britain the unemployed felt abandoned and forgotten. Jarrow Labour MP Ellen Wilkinson resolved that Parliament should not forget them and organised a march from Jarrow in County Durham to London.

While all these things were happening, or about to take place, the British people waited for the Coronation of George V's successor, Edward VIII. They had no idea that the line of continuity between past and present, which the monarchy represents, was in jeopardy. A King had not abandoned the Throne since 1688, when James II fled from the advancing army of William of Orange. By one of those ironies of history, a

Dr Blunt played a key role in forcing moment

provincial man of the cloth, the Bishop of Bradford, was to play a key role in forcing the moment to a point of crisis.

The Right Reverend Alfred Blunt claimed he had never heard of Wallis Simpson, the American divorcee with whom Edward VIII had long been obsessed. But as a member of the House of Lords it is inconceivable that he was unaware of the tension between 10 Downing Street and Buckingham Palace concerning the King's determination to marry Mrs Simpson - once her second divorce had been granted.

The Prime Minister Stanley Baldwin was intent on keeping the matter as quiet as possible at home, though in high society circles abroad Edward's love affair with a married woman was the currency of gossip.

British Press barons were certainly aware of what was going on, but as members of the establishment they felt constrained to wait upon events; and

so the newspapers, which were also aware that something was going on, said nothing.

On the eve of Bishop Blunt's speech to the Bradford Diocesan Conference on December 1, Britain was at the point of a constitutional crisis. Edward VIII had given Stanley Baldwin an ultimatum: either Mrs Simpson became his Queen or he would abdicate.

Enter the Bishop and former T&A journalists Ronald Harker and Charles Leach (the latter was to become Editor).

Harker was sent to cover the Diocesan Conference and reported the Bishop's speech in great detail. His massive opening paragraph - nearly 120 words - touched on the matter of the moment and quoted Dr Blunt verbatim.

"The benefit of the King's Coronation depends under God, upon two elements: first, on the faith, prayer, and self-dedication of the King himself; and on that it would be unproper for me to say anything except to commend him, and ask you to commend him, to God's grace, which he will so abundantly need, as we all need it - for the King is a man like ourselves - if he is to do his duty faithfully. We hope that he is aware of his need. Some of us wish that he gave more positive signs of such awareness."

The last comment was the stick of

Continued on Page 65

Without the bond between the monarch and his people, a king could not undergo the rites of a Coronation

Continued from Page 64

dynamite: it implied that the King had become detached from grace - the spiritual bond uniting God, the monarch and the people - and that without this bond a king could not undergo the rites of Coronation. The subsidiary headline in the T&A spelt it out: "True Aspect of the Coronation".

Ronald Harker understood the nuance of the Bishop's remarks but sought corroboration from his colleague Charles Leach. The latter agreed with the former that the national media might be interested in the speech and so it was sent over the wires to the Press Association.

Nine days later the King took his irrevocable step. In a broadcast to the nation he declared that if he could not reign side by side with the woman he loved then he had no wish to reign at all. On December 11 the Abdication Act was passed by Parliament, and Edward and Mrs Simpson stepped into history as the star-crossed lovers, the Duke and Duchess of Windsor.

For years their story appeared the very stuff of romantic fiction; women especially felt for the Duke as though he was a tragic hero. That was not the view

PUSH: *The Bishop of Bradford, Dr Alfred Blunt, whose speech to the Bradford Diocesan conference played a key role in the downfall of King Edward VIII and his bride Wallis Simpson*

taken by Wartime Prime Minister Winston Churchill, nor was it the view of the wife of the Duke of York - George VI as he reluctantly became.

To Churchill, the Duke of Windsor, with his overt admiration for Hitler and desire to bring about a rapprochement between Britain and Nazi Germany, was at best an embarrassment and at worst a diplomatic menace.

The burdens which fell upon George VI's shoulders, especially during the War, took their toll of his health. His

wife, our present Queen Mother, blamed her husband's death in 1952 on his brother's selfish decision to put his own desires before his obligations to the nation, the Empire and the Commonwealth.

Alfred Blunt remained Bishop of Bradford for another 20 years, until his retirement in 1956. The Duke of Windsor died on May 28, 1972, at the age of 77. His wife lived on for another 14 years, dying in Paris on April 24, 1986. She was 89.

T&A

1937 *People made merry, despite rain – and the Great Depression*

Deck the streets in regal bunting!

The Merrie England pageant was among the casualties on Coronation Day, 1937.
The Lord Mayor of Bradford, Alderman George Carter, had been in charge of the arrangements for celebrating the crowning of George VI and was himself at Westminster Abbey on Wednesday, May 12, representing the city.
Other events, like a gymkhana at Baildon, were dropped because the weather was less than festive, but schoolchildren enjoyed the holiday feel of the day, as well as admiring their Coronation mugs and books.
Parades and processions went ahead regardless - it was, after all, only rain, and this was, after all, the West Riding, where we breed 'em tough…school halls were shushed to silence to hear the ceremony broadcast on the wireless from London. Apart from those inside the

Wednesday, May 12, 1937

abbey, only a tiny handful of very lucky people actually saw the Coronation.
The BBC's television service was not yet a year old, and nobody north of Potter's Bar had a set.
But Bradford was ready to celebrate, even if it hadn't seen. Bonfires, bunting, souvenirs, illuminations, flag-waving and an open-air stage constructed in Peel Park all helped to set the seal on the day.
The afternoon pageant performance in the park was washed out, but the evening one went ahead defiantly.
Busby's staged a giant firework display at Northcliffe playing fields while those who could afford it - Britain and most of the western world was in one of the worst depressions it had known - made merry.
In Bradford there may have been more than a tinge of sympathy for the new king. He hadn't wanted the job and, but for his brother's affair with Wallis Simpson, bringing about the abdication,

LONG TO REIGN: *The new King George VI with his Queen Elizabeth, and daughters the Princesses Elizabeth and Margaret after the glittering Coronation ceremony. Below, how the T&A reported the mood of the city at the joyous occasion*

he wouldn't have got it.
But fate's an odd thing. The Duke of York, a diffident, rather dull family man

Continued on Page 67

LONG TO RAIN: *The bunting was strung out across the streets of Bradford despite the rain as the loyal citizens of the city celebrated the coronation in the rain*

Continued from Page 66

afflicted with a stammer, was just what the nation needed with war less than three years away. He had also a wife who was made of two metals - solid gold most of the time, and stainless steel when necessary. The word 'duty', not a fashionable one these days, was to characterise the reign of George VI, through the war years until his early death in 1952 from cancer at the age of 57.

He may have been dull but he was, as far as his people were concerned, dependable.

All this was in the future on that rainy day in 1937.

A T&A photographer was posted at St Luke's Hospital to catch the first 'Coronation Babies'. There were four, two boys and two girls. Both the boys were called George - though the new king was always Bertie to his family - and one was given the middle name Rex, while one of the girls was Elizabeth Margaret (thus taking in both the new queen and her two daughters). The fourth girl would have been Elizabeth too, but her parents already had a Betty.

The T&A also pulled out all the stops to get pictures from around the West Riding of the celebrations, though each showed a sombre picture of rain weeping from leaden skies.

It was a pity - Bradford's budget for the celebrations was £6,500, a tidy sum, and maybe half a million at today's prices.

But children went home clutching their gleaming mugs - there must be thousands still wrapped in newspa-

per at the backs of cupboards in homes around the place even today.

And there was always the exciting prospect of seeing the Coronation at the cinema - as soon as the film had been processed and printed and put on the train.

The next Coronation, just 16 years later, was the event which first alerted the nation to the possibilities of television.

T&A

1938 *Basque refugees given shelter in Bradford from Franco regime*

YOUNG BASQUES AT RUGBY LEAGUE FOOTBALL MATCH.

Basque children, refugees from Spain, who are being cared for at Morton Banks, among the spectators at the Keighley v. Bramley football match at Lawkholme on Saturday.

LONG WAY FROM HOME: *Refugees from the Basque region of Spain are treated to a seat at a rugby league match during their stay in the area*

Flight from a dictator

Bradford has been a haven for generations of refugees. Latterly, Kosovans and Bosnians fleeing Serbian ethnic cleansing in former Yugoslavia.

After the Second World War, thousands of Poles, Ukrainians, Estonians, Latvians and Lithuanians made a home here because their respective homelands were under the political domination of Soviet communism.

Before them, Basques from Northern Spain came here rather than live under the political rule of the country's fascist dictator General Franco.

Franco, it may be remembered, led an Army revolt in July, 1936, against the democratically-elected Popular Front Government, which gained power in February of that year by promising social reform and especially land redistribution. This proved too much for the Roman Catholic Church and the Spanish Army. In the summer Franco invaded Spain from Morocco, and for the next three years savage civil war ravaged the country until the surrender of Madrid in April, 1939. During the course of the war cities sympa-

Monday April 4, 1938

thetic to the Government were bombed with the help of the Condor Legion - warplanes and pilots loaned by Nazi Germany. Guernica was one victim, Bilbao in the Basque country was another. The civil war roused many non-Spaniards to actively lend a hand against fascism. While most European governments preferred not to get involved, local communities organised their own Spanish Relief Committee and offered what aid they could to Spanish refugees.

Basques started to arrive in Bradford in 1937. There were up to 100 children in camp at Morton Banks Sanitorium,

POWER: *General Franco, who forced families to flee Spain after his invasion from Morocco that ended in his taking control of the country*

Riddlesden, for example. Keighley families were encouraged to invite them home to tea. Two of these children were nine-year-old twins Araceli and Alicia Morales, who became members of the T&A's Nignog Club for youngsters.

Other Basque refugees lived in the old Dr Barnardo's Home in Manningham - a leafy, middle-class suburb in those days. The plight of the Basques touched all classes of people. On November 21 the Duchess of Atholl addressed a mass

meeting at Keighley on the Spanish relief work being done in the country, and appealed for even more gifts of clothing and money.

Some of the exiles made a life for themselves as best they could. Luis Bersaluce, the camp chef at Riddlesden, married Maria Allende, one of the assistant cooks, at Keighley's Devonshire Street Congregational Church.

And then, on Monday, April 4, 1938, these beleaguered people either read or heard the news from Spain: Franco had followed up his air raids of two years before with a heavy artillery bombardment.

"Many Babies Among Victims," reported the T&A. "Families Surprised Walking in Bright Sunshine." Isn't that the way disaster happens? Not when you expect it, but out of a clear blue sky when you're thinking about something else.

The presence of artillery round Madrid meant that Franco's troops must be in a position of control: the end was in sight. Eighteen months after the Spanish capital surrendered, Nazi Germany invaded Poland on a trumped up pretext and Britain declared war. For the next six years the world had no time to worry about the fate of the Basques.

T&A

1939 *City folk awoke to read about the outbreak of hostilities*

Bradford at war

If the first casualty of war is truth, the second seems to be hard information. As Monday, September 4, 1939 dawned, both the Telegraph & Argus and its sister paper the Yorkshire Observer devoted space to fighting words...and the importance of the good old vegetable. 'Declaration Of War Found City Almost As Usual' read the banner headline on the back page of the Observer (the front was given over to the international situation). There was a picture of a newspaper seller

Monday, September 4, 1939

handing out copies of the T&A's special Sunday edition, but that in itself had dealt with only the Sunday sitting of the House of Commons.

The Prime Minister, Neville Chamberlain, had announced the outbreak of war to Parliament and then to the nation on the wireless just after 11am - too late for

newspapers.So it was left to the morning Observer to bring the West Riding up to date.

There was a map of Poland on page one, a useful contribution because there were many who weren't too sure where Poland was, rather like, 40 years later, the Falklands crisis had many people hunting for the atlas.

There was news of local children who had been evacuated and there were plenty of

Continued on Page 70

READ ALL ABOUT IT: *Anxious readers gather round the T&A paper seller as he hands out copies of the paper's special edition*

The vision was of a land laid waste by bombs

Continued from Page 69

hints about what to do in the event of air raids.

Air raids, popular opinion held, would be the key to the whole thing. The bomber would be the crucial weapon in the coming conflict. Stopping it, or at least minimising its effect, would be the main priority for the nation.

As it turned out, the key weapons would be scientific - things like radar, asdic for submarine detection, improved radio communications, better rocketry. And the war-winner in the air would be the fighter in its various guises, as interceptor stopping bombers, as ground-support, firing tank-busting rockets, or as reconnaissance platform, pinpointing submarines or watching troop build-ups.

But in 1939 the vision was of a land laid waste by bombs, its people poisoned by gas, overrun by invaders. Indeed Neville Chamberlain, pictured waving to the crowds as he left Downing Street for the Commons, had his secretary with him, carrying his gas mask.The secretary was the young Lord Dunglass, later to renounce the title of Lord Home to become Prime Minister himself, as Sir Alec Douglas-Home.

There was another face on that front page - the new First Lord of the Admiralty, Winston Churchill, who had been invited to join the War Cabinet. And it was the Admiralty who had the first bad news of the war - within 24 hours of hostilities beginning, the passenger liner Athenia was sunk by a submarine off Ireland with 1,400 on board. Most were saved but many were lost. Survivors from the West Riding were soon able to tell their tale to the T&A.

Continued on Page 71

DOING THEIR BIT:
Men report to the recruiting office in Bradford to join up following the declaration of war. The mood of the times was even captured in advertisements carried in the T&A, left

FINAL WHISTLE:
Day one of the war - and sport is already counting the cost of impending battles with Germany

SUNDAY, 1939.   SPORTS SECTION.   7

Still No Gleam For Football.

All League Football Is "Off."

PROFESSIONALS TO DISPERSE.

THE English Football League and the Scottish Football Association held special meetings yesterday, and both left that all contracts between clubs and their professionals shall be suspended. Thus all organised football is in abeyance.

The Football League Management Committee met at Crewe, and Mr ... the secretary ...

BUT MORE MEETINGS COMING.

West Riding F.A. Advice For Leagues.

By George M. Thompson.

THERE is still no hint that football will be resumed even ... scale.

Huddersfield Cricket Decision.

Outstanding Game Cancelled.

A MEETING of the Huddersfield & District Cricket League was held last night to decide something in regard to the outstanding fixtures of the season. Most of the clubs still have three matches to play.

The president, Mr. W. H. Bolt, after expressing his sorrow that they should have to meet under such depressing ...

How we reported the news

England and France together have honoured their bond to Poland. Come what may, we stand committed to fight for the cause of freedom, individual and national. For the rights of the person against the tyranny of force. For the sanctity of the pledged word against the violation of engagements. For the supremacy of

Telegraph & Argus

Yorkshire Observer leader article, September 4

democracy against the onslaught of 'the pestilence of Nazi tyranny...' '...there is much to do. The grim realities of conflict have already entered millions of homes. The call to sacrifice has been made and answered, in part, by young and old. Never before has the personal contribution of people of all ages and degree been so widely spread. As we value our homes, our families, our heritage and our beautiful country, so shall we make that contribution which may enable this solemn task to be accomplished soon.

CITY TO FARM: *Bradford evacuees Eric Hartley, centre, of Ashbourne Way, and Billy Walton, right, of Peterborough Terrace, with Billy Worsley, whose family's farm in Hebden, Upper Wharfedale, had become their home*

Continued from Page 70

The ship, they said, had been sunk without warning by a U-boat which then surfaced and fired on the Athenia.It was, it was felt, about par for the course with the Germans. Memories were stirred of 'Hunnish beastliness' from the First World War.

But the horticultural shows went on, and with added vigour - Dig for Victory would be the slogan for allotment holders, and austerity and plain, hard slog would be the key to victory.

So would fair shares for all, and within two days of the outbreak, shopkeepers were urging customers to register with them for the purposes of rationing. But the Yorkshire Observer's own flower show was put on hold, and many sporting fixtures were cancelled. Children, moved out of the city away from the bombers, were pictured splashing in the River Wharfe.

And still the real news failed to come in...France was said to have invaded Germany (which technically it had, establishing a toehold on what was once again being called the Western Front) and Polish bombers were said to have bombed Berlin (which was complete fiction).

The horticultural shows went on... with more vigour

By the end of September, Poland would lie shattered, split between Hitler's Germany and Stalin's Russia. The two dictators had signed a peace treaty earlier in the year. Britain's idea that Germany could ever be starved out of the war became fantasy at that point - Russia could supply Germany with grain, oil, metal, in fact just about anything it could pay for.

Poland was why Britain went to war. It was a guarantor of the central European's state's neutrality and, when Germany invaded it, had little choice but to declare war. But where to fight?

This was a problem throughout the first

Continued on Page 72

CASUALTY: *Within 24 hours of hostilities starting a U-boat sank the liner Athenia off the coast of Ireland. Survivors from the West Riding were soon to tell the T&A of their ordeal*

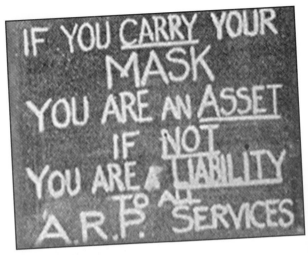

BE PREPARED: *The slogan in front of an ARP post in Bradford and, right, office girls taking heed of the message during a lunchtime stroll. Below, the brave view of a French newspaper, repeated in the T&A*

If Hitler Wants Peace He Must Put His Cards on the Table

" IT is up to Hitler now to lay his cards on the table. Then the Allies will give their decision," remarks the French newspaper, "Petit Journal," commenting to day on Mr. Chamberlain's reply in the House of Commons yesterday to Hitler's "peace offensive" moves.

" Chamberlain's speech sounded to us like an 89 per cent. No."

As war went on, the grimness of the situation was apparent

Continued from Page 71

year of the war - everybody knew where the bully was, but nobody could get within punching distance. Hitler held a potentially-winning hand.

As the war went on, the grimness of the situation was apparent. Two things were to change all that.

First Hitler, emboldened by his hatred of 'Bolshevism', would perform the stupidest act of his life - invading Russia.Then Japan, flown with its successes in the Pacific, would do something equally stupid - bombing Pearl Harbor and bringing America into the war.

From that point the Axis forces were doomed. It was just a matter of time before the democracies, fuelled, fed and armed by the USA, gained the strength to invade mainland Europe, signalling the end for Hitler's brand of Fascism.

And Anglo-American co-operation on a newly-discovered form of energy would bring Japan, two of its cities reduced to piles of radioactive ash, to the brink of ruin.

But that was years in the future in 1939, as Bradford sat down to its newspapers and wondered what the future held.It might not have known what had happened, or what was going to happen, but it knew where its duty lay.

TRYING TIMES: *Bradford parents learn how to use gas helmets for babies at a demonstration at St Oswald's School, Little Horton*

T&A

Defiant spirit as

the bombs fell

AIR RAID: *The Bradford skyline is lit up by fires from the bombing raids. Below: Picking up the pieces in Brunswick Place*

The Battle of Britain took place over the skies of South-East England in the summer of 1940, after the fall of the Low Countries and the capitulation of France.

On June 23, Hitler took time out to play the tourist in Paris visiting, among other places, the Eiffel Tower and Napoleon's rose-coloured sarcophagus at Les Invalides. All that remained between him

Saturday, August 31, 1940

and total victory in the West was Britain.

Invasion barges were massed in France's Channel ports; merchant ships were converted by teams of ship-builders. Operation Sea Lion, the invasion of Britain by sea, merely required the German Luftwaffe to knock out the Royal Air Force. But there was a time limit; Hitler was keen to turn his victorious forces East to strike at the real enemy - Stalin's communist USSR.

Nazi occupation of Holland and Belgium gave Germany's pilots access to the airfields of Northern Europe; their bombers could raid more of Britain simply by flying across the North Sea and then striking 60 to 70 miles inland. The coastal ports and

the manufacturing cities between them became vulnerable.

Bradford experienced four raids between August 22, 1940 and March 14, 1941. The first, at 11.13pm on August 22, resulted in three bombs falling on Heaton Woods.

The second, six days later, came at 1.30am. Four bombs hit Bradford, but the damage was minor and the six casualties were only slightly injured.

The third, on Saturday night and Sunday

Continued on Page 74

Continued from Page 73

morning of August 31 and September 1, 1940, started at 11.13pm and ended at 2.40am, during which time 116 bombs caused considerable if random damage in and around the city centre and over a broad area beyond. One woman died and 111 other people were reportedly treated for injuries.

On Monday, September 2, the Telegraph & Argus was only able to report in general terms that a North-East town had suffered bomb damage. Naming specific locations and buildings was considered advantageous to the enemy and so was not allowed.

At a time of tension, with the outcome of the Battle of Britain undecided and invasion expected soon after, the T&A leader column took a defiant stance.

"If the Germans think they are going to win the war by setting departmental stores on fire and dropping bombs on shops, then they are going to be very much mistaken…Why play the German game by magnifying the effects of an attack which, taking into account its duration and severity, caused comparatively little damage?"

A confidential report listing the damage in Bradford runs to 15 paragraphs. The biggest fire gutted Lingard's departmental store in the city centre. The adjoining Kirkgate Chapel was also gutted. A bomb tore through the roof of the Odeon cinema and landed in the stalls. A five-storey slice was blown out of a wool warehouse packed with bales in Crossland Street, off Manchester Road.

In Rawson Market the fruit section was squashed and gutted by fire; part of the meat section got a roasting too. Sharp's carpet and lino shop was burned out. After the raid delayed action bombs exploded, one of them in the middle of the city near a church.

Everywhere, windows were smashed, blown out, or cracked. Tramlines were down in places as were telephone lines. Smouldering rubble and the lingering acrid smell of smoke greeted Monday morning's commuters.

A high-explosive delayed action bomb blew up that morning in the garage of a bus company.

DAMAGE: *Lingard's departmental store is badly damaged in one of Bradford's raids, and, above left, the bus depot is similarly affected. Below, broken windows in the Halifax Building Society branch office*

The building and a number of vehicles were damaged, and a crater 30 yards in diameter was left into which curious onlookers peered. Tyrrel Street, Aldermanbury, Sunbridge Road, Upper Millergate, Northgate, Otley Road, Wapping Road, and Laisterdyke all received major and minor damage.

Windows were smashed, blown out or cracked

By the time the bombers returned - at 8.46pm on March 14, 1941 - the war's course had altered. The RAF's victory in the Battle of Britain ensured that invasion via the English Channel was no longer a realistic threat. The Luftwaffe, which had come within a week of destroying the RAF on the ground (by bombing Fighter Command's bases and coastal radar stations), was redirected to blitz British cities, principally London, by night.

The raid on Bradford that March night seems to have been the heaviest in terms of the number of bombs dropped - reportedly 595. Few, if any, would have been the kind of high-explosive blockbusters unleashed on the capital. The damage appears to have been slight: two houses demolished, eight others damaged, plus a railway cabin in Clayton. Casualties were light.

Nearly two months later a German bomber on fire crashed in Idle and burned out. Three people were killed and five seriously injured. Two cottages were demolished, and two more badly damaged.

The pilot landed in Bradford and was captured. The three remaining crew members were captured in another part of the West Riding.

That, more or less, was Bradford's war.

1941 Food became a luxury as rationing imposed

FOOD RATIONS: *You didn't get much on your plate with the weekly rations*

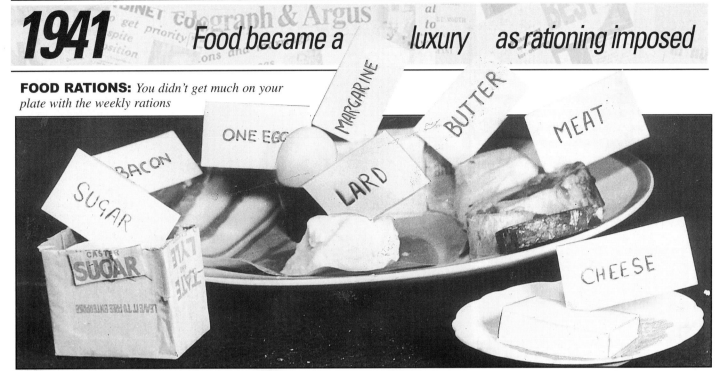

A struggle to survive

T he advert in the window at the Farmer Giles Milk Bar in Tyrrell Street left a lot of questions unanswered.

It was, after all, April 1, 1941 - All Fools' Day and with the Second World War well into its second year.

'The Walnut Wonder Sundae' had probably one accurate word in its title - the word 'The'. The chances of there being a walnut in this confection were pretty low - which was where the Wonder came in. The buyer was probably left wondering where the nut was.

The word Sundae suggested some glorious confection of ice cream and fruit. Fat chance, with rationing beginning to dominate the national diet.

Hitler's ships and submarines were sinking

Tuesday, April 1, 1941

British ships carrying vital supplies. Things like rubber, oil, steel and minerals were at a premium. So was food - but there was no room in cargo holds for luxuries. Oranges, bananas and peaches were off the national menu for the duration for most of the population.

Gardens became food factories. Anything which you didn't grow yourself was probably rationed. Each citizen was issued with books of coupons and each coupon represented a certain number of 'points' - and if you didn't have the points, you couldn't buy the goods, no matter how much money you had.

Butter and bacon were among the first things to be rationed, within a couple of weeks of the war starting. By 1942 the

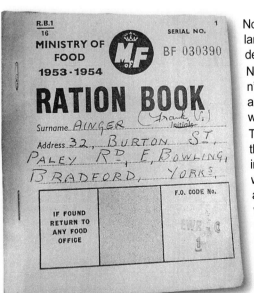

ration system had been developed into a fine economic art. Buyers had to be registered with retailers - special dispensation from the Ministry of Food was needed to change shops.

Nobody could describe the system as popular - but at the same time nobody could describe it as unfair.

Naturally there was favouritism, and it wasn't long before the black market emerged, along with a new name - Spiv - for those who operated it.

The one thing which was not rationed throughout the war was bread - although in the bankrupt aftermath it was for a while. But the Ministry insisted that more and more of the whole grains of wheat went into the flour - bad news for a nation which associated white bread with gentility and purity.

By the end of the war, some of the bread would make today's heavy-duty wholemeal look like stuff for people without teeth.

The war produced a healthier, if rather emaciated, nation - and the idea of fair shares of both the burden and the benefits was to help the Labour Party to overwhelming victory in 1945.

T&A

1942

King and Queen paid surprise visit to Bradford area

The abiding memory of King George VI and his wife Queen Elizabeth (now the Queen Mother) is their presence in wartime London during the Blitz.

This may now seem quaint, like folk-lore, but during the Second World War the King and Queen meant a great deal to the majority of British people. They were the embodiment of

Looms Clatter While King and Queen Tour Bradford Works

Hundreds of Our Bomber Raided...

the unified nation to whom the men and women of the armed forces swore allegiance - unlike Nazi Germany where soldiers, sailors and airmen had to give an oath of loyalty to a politician, Adolf Hitler.

King and country were two sides of the same coin. King George and Queen Elizabeth felt this deeply, which is why they made a point of going out into the bombed streets of the capital and visiting the industrial cities of the North.

Thursday, March 26, 1942

When the royal train steamed into Forster Square Station at 10am on March 26, 1942, the people of Bradford were surprised - the visit had not been announced in advance for security reasons.

Evidently they were also pleased for, although life goes on whatever the crisis, Britain had not had much to feel glad about.

Fighter pilots of various nationalities had given the Royal Air Force the ascendancy in The Battle of Britain, as Churchill called it; but Hitler's Panzer Divisions had bulldozed the Allies out of mainland Europe on to a strip of beach at Dunkirk, from which 330,000 were rescued by sea.

Montgomery's defeat of Rommel's Africa Korps at El Alamein was still months away.

King George wore the uniform of the RAF. The Queen wore a long coat of fine woollen material in Parma violet. Her matching felt hat had a wide ribbon and a wide brim turned up at the front.

FLYING VISIT: *King George VI and Queen Elizabeth are greeted on their arrival in Bradford on a surprise visit to the city in wartime Britain*

A boost to morale

The royal couple were driven to a factory - not named for security reasons at the time - where they watched uniforms being made. They chatted to the workers.

"I think she is lovely - they are a beautiful couple," said machinist Freda Moore.

"I think the King is grand. He is worth fighting for," said William Skinner, of Mannheim Road, Heaton. He was later called up to serve in the RAF.

After visiting another part of the premises being used by the Regional Blood Transfusion Unit, the King and Queen spent nearly an hour in Lister Park, inspecting and talking to 700 Civil Defence workers and 300 members of

the National Fire Service. The City Police Band played the National Anthem.

A big crowd gave the King and Queen a rousing send-off as they headed for the Keighley area, where they went on to inspect a munitions factory at Steeton.

All in all it was a cheering, morale-raising visit for the people, some of whom may have remembered the couple when they last visited in April, 1928, as the Duke and Duchess of York. The Queen Mother returned to Bradford on March 29, 1962, to attend the gala performance of the opening concert of the Delius Centenary Festival at St George's Hall.

T&A

1943

It was queues all the way for exodus to the seaside

All aboard for a day of fun

When Bowling Tide week came around in 1943, things were definitely looking up.

The Allied invasion of Sicily had been successful and Italy was teetering on the brink of surrender. America was in the war and acting as both the arsenal and the larder of democracy.

The Sicily invasion, said the pundits, was a dress rehearsal for sea-borne landings on the coast of western Europe, and for once the pundits were right. D-Day came less than a year later.

So Bradford decided it was holiday time at last - even if it amounted only to a day in Morecambe or Blackpool. The 7.28am train from Bradford Exchange on Saturday, August 14, took 800 revellers to Blackpool. By the time the 9.10 train left, there were 1,100 on board and 50 hopefuls left behind on the platform - even though wartime had turned the British talent for cramming people onto a train into an art form.

Across the way at Forster Square,

QUEUES, BUT NO BIG RUSH

Blackpool and Morecambe the Most Popular

BLACKPOOL and Morecambe are always popular resorts at Bowling Tide, and to-day Bradford holiday-makers poured into both these places in their hundreds.

EXODUS: *Trippers queue at the Exchange Station in Bradford for trains to Blackpool as a break from wartime city life*

For many in the stations queue there would be an introduction to another wartime joy - Z-class travel. This was railway jargon for carriages so full that you couldn't get another body in with a shoe horn.

By midday it was getting fairly frantic. The 12.45 to Morecambe from Forster Square was reported as 'Z-class' by 12.30. Passengers for Birmingham, Bath, Bristol and Bournemouth also found themselves standing. Those boarding London trains at Leeds felt a prickle of irritation that the old rivals from Bradford had bagged all the seats.

Accommodation at Morecambe's boarding houses was 'pretty tight' according to the Information Bureau, and eating out was a bit of an ordeal. Lunch meant waiting in a queue from 11am to 1pm, then getting back in the queue for tea at 3.30pm. There were, in fact, queues everywhere, but by

Saturday, August 14, 1943

Morecambe trains were less crowded - possibly because 'Bradford-super-Mare' was renowned more for peace and quiet than its neighbour down the coast. Blackpool didn't offer bright lights (the blackout was still in force) but it offered a brash cheeriness that would be a perfect antidote for wartime shortages, long hours, income tax at ten bob (50p) in the pound. It offered the tower, as well, and a beach.

1943 queues had become so much a way of life it probably made the resorts a real home from home.

Ration books, of course, had to be handed over to the landlady of the boarding house. Food restrictions didn't have holidays. For those who stayed at home there was a lot going on - concerts and beauty contests, donkey rides in the parks, sporting contests around the city and the chance to see some quality cricket.

The Bradford League, during wartime, could boast such players as the great Leonard Hutton, Notts fast bowler Bill Voce, A V Pope of Derbyshire, and Yorkshire's Alex Coxon, Wilf Barber and Arthur Booth.

But a great pall fell over cricketers and cricket lovers, not only in Yorkshire but all over the world, with the news, on September 1, 1943, of the death of Hedley

Verity, left. The Yorkshire left arm bowler, a Captain in the Green Howards, had been wounded in action while leading his men across a blazing Sicilian cornfield, and died later as a prisoner of war.

At a time when the Telegraph & Argus was allowed to print only a four-page paper, Verity's death was given a whole column. It is a mark of the true sense of loss that was felt. Anything less than a whole column would simply not have done.

T&A

1944
The end for Bradford's legendary pie

Crusty old friend!

It was an unlikely national symbol. We had the bulldog, of course, and the Union Flag. And there was Winston Churchill himself, who was a bit of the former and a proud symbol of the latter. But a meat and potato pie…? It's funny what sticks in the national consciousness.

The pie was in the window of Arthur Roberts's food shop in Godwin Street and had been there for about 40 years. Not the same pie, of course. Its crust was regularly renewed and there wasn't

Monday, April 17, 1944

actually anything inside it - except the secret mechanism which had kept it puffing steam over the years.

And it was this which caught the imagination of J B Priestley, who in the war years became the nation's favourite Bradfordian when he gave a series of Sunday evening radio talks called postscripts.

Roberts's pie shop had its front blown off in an air raid and Priestley, visiting his native city, passed the partly boarded-up window and saw the pie still doing its stuff. Or, as he put it, 'a giant, almost superhuman meat pie, with a magnificent brown, crisp, artfully wrinkled, succulent-looking crust ... giving off a fine, rich, appetising steam to make your mouth water … a perpetual volcano of meat and potato'.

At a time of food rationing, this was not only evocative, but probably quite painful to listeners. And the pie, he reported, was still steaming - 'every puff defying Hitler, Goering and the whole gang of them'.

This was at the end of September 1940, when the Battle of Britain had just been won. It became one of his best-remembered broadcasts - much to both his own and Arthur Roberts's annoyance.

Mr Roberts, who died on April 17, 1944, got fed up of people coming to rubberneck at his creation, while JB got fed up of people asking him about the pie.

It was nicknamed Bertha and had some sort of steaming kettle device, or a pipe

Bradford's "Dickensian" pie shop to close after 50 years

STEAM DREAM: *Mrs Roberts (left) with Bertha, the famous tantalising pie which for years had pride of place in her husband Arthur's shop window in Godwin Street. J B Priestley (left) was one of the pie's biggest fans*

connected to such a kettle, under the plaster of paris crust. Though even here, there is conflict. One school of thought said that the crust was real, and renewed frequently on Wednesday, which was half-day closing.

When Mrs Roberts retired in 1955, the secret went with her. And Bertha disappeared, despite one or two ideas about

putting her in a museum. Among the sceptics who mocked this idea was the man who made the pie famous.

J B, writing in the Yorkshire Observer, said: 'If the pie, the steaming window, the old eating place itself, will soon vanish for ever, then I am genuinely sorry. But not because there was once a Sunday night in the war when millions heard about the pie and talked about it for some days.

'No, I regret its disappearance because, like its owner, it had character…I do not see it as a museum object, which might turn up one night on Animal, Vegetable or Mineral … Let it steam, especially when we are feeling peckish, in our memories'.

1945

The nation went wild as the horror of total war ended

Yorkshire VICTORY Observer

6-A.M. EDITION

Plaza UTILITY STOCKINGS

No. 25,382. BRADFORD. TUESDAY, 8 MAY, 1945. ONE PENNY

European War Will End Officially This Afternoon

IT'S VE-DAY—AT LAST

Broadcasts By King, Premier and Victorious Generals

2 DAYS' NATIONAL HOLIDAY FOR PEACE CELEBRATIONS

Churchill's Luncheon Party

By Our Political Correspondent

THE WAR IS OVER. TO-DAY IS VE-DAY. TO-DAY WILL BE PUBLIC HOLIDAYS.

THE official announcement of the end of hostilities in Europe will be made in this country to the House of Commons this afternoon. Then Mr. Churchill will go to the microphone at 3 o'clock and broadcast the official statement which will be made simultaneously in London, Moscow

THE KING'S MESSAGE TO EISENHOWER

King last night sent the following gram to General Eisenhower, Supreme ander, on the Allied victory :—

teen months ago you led the Allied ionary Force across the English Channel, with you the hopes and prayers of of men and women of many nations.

It was entrusted the task of annihilating the armies in Western Europe, and of thus liberating the peoples whom they had enslaved.

★

" All the world now knows that, after fierce and continuous warfare, this force has accomplished its mission with a finality achieved by no other such expedition in history.

" On behalf of all my peoples, I ask ... Supreme Commander, will ... deeply.

Oslo Radio Proclaims "Peace"

GERMAN S.S. MASSACRE IN PRAGUE—CZECH AIRBORNE AID RUSHED FROM BRITAIN

WHILE the calm of peace spread over Europe yesterday, German S.S. men in Prague, capital of Czecho-Slovakia, last night abandoned all normal conduct and in lawless frenzy were shooting down Czechs in the streets, while bombs from German 'planes rained down on the city.

TWO columns of General Patton's Fourth Armoured Division were dashing for the city. They were only seven miles mown down by other S.S. men with machine-guns. Refusing to recognise the Flensburg surrender announcement, the commander of the German troops in Czecho-Slovakia had issued a " fight on

"MONTY" MEETS ROKOSSOVSKY

FIELD-MARSHAL MONT-

IT'S OVER: *King George VI and Queen Elizabeth gather on the balcony of Buckingham Palace with daughters Princess Elizabeth and Princess Margaret to greet the jubilant VE Day crowds*

An end to blood, toil and sweat

After six years of blood, toil, tears and sweat, war for Britain and her Empire ended on two Tuesdays in the spring and summer of 1945.

On May 8 Nazi Germany - its capital in ruins, its leader dead, and the country over-run - unconditionally surrendered to the Allies. The war in Europe was over.

Three more bloody months were to pass before the war in the Pacific was resolved by the explosion of two atomic

Tuesday, May 8, 1945 and Tuesday, August 14, 1945

bombs above the Japanese cities of Hiroshima and Nagasaki, on August 6 and 9 respectively. On August 14, Emperor Hirohito announced his country's capitulation.

The Japanese reaped the whirlwind they had sewn nearly four years earlier at Pearl Harbor. The decision to use the A-bombs was taken after the Americans took nearly three months and suffered 12,000 casualties in taking the Pacific island of Okinawa.

Nearly 51 million men and women had served in the armed forces of the main protagonists. After the last shot had been fired the number of dead - men, women, and children, soldiers and civilians - was estimated at 55 million, roughly the entire population of Britain today.

War had inflicted suffering upon civilian populations count-

Continued on Page 80

REMEMBER: *Children are gathered for a party to celebrate a day that will live with them forever as crowds gather round Bradford's cenotaph on the night peace was declared in Europe, below*

Continued from Page 79

less times before; but total war took on a new meaning in World War II, as Allied and Soviet troops discovered when they passed through the gates of Belsen, Auschwitz, and Changi Jail.

In North Germany and Eastern Poland the Nazis had set up concentration camps and killing centres to deal with social and political undesirables, and those considered to be less than human under the ethical code of National Socialism - Jews, gypsies, Slavs. Millions were rounded up and systematically beaten to death, shot, or gassed. Others were burned alive in churches. Thousands of miles away in the Far East the Japanese Imperial Army had also shown that in victory it felt no obligation to treat the defeated with anything other than contempt and cruelty. Thousands of captured Allied troops were systematically worked and starved to death on the Burma railroad.

But on Tuesday, May 8, the grisly accounting had yet to be done. Germany's surrender was something to be celebrat-

It was relief rather than triumph

ed, although the banner headline across the front of Bradford's Yorkshire Observer - IT'S VE-DAY - AT LAST - expressed relief rather than triumph.

It was a day of announcements and broadcasts, in the House of Commons, over the radio. Prime Minister Winston Churchill, King George VI, General Dwight Eisenhower, supreme Allied commander in Europe, and Field-Marshals Montgomery and Alexander, all addressed Britain, the Empire and the Commonwealth.

Hundreds of thousands jammed the streets of London. Flags waved and beer flowed. In Bradford the bells of victory echoed and floodlights lit up the town hall. Thousands crammed the open space between the building and the surrounding warehouses (the latter were later demolished). Mrs Lillian Bailey was 18 at the time. "At first my friends and I tentatively joined in the singing, but as the crowds and the atmosphere grew we let our hair down and sang and danced with abandon. It was a wonderful feeling of sharing an experience that had prevailed all through the war

Continued on Page 81

Continued from Page 80

years, a feeling that sadly was not to last," she wrote to the T&A in 1995, on the 50th anniversary of VE Day.

Mary Pinkney was serving with the Women's Auxiliary Air Force (WAAF) at a Bomber Command base in Lincolnshire. She too recollected her experience of the first night for six years without war.

"A large group of us went out into the nearby village of Barnetby, where flags of every colour were being hung everywhere. Blackouts were torn down and the lights were an amazing sight. Doors were open, and I thought the hugging and kissing would never end.

"The laughter was helped by an endless supply of rhubarb and gooseberry wine. There was food everywhere despite rationing. We sang until we were hoarse and danced the night away in the streets.

"But there were many tears shed, too, as we remembered the boys who never made it. We prayed for the 1,000 air crew from Elsham's base whose Lancasters failed to return. And our hearts went out to the boys who were still fighting in the jungle in places like Burma, and to the many who were still Prisoners-of-War."

VE Day was a time of very intense but mixed emotions for thousands of Poles who were living in Bradford. Some had fled from the Nazis after the 1939 Nazi-Soviet Pact had removed Poland from the map of Europe and the Nazi war machine had crushed Polish armed resistance in three weeks. Others had fought in the Battle of Britain in 1940.

Ukrainians were here too, those who had managed to escape both the Nazis and Stalin's avenging Red Army.

The story of how the Poles came to Bradford actually goes back to World War I. During the First World War, Bradford man Tom Neale had been captured and put to work on a farm run by a Pole sympathetic to the Kaiser and the Central European powers. He had been treated kindly, and so when the same Pole turned against Nazi Germany in 1939 and became a fugitive, his Bradford friend offered him a refuge.

Tom Neale, who ran a sweet shop in Idle, started an Anglo-Polish Society in Bradford. Other people followed his example so that by 1941 some 600 Polish airmen had been 'adopted' by Bradford families. For thousands of others home was a resettlement camp in Yorkshire.

For the Poles and the Ukrainians the end of the war did not mean that they could

PARTY TIME: *Street parties break out for young and old alike all over Bradford like these in Odsal, above, and in Wilsden, left*

go home; what home was left for them to go to?

When Stalin, Churchill and President Roosevelt met at Yalta in the Russian Crimea in February, 1945, to discuss the shape of the world after the war, Poland had been ceded to the Soviet Union's sphere of influence. Winston Churchill reluctantly agreed to this, recognising that Stalin would not co-operate unless he could protect the USSR's western border with a buffer zone.

But many Poles in Bradford did not want to live under a totalitarian regime, especially one which had so readily agreed to carve up Poland in 1939 and share it with Nazi Germany. So they stayed. By 1950 the city had up to 5,000 people of Polish origin - double the number here today.

Few people understood the implications of the Atomic bombs which the Americans exploded above Hiroshima and Nagasaki. Most people were just

glad to accept that they had brought about the abrupt end of a war against a brutal and defiant enemy.

VJ Day on Tuesday, August 14, again brought out the bunting and the people into the streets, although it was an understandably bigger event in America which had remained on the sidelines until December 7, 1941, when Japan had launched its surprise attack on the US Pacific fleet in Pearl Harbor, Hawaii. Possession of the A-bomb made victorious America the world's pre-eminent super-power. Stalin, ever suspicious of his allies as he was of his comrades in the Kremlin, regarded this as a threat to the security and influence of the USSR. For another 40 years a different kind of war, the Cold War as it became known, was to lock the USA and the USSR into a diplomatic and armed confrontation in Western Europe and in other parts of the world.

T&A

1946 *Landlords forced to restrict drinking as beer ran short*

**NEW DRINKING TIMES PLANNED—
EIGHT-HOUR WEEKLY MINIMUM**

BREAD RATIONING RIDDLES

IF Bradford licensees carry out the recommendation of their association, the city's public-houses will be open for a minimum of eight hours a week.
Proposed hours are :—
8 p.m. to 10 p.m. on Friday, Saturday, and Sunday.
Noon to 1 p.m. on Saturday and Sunday.
Mr. Herbert Stephenson, secretary of Bradford and District License-Holders' Association

WANTED STOCKS TO SELL TO PAY HIS RENT

DRY RUN: *Pubs like the Craven Heifer in Manchester Road, now demolished, had to severely restrict opening hours*

Short time in the pubs

The war was won but Britain was broke. To make things worse it was a miserable, wet summer, brightened only by Yorkshire winning the county championship.

Bread, which had gone through the war unrationed, finally went 'on points' as the peace began in a mood of unrelieved austerity.

Everything was in short supply, it seemed -

Tuesday, July 2, 1946

fuel, food, tobacco, clothes. This was to make the winter of 1946-47 a truly terrible one. It was to be exceptionally cold, and with coal hard to get because fuel to transport it was in short supply, it is now regarded as probably the toughest winter of the century to survive.

As the middle of the year approached, there was another blow. On top of all the other scarcities, beer was now declared to be in short supply. On July 2, 1946, Bradford's licensees got their heads together to decide what to do about it.

It was during the First World War that Britain's strict licensing hours had been introduced to stop munitions and other vital workers turning up for work plastered. The control provided by this appealed to the puritanical streak in the British, and the restricted hours remained for another seven decades.

But in 1947 things got really tight - which is

more than you can say for the pub customers. Licensees decided to adopt a minimum eight-hour week which was to work like this: Open from 8-10pm on Friday, Saturday and Sunday, and from noon to 1pm on Saturday and Sunday.

The rest of the week depended entirely on whether customers had supped their regular waterholes dry or not. There were long faces among the drinking classes. The publicans decided to stick together on the hours, so there was no prospect of 'pub-hopping' from a closing pub to one which was still open.

The Bradford Brewers' Association ordered a set of slip-in cards for pubs, to display opening hours, and to let the public know when there was ale to be had.

Herbert Stephenson, secretary of Bradford and District Licence-Holders Association, said most licensees had only enough beer for eight to 12 hours a week, but he hoped that landlords wouldn't open until sold out, then close for the rest of the ration period.

But one landlord was more optimistic - by opening from 11.30am to 2pm, and from 6pm to 8pm, he reckoned he could make his ration last for six days, and would have to close only on Sunday (a number of Bradford's pubs, particularly in the city centre, stayed shut on the Sabbath).

On the whole, with no new clothes for the season and ale in short supply, a long, hot summer was probably the last thing on people's minds in 1947.

T&A

1947

Odsal men's Challenge Cup victory

Wembley wonders!

Northern put rivals Leeds to the sword

Great was the fight and great was the victory! proclaimed the triumphant leader article in the T&A, the Monday after Bradford Northern had won the silver Challenge Cup at Wembley.

To be exact, Northern beat Leeds - always a cause for satisfaction - and were, admitted the Leeds skipper Ike Owens, the better side.

Northern won 8-4. That might not seem much of a score, but in their preceding

Saturday, May 3, 1947

four cup matches against Barrow, Hunslet, Wigan and Wakefield, the Leeds players had not conceded a single point. By contrast, Northern's opponents - Salford, Huddersfield, Workington, and Warrington - had scored 15 between them.

Although Leeds started as favourites they failed to penetrate Northern's defence and cross the try-line. Willie Davies, Northern's Welsh International stand-off half back, had a particularly brilliant game, and won the Lance Todd Trophy after being voted Man of the Match.

As Northern's skipper Ernest Ward walked off the sunlit pitch holding the trophy he may have cast his mind back

TROPHY TIME: *The Northern players show the cup off to the crowds from an open-topped bus as they travelled to a civic reception at the City Hall. Left, skipper Ernest Ward leads his triumphant team around Wembley after their victory*

Continued on Page 84

PRIDE OF THE CITY: *Bradford Northern players and officials, with the Lord Mayor, Alderman T I Clough, and the Lady Mayoress, show off the trophy at the New Victoria Cinema. Below, Northern fans up for the cup at Wembley*

Fans could buy a copy of the 'Pink' in London!

Continued from Page 83

to less bright days in the past. If he did not, the T&A certainly did.

"Bradford Northern have travelled a long way from the uncertainty and gloom of the Birch Lane days. But the faith which was flickering and only just kept alight in those seasons of travail has now, at long last, burst into the effulgence of victory, and the club justly and rightly claims its due reward."

Well, not quite. Of the record gate receipts of £17,500, Northern's share was reportedly just £750 - hardly a king's ransom for five cup victories and beating Leeds into the bargain to claim the trophy.

Bradford was delighted to have something to celebrate. The T&A was plugged into the collective spirit of the occasion too.

The paper not only printed the story and result in that evening's Yorkshire Sports, it arranged to have several thousand copies of the pink supplement flown from Yeadon to Croydon airport, and then transported to central London for sale among celebrating Northern supporters. By 10pm not a copy remained unsold.

The team was given a civic reception on the Monday evening. As the players arrived at the Town Hall they were greeted with a trumpet fanfare, three cheers, and a rendition of See The Conquering Heroes Come.

It was the start of a memorable three years for Northern. In 1948 and 1949 the team won through to Challenge Cup finals against Wigan and Halifax respectively, losing 8-3 to the Lancashire side but beating the Yorkshiremen 12-0.

T&A

1948

Outspoken Tyke who was loved   by millions

Wilfred, darling of the radio

T he year of 1948 is usually associated with the Berlin Airlift, when America and Britain beat the Communist blockade of West Berlin by flying in thousands of tons of food, coal, medicine and clothing and other essentials.

At least the first month or two of that year are special for Bradford for an entirely different reason. A very great broadcaster, revolutionary in his own Yorkshire way, was starring at the

Wednesday, January 21, 1948

Alhambra with a young woman who went on to become Britain's most popular comic actress.

The broadcaster was Halifax-born Wilfred Pickles, whose travelling radio programme for the BBC, Have a Go, regularly attracted a listening audience of 18 million and upwards. The young woman was June Whitfield. He was Buttons and she was Cinderella in Francis Laidler's marvellous pantomime which bridged Christmas 1947 and the New Year. The panto was broadcast on the BBC Home Service on January 21, 1948.

Pickles, the Michael Parkinson of his day, was revolutionary because he refused to disguise his distinctive Yorkshire accent. He fought successfully against attempts within the BBC hierarchy to use the bland Received Pronunciation which broadcasters were expected to use.

"There has been a gradual standardisation of spoken English. Too many

"ROYAL" SEND-OFF FOR 'CINDERELLA' IN BRADFORD

THE only joy one may be certain of seeing in "austerity" is when it is lit up with coloured ...nts and turned into comedian-fodder by such ..pular Yorkshiremen as Wilfred Pickles, who, as Buttons, set off with a bang the opening of Mr. Francis Laidler's "Cinderella" at Bradford Alhambra last night.

THE BARON

Rich is at ease as the and particularly good in ...g parody with Marion ...n, an Ugly Sister. Her ...ly droll companion is ... Milner.

Barbour, junior, and Barbour are an engaging ...ersatile pair of brokers' introducing a ...

With Wilfred, in turn the mischievous "spoker" of everybody's wheel, and the sympathetic gallant to lonely Cinderella, the audience was at once put into the mood to give a "Royal" reception to the

Northerners, I'm afraid, are ashamed of speaking the language their forefathers spoke," he said.

In 1948 Pickles read Shakespeare's sonnets in his own voice on the radio. The public loved it, and they loved him and his wife Mabel for taking Have a Go out into villages, towns, and cities beyond London to "let the people meet the people". Have a Go was first broadcast from Bingley on March 4, 1946. It was a cheerful neighbourly sort of programme, a precursor of Down Your Way, exactly suited to Wilfred Pickles' personality. He made people laugh by asking "Are y' courtin?"

His fan mail was colossal, more than 1,000 letters a week. He employed three secretaries to deal with it, and ordered signed photographs of himself 10,000 at a time. He thrived on getting out and about.

Hospitals were regular venues for his radio show. At 2.15pm on Christmas Day, 1947, dressed up as Santa Claus and accompanied by June Whitfield and other members of the Cinderella cast,

he broadcast a special show for the Light Programme direct from Bradford Children's Hospital, Manningham.

The Yorkshire Observer reported: "While the millions who heard little Harvey Matthews, aged 11, of Torre Crescent, Bradford, sing from his bed the second verse of Away in a Manger, and the third verse by eight-year-old Jean Scotcher, of 8 Bowling Alley Terrace, Rastrick, accompanied by Jack Harvey's Orchestra, must have immediately understood the whole spirit of Wilfred's party."

The pantomime stars in their stage costumes brought gasps of surprise and pleasure from the children. But there was more, a link from the hospital to Walt Disney in Hollywood, who persuaded Donald Duck and Mickey Mouse to send their Christmas greetings to that hospital in Bradford.

That was Wilfred Pickles all over. The loss of his son at the age of seven had the effect of making him go out of his way to do something for children.

Like Freddie Trueman and Jimmy Savile, Wilfred Pickles was an unapologetic Yorkshireman. Pride in his roots, however, did not make him small-minded or one-dimensional.

His career was multi-faceted. One newspaper described him as "a superb actor of startling versatility".

He brought cheer, fellowship and a bit of silliness to the nation during the years of rationing after the war.

T&A

1949 Duke of Edinburgh delighted crowds as he toured district

Prince opens new Grammar School

CHAT: *The Duke at Leafield Mill in Yeadon chats to one of the workers*

The Duke of Edinburgh arrived in Bradford on January 12, 1949, when his wife - yet to become Queen - had just given birth to Prince Charles.

He was here to open the new Bradford Grammar School, opposite Lister Park. It had been a long time in the building, which was interrupted by the war.

The foundation stone had been laid in 1937, but the unopened school was taken over by the army for the duration. There was pride in the air when opening day came around. Head boy Colin Pearson referred to the day as 'the glorious twelfth'

Wednesday, January 12, 1949

in thanking the Duke on behalf of the school.

Prince Philip arrived by train at Apperley Bridge and one of his first stops was at a Leafield Mill, Yeadon, where he met young mender Betty Jackson. Watching her doing her intricate job the Duke asked: 'Doesn't it give you spots before the eyes. It would be a bit awkward if you had been out the night before.' Miss Jackson simply said: 'Yes, rather', so the Duke called over his equerry, Lt Michael Parker, to share the joke.

The Duke had arrived in Bradford quite

early - his special train pulled into Forster Square at 6.55, but he remained aboard for breakfast before travelling back to Apperley Bridge to start the tour proper.

There were cheering crowds in bright winter sunshine when he returned to Bradford and appeared outside the Town Hall on a platform before moving to Frizinghall to open the £250,000 school. One thousand five hundred parents, staff and boys were waiting for him, and there had been large crowds gathered along the route from Bradford.

The procession went through Lister Park where schoolchildren, who had been given the day off, lined the path. After the opening, the Duke was given a present for his new son, Prince Charles - a rectangular shawl in Bradford-processed wool, with a leaf pattern, knitted by women at the Bradford National Institute for the Blind.

After the Duke's departure, headmaster Mr R B Graham referred to 'that nice young man' who had opened the school. 'He was just as we all hoped he would be' said the head.

Later the Duke's equerry wrote to the Lord Mayor, Alderman F J Cowie, thanking everyone for the wonderful day.

'His Royal Highness was very moved by the splendid reception the people of Bradford extended to him' said the letter.

T&A **BIG DAY:** *The Royal motorcade leaves Lister Park en route for the ceremonial opening*

1950

The classic cars made in Bradford

A real good sport

HOT MOTOR: *In three consecutive years the Jowett Jupiter won its class in the Le Mans 24-hour Grand Prix*

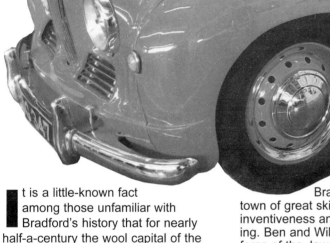

Javelin Jupiter on its way in 24-hour road race

NEARLY 100 m.p.h.
UP TO 30 m.p.g.

I t is a little-known fact among those unfamiliar with Bradford's history that for nearly half-a-century the wool capital of the world also manufactured motor-cars.

That this should be so may be attributed to two reasons. Firstly, those writing about or promoting Bradford's history invariably focus on textiles or culture - the latter usually means the Brontë sisters. Secondly, engineering, for which the Bradford district is or ought to be

Friday, June 16, 1950

equally famous, is not an exciting subject, especially for those with an arts bent.

And yet textile manufacture itself would have foundered in Bradford but for the presence of skilled artisans able to design, make, and maintain precision machines. Marine engineering, for example, used to be important in Bradford.

British Aerospace used to have a factory here, as did GEC, Bairds, and International Harvesters. These major manufacturing concerns would not have come at all without a long tradition of engineering expertise to attract them.

Bradford used to be a town of great skills, craftsmanship, inventiveness and entrepreneurial daring. Ben and Willie Jowett, the driving force of the Jowett Cars company, moved from back-street Manningham to a big site at Idle after the First World War.

The brothers set out to be manufacturers of quality vehicles and for many years insisted that each car must be individually made. Until the Second World War only about 25 cars a week came off the Jowett production line.

During the Second World War the company adapted to the needs of the military and produced a total of £5m-worth of goods for the Ministry of Supply and the Admiralty.

Post-war, new designs were required for new vehicles. In 1947 the company launched the Javelin, a compact, streamlined car with a seating capacity for six and a top speed of 80mph. In six years until 1953, the company mass-produced (a new development) 23,000 Javelins.

However, the car was under-priced, the gearbox was found to be unreliable, and the bodies were made by a Doncaster firm at a pre-determined rate.

Although there were problems selling the vehicles in sufficient quantity to the public, the Javelin was so successful in international competitions like the Monte Carlo Rally that the decision was taken to manufacture a high-performance sports car.

The 1.5 litre Jupiter was launched in 1950. In three consecutive years it won its class in the Le Mans 24 hour Grand Prix and captured first prize in the 1.5 litre class in the 1951 Monte Carlo Rally.

But the car proved too sophisticated and expensive to sell to the public in any cost-effective quantity. Only 1,000 were built between 1950-53. An improved version, the R4 Jupiter which was to have been priced at £707 - £80 cheaper that the Triumph TR2 - never got further than the prototype stage.

Having adapted from peace to war, Jowett Cars evidently had difficulties adjusting itself to the mass production of what it used to make individually. In 1954 the Idle factory was sold to International Harvesters. All creditors were fully recompensed. About 100 staff moved a vast stock of spares to Batley where until 1963 they ran a spares and servicing service.

T&A

1951 Bradford switched Britain on to the 20th century!

Northern lights...

I t took the Second World War to drag Britain into the 20th century. Before 1939 the country had an oddly outdated feel, as though Edwardian England had not ended.

The movies made by Ealing Studios in the 1950s show a country where starched collars were still in fashion and young men were expected to behave like deferential schoolchildren to anyone

Wednesday, October 24, 1951

old enough to remember Queen Victoria. Indeed, going to the movies was regarded as a suspect activity in some quarters.

We must have been about the last major European country to consider playing football under floodlights, and did not get around to it until six years after the war. The idea of playing rugby league under lights became reality in 1951, and it was our very own Bradford

Northern club which led the way.

A week before the New Zealand tourists were due to play at Odsal - a vast stadium in those days - Northern put on a preview which was attended by rugby league officials, journalists, and curious members of the public. This took place on the night of October 24.

The oval area containing the pitch was illuminated by 43 lamps additional to the ones used for nocturnal speedway meetings. In all, Odsal was lit up by a total power of 43,000 watts. The cost of floodlighting a match was estimated by lighting technician Mr A E Wilkinson at about ten shillings (50p).

Jack Burns, the T&A's sports editor, reported: "One who knows from experience told me that this Odsal floodlight-

ing was superior to that which he had seen in Chicago and Los Angeles. My own view is that those who see it for the first time are going to be impressed by it."

They were. A floodlit match has a certain magic to it, especially if the game itself turns out to be exciting. Mr Bill Fallowfield, secretary of the Rugby League, was so stirred by the preview that he ventured to declare that he could see no reason why floodlit rugby should not be a regular feature on BBC television.

The most unequivocally enthusiastic voices belonged to New Zealand managers Bill McKenzie and Dave Wilkie.

"I can see no reason why it should not be a terrific success after a few minor adjustments. Our lads are looking forward to playing under these conditions," Mr McKenzie said.

And so Britain began to light up its sporting darkness - and Bradford was one of the pathfinders.

T&A

1952

Bradford actress sets off on road to fame

First rung to fame

The late Samuel Beckett's favourite actress was Billie Whitelaw. The reclusive author of the plays Waiting For Godot, Endgame, Krapp's Last Tape and the novels Molloy, and Malone Dies, greatly admired her skills, her dedication to the performance.

She learned the basics of her craft in Bradford, where she came as a nine-year-old wartime evacuee. Billie Whitelaw was born on June 6, 1932, in Coventry.

Her parents, Perceval and Frances, lived at 3, Ruskin Avenue, Heaton, and later moved

Monday, March 28, 1952

to Eldwick. The young Billie attended Thornton Grammar School and started her acting career at the age of 12 broadcasting on the BBC.

She also joined the Junior Drama Class at Bradford's Civic Playhouse - now the Priestley Centre for the Arts, and appeared on stage at the Playhouse with Mildred Dyson.

By the time she was 15, Billie Whitelaw's voice had been heard on the wireless more than 100 times. At the age of 19, when she joined the cast of the Penguin Players for a production of His Excellency at the Keighley Hippodrome, she was a veteran of the airwaves with nearly 400 broadcasts to her credit.

Most of them were made for Children's Hour, a 60-minute programme of talks and stories, for which she created a character called Bunkie.

She reportedly obtained her first stage job through the Penguin Players' Richard Burnett; he gave her an audition while he was a producer at Bradford's Prince's Theatre. As a result she appeared in several plays in her adopted home town and in Leeds.

The play at Keighley Hippodrome had its first night on Monday, April 7, 1952.

The year of 1952 turned out to be significant for her personal life too. In November she married her first husband, West End actor Peter Vaughan.

In 1961 her work was recognised with two awards: the Silver Heart Variety Club Award, and the TV Actress of the Year (which she

BRADFORD ACTRESS

WHEN repertory returns to the Keighley Hippodrome Monday week, among the cast the Penguin Players will be Bradford girl, Billie Whitelaw.

She is a young girl who ha acked a great deal of experien to a very short time. She entere e profession by way of lade her first broadc twelve. She had 100 ti

eated hildren's her first Richard ed a greenguin icked a greudition was to a very sta the heatre, e profession and as she appeared in several Bradford and Leeds. has since played a wide of parts in repertory in ury, New Brighton and ster, and is now delighted to me associated with Mr. nett once more in this new nture so close to her home.

STAGE STRUCK:
Actress Billie Whitelaw, whose career took off in Keighley, and left with her mother Frances at Eldwick in 1964

won again in 1972). Her big theatrical break followed in 1964 when she took over the role of Desdemona from Maggie Smith in Laurence Olivier's memorable production of Shakespeare's Othello for the National Theatre.

The T&A's theatre correspondent, the late Peter Holdsworth, described how an excited Billie had rung her parents in Eldwick at 1.30am to tell them how thrilled she felt after her first night on the same stage with Olivier as Othello, and Frank Finlay as Iago.

Four years later Billie Whitelaw won a British Academy Award. She went on winning awards for her work until 1988. In 1991 her career on radio, TV, the stage and the screen was acknowledged with a CBE.

But it is her association with Samuel Beckett's plays which marks her out from more popular contemporaries such as Judy Dench, Maggie Smith, and Thora Hird. She said in 1986 that her meeting with Beckett was the most significant of her life. "When we met I came under a marvellous umbrella of empathy and love…I think he demands more concentration from the actor than any other writer I know," she said. For her role in Beckett's Not I at London's Royal Court she had her entire body blacked up; all that was visible was her mouth, illuminated by a spotlight. At one point Beckett drove her so hard - unaware that he was - that she momentarily broke down. Beckett, who had a fiercely sharp mind but a kind heart, was distraught. Once in a while she returns to Bradford - usually photographed at the Priestley Centre, where she learned her craft, or Pictureville.

T&A

1953 1,200 flocked to annual social bash to see Harry Secombe

Goon to the Press Ball!

"Sideline" at Press Ball

Once again, Bradford's Press Ball—held last night at the Windsor Halls—proved one of the year's most popular social functions. The 1,200 guests included the Lady Mayoress of Bradford (Miss Annie Crowther). Dance music was provided by the orchestras of Ambrose and Ken Swaine. Prizes, of which there were more than a hundred, varied from suit lengths to a stand pie. Hundreds of balloons floated from the ceiling at midnight. Proceeds were for Press charities. Picture shows Harry Secombe, the comedian, who presented the prizes, busy signing autographs.

Big, formal nights out are becoming a thing of the past. The firm's dinner dance has all but ceased to exist, and fewer and fewer people these days can actually do a recognised dance like the waltz or the foxtrot.

That's one of the reasons why there hasn't been a Bradford Press Ball for more than 20 years.

But for a long time it was a genuine highlight of the Bradford social calendar - and no aspiring journalist could really claim to be properly in the business until he or she had spent many hours writing begging letters to pals and contacts and perfect strangers asking for tombola prizes to raise money for the National Union of Journalists' Widows and Orphans Fund or the benevolent society which looked after old news vendors.

Tickets for the ball weren't cheap, but the organisers always liked to think the paying guests got their money's worth.

They did on November 4, 1953, when 1,200 flocked to the Windsor Halls for what turned out to be one of the year's most popular social events.

MADCAP: *Goon Harry Secombe is happy to sign autographs for admirers at the Press Ball in the Windsor Halls, Bradford, the highlight of the social calendar*

It was partly thanks to the Moss Empires theatre people, who had had on their books for two or three years an aspiring comic from Wales called Harry Secombe, who was still touring in what had once been called music hall, but had evolved into variety.

The tour brought the young Secombe to

Thursday, November 4, 1953

Bradford at the right time. By now, thanks to a wartime meeting with Spike Milligan, Secombe was one of the Goons, rising stars of comedy thanks to the writing of Milligan, arguably the most influential British comic genius of the century.

By the time he got to Bradford nearly everybody was wild about Harry. He plunged in,

sold tombola tickets, told jokes and filled the place with that piercing giggle and - along with the music of Bert Ambrose and his Orchestra - made it a memorable night.

Ambrose was quite a catch, too. Well known from the wireless (it was a few years before the word radio would catch on, partly thanks to the arrival of the transistor), his orchestra wasn't quite on a par with, say, Henry Hall or Victor Sylvester, but was certainly in the top rank of British swing and dance bands.

Balloons floated from the ceiling at midnight onto the heads of the dancers, replete with a good supper (rationing had just ended, with meat one of the last things to come off 'points').

Somehow the modern equivalent - a disco with doner kebabs afterwards - doesn't have the same kind of style.

T&A

1954
The world's biggest-ever crowd for an RL match

Full to bursting...

FAN-TASTIC: *Almost every inch of Odsal Stadium is covered by spectators for the Challenge Cup final replay between Halifax and Warrington*

Telegraph & Argus

Lighting-up Time: 9.46 p.m. to 4.20 a.m.   BRADFORD, THURSDAY, 6 MAY, 1954   Broadcasting on Page 6

THIS WAS THE ODSAL "FULL HOUSE" RECORD 102.575

Football was big news in 1954. The magical Magyars of Hungary, including Puskas, Czibor, Koscis and Hideguti, crushed England 7-1 in Budapest, and then controversially lost 3-2 to West Germany in the World Cup final in Switzerland.

Rugby football was in the news too, and Bradford's gigantic Odsal Stadium made history on the night of Tuesday, May 4, by hosting the world's biggest-ever crowd for a rugby league match - 102,575. And Bradford Northern weren't even playing. What drew such a multitude was the clash between Halifax and Warrington in the Challenge Cup final replay. Both teams were contenders for the Championship that year and this factor added extra interest to the showdown at Odsal.

Halifax lost the replay 8-4. They also lost the Championship decider that Saturday in Manchester by the narrower points margin of 8-7. So the Lancashire side ended the 1953-54 season with the double.

But back to that record-breaking crowd. It

Wednesday, May 5 1954

surpassed the expectations of ground officials principally because they opened the gates to admit bus-loads of late arrivals and then decided to leave them like that.

More swarmed in, although just how much of the game they got good sight of is debatable.

If only a fifth part of a crowd of that size turned up at Odsal today the traffic chaos would be enormous. But 45 years ago few families owned one car let alone two. The T&A was able to report that by 10pm - an hour or so after the final whistle - all traffic had been dispersed from the Odsal area.

That day's paper also carried another story which, one way and another, was to have repercussions for more than 40 years.

Stanley Wardley, Bradford's all-powerful

city engineer and surveyor - the man responsible for the city's central road system and the demolition of Swan Arcade and much else - had drawn up plans to redevelop Odsal into the 'Wembley of the North'. The estimated cost of £225,000 would provide space for between 93,000 and 100,000 if necessary.

Just two small stands were proposed with covered accommodation for 8,000.

Bearing in mind that within 12 years the whole of Wembley Stadium's seating and terracing was covered, Mr Wardley's plan seems somewhat short-sighted.

However, it became just another idea. Apart from refurbishment in the mid-1980s for the World Speedway Championship, the stadium remained badly in need of an overhaul that was both sensible in scale and, above all, affordable.

The Superdome project, proposed in 1993 by former Bradford City director John Garside, was to prove neither although the scheme was not abandoned until 1998.

T&A

1955

Bankfoot scene of clash with the police

Five of 17 who appeared in court

No. 27,231

BRADFORD, MONDAY,

₃AOL SENTENCES AFTE₁
BANKFOOT DISORDERS

ounding
f girls

Bradford–Keighley
Teddy gang fight

THE 17 WHO
WERE CHARGED

The following 17 men appe
in cour₁

William Finan (19), app
r. of 69, Walker

COURT CLAMPS DOWN: *The T&A's front-page report on the court cases which followed the 'Battle of Bankfoot', which only ended after a police baton charge. The faces of the defendants pictured at the time have been obscured to protect their identity*

Teddy boy battle

Teddy Boy trouble was commonplace in British towns and cities in the 1950s, and Bradford was no exception. Rivalries ran high between gangs of young men and youths from different districts.

Dressed in their Edwardian attire of drainpipe trousers, fingertip-length jackets and bootlace ties, and often armed with knives, razors and knuckle-dusters, they would raid each other's territories

Saturday, November 26, 1955

and challenge each other to gang fights. The most spectacular of these in Bradford was the Battle of Bankfoot, which took place on the night of Saturday, November 26, 1955. When it finally ended after a police baton charge, three teenage girls had suffered

knife wounds, 17 Teddy Boys were arrested, and several policemen's helmets had been badly damaged.

At the height of what was in effect a riot, a crowd of more than 200 people were milling about outside the Ideal Ballroom and the road was blocked to traffic. Eye-witnesses described it as "just like a rugby football match out of control".

Continued on Page 93

SCENE OF THE CRIME: *The Ideal Ballroom in Bankfoot where dozens of Teddy Boys fought a pitched battle with the police*

How we reported the news

As the result of an incident inside, the management promptly called the police and certain youths were told to leave the premises. They did so, but one of them was taken into custody on a charge of being in possession of an offensive weapon.

"Later trouble broke out outside the hall and the road was quickly blocked by groups of youths engaged in fighting and altercation. The three girls, who were leaving the dance hall, received their injuries

Telegraph & Argus

From the T&A of November 26, 1955

in the melee, which at one time threatened to assume the ugliest proportions. "Two of the injured girls were taken to Bradford Royal Infirmary and later discharged. The third girl went to St Luke's Hospital for treatment.

What the T&A said

The vast majority of the citizens of Bradford are not prepared to regard these 'Teddy Boy' gangs, or the melees to which their existence inevitably leads, as a mere outbreak of animal high spirits. Gang warfare conducted with fists and non-lethal weapons differs only in degree from the shooting war that has for so long terrorised some areas of the United States.

There must be disappointment that the opportunity was not taken by the Bradford magistrates to indicate in the most unequivocal terms that a repetition ofthe Bankfoot affair will not be tolerated. Physical violence, whatever its form, is one of the gravest crimes against the community.

- Comment column on Tuesday, November 29

Continued from Page 92

The trouble began inside the dance hall and was part of a feud between Bradford and Keighley Teddy Boys. Police were called when about a dozen youths began fighting on the balcony. It was in the aftermath of this initial trouble that the three girls, who had the misfortune to be in the wrong place at the wrong time, received knife wounds - one in the wrist, one in the arm and the third in the back.

The dance hall was cleared and police reinforcements were summoned, but by the time they had arrived the trouble had escalated in the street.

A large crowd gathered and clearly did not appreciate the police presence. Soon it was not only Teddy Boy against Teddy Boy, but Teddy Boys against the 20 officers who had been sent along to deal with the disturbance and were hopelessly outnumbered.

The fight that followed was so fierce that helmets were knocked in, uniforms were damaged and staffs had to be drawn before order could be restored and the road reopened to traffic.

At one point several arrests were made and the drunken youths were put into a police van. A roar went up from the crowd and other youths charged the van in an unsuccessful bid to release them. When the 17 arrested youths

appeared in court the following Monday, three were given short prison sentences for offences including being drunk and disorderly and behaviour likely to cause a breach of the peace, with one of them also being convicted of "possession without reasonable excuse" of a knuckle duster. A further 14 were fined and bound over.

The proprietor of the dance hall, Mr Bert Shutt, told the T&A afterwards that he had been warned in an anonymous telephone call that there was trouble brewing among the Teddy Boys and had taken steps to prevent "what might have been a very serious situation."

T&A

1956

Bradford's new bishop had upbeat message

HOP OF BRADFORD
THRONED
ned in loyalty'

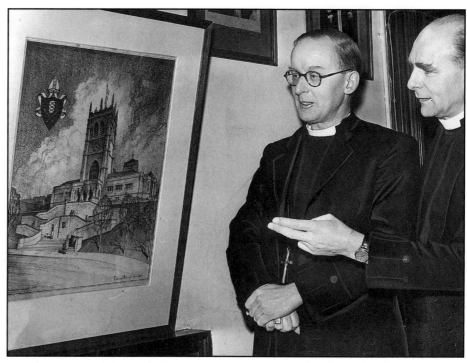

NEW ERA: *Dr Donald Coggan views a picture of Bradford Cathedral the day before his enthronement, left, in the cathedral in front of 1,000 people*

Great time to be alive!

Friday, February 3, 1956

In the momentous year of 1956, the year of the Suez Crisis, the Hungarian Uprising, and John Osborne's Look Back in Anger, Bradford got a new Bishop, the Right Reverend Donald Coggan.

His predecessor, the Rt Rev Alfred Blunt, who resigned at the end of October, 1955, had inadvertently made history in 1936 by publicly speaking about Edward VIII's need for grace which led, indirectly, to the King abdicating in order to marry American divorcee Wallis Simpson.

The new bishop was ordained in his 47th year in front of more than 1,000 people at Bradford Cathedral on February 3, 1956. In his sermon he said he believed that he was alive at a most thrilling time.

"I cannot align myself with those, wistfully looking back to the Victorian era or some other bygone age, dismally hankering for the good old days. This is the day which the

Lord hath made; we will rejoice and be glad in it. Behold, now is the accepted time; behold, now is the day of salvation…
"Something of that old lethargy which marred the work of the Church, and the old apathy which strangled the spiritual life of the country in the 'thirties and the early 'forties of this century is beginning to pass.
"Slowly men are coming to see that they cannot live by bread alone," he said.
Bishop Coggan, who gained a Double First in Oriental Languages at Cambridge University in 1931, had spent the late 1930s and early 1940s beyond the reach of the apathy he identified in his sermon. From 1937 to 1944 he was New Testament Professor at Toronto University, Canada,

training men for the priesthood.
Married with two teenage children, he was an academic essentially. He had lectured in Semitic languages and literature at Manchester University and during his career wrote 19 books and received 19 honorary degrees from universities and theological colleges in Britain, the United States, and Japan. But his faith was heart-felt.
"If Bradford Cathedral or York Minister had a bomb dropped on them, that wouldn't be the end of the Church of England. The laity is 95 per cent of the Church; they are the body of Christ, they will still be there," he told the T&A during a visit to Bradford in 1988.

His career in Bradford ended in 1961 when he moved on to become Archbishop of York, a position he held until 1974 when, at the age of 65, he was enthroned as Archbishop of Canterbury. Dr Coggan retired in 1980 and was made a Life Peer.

T&A

1957

Let the young folk jive, said minister

The Rock Gospel

When the Rev John Harwood preached a sermon in favour of the latest musical craze, Rock 'n' Roll, to Eccleshill Congregational Church on March 10, 1957, he was unwittingly passing a baton into the future.

In the 1980s it would be seized enthusiastically by another Eccleshill vicar, the Rev 'Rockin' Robin Gamble, who energetically and theatrically preached values of the New Testament through the music of The Beatles, and Queen.

"Let the young folk dance, let them jive, let them rock 'n' roll," said Mr Harwood, inno-

Sunday, March 10, 1957

cently unaware of the origin of the phrase Rock 'n' Roll - Black American slang for sexual intercourse.

"Impulses, instincts, personality needs, all find themselves ventilated at this level. Anything which sublimates grosser tendencies and by-passes brute nature is not evil. It is positive, not negative."

If Rock 'n' Roll was dimly perceived as a threat by the more timorous among Mr Harwood's congregation, there was little evidence of its presence in the UK. The Top 20 chart for January through to March makes interesting reading. Eddie Calvert (Oh Mein Papa), Winifred Atwell (Let's Have a Party), Mantovani (Swedish Rhapsody), the Beverley Sisters (I Saw Mommy Kissing Santa Claus), the Obernkirchen Children's Choir (Happy Wanderer), Norman Wisdom (Don't Laugh at Me), Dean Martin (That's Amore), Bing Crosby (Changing Partners), and Eddie Fisher (Oh! My Pa-Pa) were hardly to be thought of as the disciples of Bill Haley, Elvis Presley and madcap Jerry-Lee Lewis.

Haley's Comets had stayed five weeks high in the chart with Rock Around the Clock the previous year; Elvis Presley had unleashed Heartbreak Hotel. However, the incursion by Rock was so insignificant that it could either be safely ignored or else embraced by liberal-minded clergymen. In other words it wasn't much of a threat to the social status quo. Youth culture, flour-

ROCKIN' IN THE AISLE: *The Rev John Harwood and his family, taken in the Sixties by which time Rock 'n' Roll had been superceded by the musical styles it inspired*

SERMON WILL BE ON ROCK 'N ROLL

...s sermon next Sunday evening will be all about his type of music.

"Rock 'n' Roll" music. He ... of Eccleshill Congrega-...

Eccleshill minister

ishing in the United States, was unknown here.

Mr Harwood rounded-off his sermon with a peroration to the mums and dads present. "Do not discourage the youngsters in their music and dancing. Encourage them and at the same time guide them through their music along the right channels."

It was his fifth year at Eccleshill. Nearly four years earlier he had created a bit of a stir by calling on churches to provide their own municipal candidates to contest seats on the city council; but that lacked the historical import of his Rock 'n' Roll sermon, bearing in mind the impact Rock was to have on music and youth on both sides of the Atlantic.

Less than five months later in July, 1957, a meeting took place at Woolton Parish Church Village Fete on Merseyside which was to lead to the revolution which changed the pulse of the world in the 1960s.

On that summer afternoon John Lennon, then 17, met 15-year-old Paul McCartney. Impressed by the latter's guitar-playing, Lennon invited him to join his group, The Quarrymen.

They came together at an important time because McCartney was still a schoolboy while Lennon was soon to join Liverpool Art College. Within six years Lennon and McCartney were on the verge of world fame.

The pounding rhythms and vocal harmonies of The Beatles were to effect all manner of changes to Britain's social fabric, changes which even Mr Harwood could not have foreseen that March evening in 1957 when he issued the commandment: Let Them Rock.

T&A

1958
Gritty northern drama blazed trail for succession of films

BRADFORD, TUESDAY, JUNE 3, 1958

Novello's
BRADFORD'S FASHION CENTRE

EPARES STAR OF FILM CHATS WI
BINGLEY AMATEUR PLAYER

THERE is going to be plenty of "Room at the Top for Bingley Little Theatre (writes Peter Holdsworth). Much of the action in John Braine's novel is centred on a similar playhouse, and the company which started shooting location scenes in the West Riding yesterday for the film of the book have recruited many players from the Bingley theatre, of which Mr. Braine is a member, to help.
Lorna Mawson, publicity manager of the Little Theatre, tells me that Jack Clayton, director of the film, has appointed her liaison officer between the screen unit and the theatre.
Yesterday she and three other performers from Bingley took...

Too proud to seek job, he stole lea from mill roof

PRIDE prevented John Wrigglesworth from seeking job at the employment exchange and registering un... Instead, he climbed six...

Room for the movies

This summer day more than 40 years ago marked the beginning of modern Bradford's involvement with the making of motion pictures.

Location shooting in the city began for Jack Clayton's movie version of Room at the Top, the hugely successful novel by Bingley writer John Braine. As the T&A reported at the time:

"Filming began today inside Bradford Town Hall. The sequence being filmed, and which was expected to take all day, was a continuation of yesterday's Town Hall arrival scene shot in Halifax.

"Laurence Harvey was still the only star to be

Tuesday, June 3, 1958

seen, although Donald Houston is now in Bradford. He enjoyed a solitary cup of coffee in the Victoria Hotel this morning, his colleagues all being at the Town Hall."

The Quality Victoria Hotel, as it is now called, was director Jack Clayton's base where he had a production office. About half the 60 members of the film unit stayed at the Victoria, which in those days faced the Exchange Railway Station; the remainder bedded down at the Midland for the three weeks of filming in Yorkshire.

Room at the Top is the story of Joe Lampton's malevolent rise from Town Hall clerk to industrial riches by marrying a millionaire's daughter, sacrificing true love along the way to reach his goal. The book was a sensation in the late 1950s. While it embraced society's common ethic - to get on and make something of one's self - it located this ambition in a handsome self-seeker. Joe Lampton, both hero and villain, broke the rules by having a passionate affair with a married woman. The film broke new ground in more ways than one.

STEAMY SCENE: *Laurence Harvey and Simone Signoret in a scene from Room at the Top, filmed in and around Bradford*

Continued on Page 97

TEAM WORK: *Film director Jack Clayton, left, welcomes actor Laurence Harvey to the Victoria Hotel in Bradford with Bingley author of the Room At The Top book John Braine, far right*

Continued from Page 96

Firstly it aimed for urban authenticity, the kind of kitchen-sink, back-street realism which Coronation Street became famous for on TV in the 1960s.

Secondly, so much of it was shot on location in Bradford, Bingley, Halifax and Keighley rather than in the studio. Thirdly, Lampton's affair with free-spirit Alice Aisgill, a drinking, smoking woman of strong opinions and fatal tenderness (one of the great Simone Signoret's best performances) was depicted pretty graphically at a time when sex was not a feature of British motion pictures.

Despite the complaints of some city centre shopkeepers - they objected to the disruption to trade allegedly caused by the presence of the film-makers - Bradford seemed to like being in the movies.

Within four years another film unit arrived to shoot the movie version of Billy Liar, the novel written by Yorkshire writers Willis Hall and Keith Waterhouse. Director John Schlesinger brought the young Tom Courtenay to the city to star as Billy Fisher, a Yorkshire Walter Mitty. The famous Wilfred Pickles played his testy father. Bingley-born Rodney Bewes, who went on to star in The Likely Lads and Whatever Happened to the Likely Lads, and a young Julie Christie teamed up with movie veteran Finlay Currie for the production.

At the time Bradford's city centre was undergoing much change, and the film captures this. Today Billy Liar remains the best motion picture record of the Bradford beloved of J B Priestley and drawn by the young David Hockney (a familiar figure pushing a con-

verted pram full of paints and artist's materials around Bradford).

In 1974 Hockney, by then world famous, was the subject of Jack Kazan's biopic A Bigger Splash.

After the release of Room at the Top and Billy Liar, the cameras kept coming back. Laurence Harvey returned for Life at the Top, the sequel to Room at the Top. The late Bob Cryer, Labour MP for Keighley and then Bradford South, was instrumental in helping to make the shooting of The Railway Children possible on the Worth Valley Railway in the summer of 1970.

John Schlesinger came back to direct Yanks in the late 1970s. Much of Alan Bennett's A Private Function was filmed in and around Ilkley in the early 1980s. Bradford-born writer the late Andrea Dunbar's Rita, Sue and Bob Too was shot on the Buttershaw estate and at Haworth, and elsewhere in Bradford. Albert Finney and Tom Courtenay teamed up for a memorable movie version of Ronald Harwood's play The Dresser, a good deal of which was filmed at the old Alhambra Theatre before its £8.2m facelift. Similarly,

part of Testament, the biopic of the Russian composer Shostakovich, was shot at the theatre. Alan Bennett came back to do location shooting for The Insurance Man, his movie about the Czech writer Franz Kafka. In the late 1990s Federico Fellini shot part of Jane Eyre on location in Bronte country - the film's premiere was held in Keighley in 1997. LA Without a Map used Undercliffe Cemetery as a location. My Son the Fanatic, based on Hanif Kureshi's novel, was partly filmed in Bradford - Oak Lane and the Midland Hotel feature prominently. The BBC2 drama Blood and Peaches, by Bradford writer Martin Sadofski, was filmed here, as was Kay Mellor's Band of Gold. The works of Bradford writers Charlotte and Emily Bronte, J B Priestley, and John Braine, have been made into 16 movies. One of Britain's most famous film and theatre directors was Shipley-born Tony Richardson, who made 23 movies including Look Back in Anger, Saturday Night and Sunday Morning, The Loneliness of the Long Distance Runner, A Taste of Honey, and the Oscar-winning Tom Jones. Another Bradford-born director, James Hill, made five movies including Born Free and The Belstone Fox.

And Bradford-born movie producer Steve Abbott had a hit with Brassed Off, starring Peter Postlethwaite and Stephen Tomkinson.

About 52 movies with a direct or indirect Bradford connection were made since that summer day in June, 1958, when Jack Clayton started filming Room at the Top at the Town Hall.

Room At The Top broke new ground for film makers in Britain

T&A

1959   *PM Macmillan enjoyed a pre-election tour in Bradford*

A rally good day!

There was a time when people got excited about elections. Canvassing, leafleting, bringing in top speakers to address meetings that were sometimes extensively reported in the Press - this was part of the warp and weft of a democratic society.

Eight days before the General Election of October 8, 1959, there was a good deal of excitement in Leeds and Bradford: the Prime Minister, Harold Macmillan, was due to fly in to rally Conservatives in both cities.

"It was a tired and drawn Mr Harold Macmillan who stepped down from a plane at Yeadon Airport yesterday afternoon. He had had a hectic morning in Glasgow, addressing six outdoor meetings, one indoor meeting and speaking after lunch," the T&A reported in its Election Gossip column.

Give a politician an audience and weariness is soon forgotten. The Prime Minister gave a 15-minute speech to a crowd of about 200 in front of Leeds Town Hall, at one point rousing himself to take on some Labour Party supporters carrying 'Ban the Bomb' banners.

The bomb in question was the hydrogen bomb which the Americans had successfully tested in March, 1954, at Bikini Atoll in the Pacific. In 1958 The Campaign for Nuclear Disarmament was formed in England to agitate for the British Government to adopt a policy of unilateral nuclear disarmament.

Lest we forget, the Cold War between East and West was a reality 40 years ago. Fidel Castro's guerrillas had overthrown the Batista regime in Cuba. Three years later this little island 80 miles or so off the Florida coast almost brought the United States and the USSR to war. The Berlin Wall was two years away from construction.

TELEGRAPH AND ARGUS, THURSDAY, OCTOBER 1, 1959

WONDERFUL, SAID THE PREMIER

GOOD DAY OUT: *The Prime Minister Harold Macmillan parades through Bradford to address a Tory party rally at St George's Hall*

After a meal and a rest at Bradford's Midland Hotel, Mr Macmillan was driven in an open-top Ford Zephyr to the big set-piece rally at St George's Hall. He

Thursday, September 30, 1959

was escorted by a double rank of Young Conservatives bearing election placards for prospective parliamentary Tory candidates.

The rally was a triumph. The Prime Minister poked gentle fun at the leader of the Opposition, Hugh Gaitskell, and had the audience in the palm of his elegant hand. At the end of it he declared: "I shall never forget this wonderful meeting."

Eight days later Bradford and the rest of the country went to the polls. Constituency boundaries were different in those days. The four Bradford seats were called East Division, West Division, and so on. Then there were the Divisions for Ripon, Skipton and Shipley. Conservatives were returned for all three of the latter.

Of the four Bradford seats, however, Labour won the East and South, while the break-away Conservative & National Liberal Party won the North and West.

Harold Macmillan's Conservative Party was returned with a majority of 100. Among the 25 women elected was a new MP for the North London constituency of Finchley - Margaret Thatcher.

T&A

1960
Labour lost its grip on power for first time in 15 years

Telegraph & Argus
The Yorkshire Observer

landslide against Socialists in boroughs as Tories make sweeping gains, capture 13 more towns

BRADFORD DEFEAT FOR LABOUR

Lose control of Council for first time since 1945

101, she lives in a world of silence

Injured girl is found in road
NEAR CAR   U.S. BALLOON

ALL CHANGE: *The T&A headlines of Friday, May 13, which proved unlucky for the Labour Party in the city*

Lucky day for some

On Friday the 13th the T&A told the public that after 15 years in office Bradford City Council's Labour Group had lost control to the Conservatives.

Of the 20 seats contested, Labour lost six at Eccleshill, Exchange, North Bierley East, North East Bierley, Bierley South, and West Bowling. The result gave the Conservatives 37 seats, Labour 34, and the Liberals nine.

Coming eight months after Harold Macmillan's Tories had gained a 100-seat majority in the General Election the result in Bradford wasn't that surprising. It

Friday, May 13, 1960

demonstrated that even in this industrial city, local politics could prove volatile.

Unlike Wakefield, Leeds, and other solid Labour power-bases, Bradford was liable to change from blue to red or, as in this case, red to blue.

Forty years ago, before the 1974 reorganisation of local government into a two-tier system of districts and counties, public services such as fire, police, water, planning, parks, and much more, were run by city councils or urban district councils.

Beyond the city of Bradford boundary, for example, satellite urban district councils existed at Ilkley, Keighley, Shipley, Baildon, Bingley, Queensbury and Denholme. These bodies with their real powers, including the power to raise a rate, had their own town halls, their own local representatives, and their own elections.

15-YEAR LABOUR RULE ENDS Lowest poll

Bradford's new councillors

In 1960 these elections took place on the Saturday, May 14, and in part reflected what had happened two days earlier. The Conservatives, who gained 23 seats across West Yorkshire, took control of Keighley, for example; but Labour, which lost 21 seats overall, held on to Shipley.

After the war the country shocked Winston Churchill by rejecting his party in favour of Clement Attlee's Labour and its promises of wholesale social and welfare reform. But by the mid-1950s the country, weary of shortages and rationing, was getting impatient for jam today and believed the Conservatives could provide the good life.

The period 1959-60 was the turning point. Nationally and locally the country had given the Conservatives a vote of confidence. Harold Macmillan, who demanded a national house-building programme of 300,000 units a year, was to say that the British "had never had it so good".

Four years later the Tories were voted out of office. Bradford sometimes reflected the national mood. At other times it did not. Take the 1970s. Nationally, Labour and Conservatives shared the decade between them. In Bradford, however, the Tories ruled right through until 1982 - the start of four years of hung-council politics. Labour won back power in 1986, probably the height of Mrs Thatcher's popularity in the country.

Now, in the second year of a Labour Government, the Labour Group's majority in Bradford has in two years gone down from 50 to 18.

Modern Bradford, unlike the city in 1960, has experienced boundary changes as well as enormous changes in the make-up of its population. That's why local politics remain volatile and fascinating.

T&A

1961

Thousands vaccinated after smallpox deaths in city

Telegraph & Argus

The Yorkshire Observer

LAST CITY

No. 29,13J   THREEPENCE   BRADFORD, FRIDAY, JANUARY 12, 1962

Bradford now has six suspect cases—five children and one nur

SMALLPOX FEAR: 2 DI

All visitors barred at Children's Hospital and St. Luke's

MOH worked through night

DR. JOHN DOUGLAS, Bradford's Medical Officer of Health, who with his deputy, Dr. W. Edgar, and members of his staff worked throughout the night in the Health Department. Town Hall telephone switchboard operators remained on duty to deal with a constant stream of calls.

WITH the death of a 49-year-old Bradford woman in the Leeds Road Isolation Hospital, Bradford has now had two deaths from suspected smallpox—and there are five child patients from the Children's Hospital and one member of the nursing staff under observation as suspected cases.

It has not yet been finally confirmed by laboratory tests that smallpox was the cause of the two death   have little doubt. The   of a 40-year   he ha

Nine years since last epidemic

*T*HE last outbreak of smallpox West Riding was in 1953 wh epidemic spread from East Lanc

In February and May of that y people died from smallpox, whic later thought to have originated cotton.

There were cases in Halifax, B Baildon, Shipley, Leeds, Lint (near Huddersfield) and Gilderso well as in Lancashire and thousa people were vaccinated.

It cost Bradford 'Corporation to vaccinate 52,000 people dur outbreak.

BARRIERS ON GATES

ck the top and
rances to St.
members
n people that
is closed to

PMG sees Premiers
Likely to refuse

anche

Bandits g £10,600 three raid

PAY-DAY bandits grabbed £10,600 in thre raids today. In the attacks they injur officials who were treated in hospital.

In the first raid four black hooded men in van rammed a wages car as it was entering a Road Services depot, smashed the windows w bars and grabbed a bag containing more than £

Raid No. 2 was outside Euston Station. Two railway employees were beaten down with iron bars and satchels holding £3,000 were taken.

The other attack was near the Central Middlesex Hospital, Park Royal.

Four cosh-wielding men attacked two wages clerks and made og with the £4,600 payroll.

At the BRS depot a car with four employees taking the weekly pay from the bank was about to turn into the gates when the van shot up on to the pavement, ramming the car's near side.

Meanwhile a Ford Zephyr rammed it from the offside, pinning it in.

The bandits leapt out, one of them grabbed the money and after a fierce struggle they drove off in the Zephyr. One of the BRS men received a hand injury.

The cashier in the car was Mr. A. Rodd, with him were Mr. F. Taylor, platform superintendent, Mr. S. Wager, traffic clerk, and Mr. G. Miller, yard foreman.

A DEPOT SPOKESMAN STATED THAT TWO OF THE CAR OCCUPANTS HAD SAID THAT AT LEAST TWO BANDITS CARRIED GUNS.

The   y car was later found in N   London.

grabbed two bags £4,600.

One of the clerks head on the other, was also hit on the h

A spokesman at said that the cash was pay-roll for the works

The two clerks had co money from the bank an in a van.

They had only walk into the offi were attacked.

The robbery was s office of a man who stores. Mr. V. Dobson his van and followe car at 50 m.p.h. but c up with it.

"One of the raider mark under his left was wearing a gr hat," said Mr. D

The car was la doned with the cos

INNER WHEEL

Members of Heckmondw Wheel have given Mrs. L. a founder-member a ha appreciation of her 24 ye ciation with the organisa founder-president, Mrs. port, made the presentat

LATE N

MAN FOR THE MOMENT: *Medical Officer of Health, Dr John Douglas, who steered the city calmly through the smallpox 'epidemic' that led to four deaths*

Calm in the face of fear

INOCULATION QUEUE: *Crowds calmly line up outside St George's Hall, next to the T&A building, for smallpox vaccinations*

The first victim died three weeks after Christmas. He was a 40-year-old abattoir worker who had been taken to St Luke's Hospital, Bradford. On the day he died, a cook on the staff of Bradford Children's Hospital was taken into isolation and later died in Leeds Road Hospital.

Friday, December 29, 1961

The medical authorities had no doubt of the cause of death - it was smallpox, and they had an outbreak on their hands.

Smallpox now no longer exists outside laboratories. Its eradication was one of the great triumphs of the World Health Organisation and its associated bodies.

Smallpox was by now a rarity, which made it difficult to spot

It was endemic in Britain up until 1935 - that is, cases were regularly reported which had their source here. In 1902 it had caused 2,600 deaths. After 1935 it was rare, and that was a problem -

diagnosis was sometimes slow because few people had seen the disease.

The first alarm bell rang on December 29, 1961, when a man recently arrived from Pakistan was taken into hospital in Bradford for isolation. He had been on a flight from Paris with another man from Pakistan, from Karachi, where smallpox was epidemic.

He was traced via an announcement in the Telegraph & Argus, came forward, but showed no symptoms. It was later shown he had no connection with the outbreak in Bradford.

On January 12, a day after the abattoir worker's death, a two-year-old girl in Wharfedale Children's Hospital, Menston,

Continued on Page 102

4

Telegraph & Argus

The Yorkshire Observer

HALL INGS. BRADFORD 1.

Telephone: Bradford 29511.

Saturday, January 13, 1962.

KEEPING CALM

BRADFORD, according to a headline in a national newspaper today, is a "frightened city."

Statements of this sort are not only far from the truth—nobody has been noticed exhibiting any trace of fear—but can cause grave uneasiness in the minds of people who read them.

Dr. John Douglas, Bradford's Medical Officer of Health, who is leading the medical campaign against the smallpox threat, has described the situation as "disquieting"

This is facing the facts as they are, but gives no reason to translate "disquieting" into "frightening."

Bradford people know that the emergency is in good hands, and that by keeping calm and following the advice of Dr. Douglas and his team they will be doing the best service to themselves and their neighbours.

The city's health department, and indeed all health authorities in the area, have been quick to launch a vigorous counter-attack on the disease.

High praise is due to those who, with the utmost speed, took the necessary steps to set the preventive machinery in motion when smallpox was first suspected in the city. This was done when a ... mortem ...

Nort...
Secre...
at 5...
car...
termi...

He...
28-ye...
Paul...
tary...
Unio...
to ta...
was...
visit...
ditio...

Af...
Mr...
flat...
bac...

un...
Pr...
Ho...
tra...
for...
th...
bra...
ser...
Ass...
spe...

H...
the...
gis...
he...
to...
car...

"I...
afte...

TE...

SI...

who...
to t...
Mon...
exp...
adm...

H...
Par...
he t...
and...
Mi...

Continued from Page 101

became a suspect. Visiting was suspended and staff were barred from using public transport.

Oakwell Isolation Hospital at Birstall was prepared for cases and was staffed by volunteers. Five young children and a nurse were taken there from the Children's Hospital. On of them, a two-year-old boy, died the same night from smallpox.

The following day the first emergency vaccination centre was opened at Edmund Street Clinic and people began to queue. Bradford's Medical Officer of Health, Dr John Douglas, a Scot whose early career had rather resembled that of the fictional Dr Finlay - small town practice, but with ambition - described the situation, with characteristic dryness, as 'disquieting'.

Douglas was to emerge as a hero in a story with no real villains. For the next couple of weeks sleep was to be a rare luxury for him and his team. He had come to Bradford in 1927 after qualifying at Edinburgh and Glasgow Universities. He became medical officer at St Luke's and medical superintendent at what was then the Leeds Road Fever Hospital before becoming the city's MOH in 1946 at the age of 45.

It was his experience with epidemic disease, garnered at Leeds Road, which made him the man for the job when smallpox arrived.

He had dealt with it before, when an outbreak from infected wool crossed the Pennines from Lancashire in 1953.

Now the race was on to find the source of the new outbreak. This was a detective story where the name of the killer was known, but the hiding place wasn't.

Then the investigators had a break - though it cost a life. A pathologist from Bradford was taken to Oakwell with suspected

smallpox. He was to die there. But it was known he had carried out a post-mortem on a nine-year-old girl from Pakistan who had died in Bradford Children's Hospital from suspected malaria. There was a problem: although the girl's father lived in Bradford, he had had her body embalmed and flown back to Pakistan for burial, and examination was not possible.

The girl had shown no signs of smallpox, but John Douglas had little doubt about the cause of death. The disease, he pointed out, was one of the most difficult to identify.

Meanwhile a second vaccination centre was to open at City Hall. And almost a thousand suspected contacts were traced, vaccinated and put under surveillance.

It was now that the politicians and some of the Press failed to distinguish themselves.

At the time, there was a Bill going through Parliament to restrict the entry of Commonwealth immigrants into Britain and a number of politicians - not all of them on the

Silliness broke out elsewhere, but Bradford stayed calm

Right - played the smallpox card as 'evidence' of the 'danger' of immigration. Meanwhile one national paper described Bradford as 'the frightened city where two people have died', while a Leeds newspaper castigated the Bradford medical authorities for playing the outbreak down. This annoyed the T&A, which has a long history of distrust of carpetbagging journalists riding into town, creating a fuss out of half-digested facts and distortion, then riding out again leaving others to clear up the mess. For a start Bradford doesn't scare easily. The man at the centre of things, John Douglas, carried on working quietly at containing the outbreak. And he advised the community: 'Go about your normal business quietly and confidently, and avoid spreading rumours'.

This was good advice.

By January 15, St Luke's re-

Continued on Page 103

Continued from Page 102

opened, with the exception of two wards in the block in which the abattoir worker had died. Over the weekend, 30,000 people were vaccinated in Bradford. St George's Hall, the school clinic in Manor Row and Central House in Forster Square all became centres, while the City Hall operation was closed down.

There was a rise in silliness. In Surrey, two students from Keighley were sent into isolation because they had attended a dance in Bradford. A Cleckheaton firm sent home a Bradford employee for a fortnight on full pay. A long-distance lorry driver who had travelled through the city was refused accommodation in Cheltenham. And there were false alarms - a case of chickenpox and one of German measles caused a few flutters.

By January 16, 100,000 people had been vaccinated in the city. The real danger was running out of vaccine, but fresh supplies kept arriving. The centres stayed open until 10pm.

What the T&A said

High praise is due to those who, with the utmost speed, took the necessary steps to set the preventative machinery in motion when smallpox was first suspected in the city. This was done when a post mortem examination was being carried out on the man who died at St Luke's Hospital.

Dr Douglas and his staff worked throughout Thursday night to deal with the immediate danger, and they will miss many more hours' sleep, along with doctors and nurses, as the lengthy but vital detective work to track down contacts proceeds alongside the work of healing.

....Bradford people know that the emergency is in good hands...

- Comment column on Saturday, January 13, 1962

Meanwhile, in Leeds, where there had not been a single case of smallpox, women tried to force their way into a clinic to have their children vaccinated, even after they were told there was no vaccine left.

In Bradford there was no panic. Letters to the T&A showed a number of people prepared to jump on the race bandwagon, but an equal number prepared to see the problem as a health matter - smallpox, after all, killed people, not racial groups.

On January 18, Dr Douglas warned: "We are entering a period when secondary cases may arise". He also recommended that sports matches be called off, and the football clubs protested that they were being picked on. Cinemas and theatres were still open.

The MOH pointed out that football matches involved large numbers of people moving around the country.

By January 20 the first round was over. It turned out to be the last round. There were just two secondary cases.

The Bradford pathologist died in Oakwell on January 23. He was the last victim. The hospitals slowly came back to life.

On January 31, Dr Douglas announced that the risk of a widespread epidemic had passed. Two weeks later, on February 12, the outbreak ended officially.

Four people died from smallpox alone. Two others died from complications following infection.

Bradford had kept its head when others all around were losing theirs. In the period of the outbreak, about 2,200 other people died in Bradford - a good half of them from the city's real mass-killers: bronchitis, pleurisy and pneumonia, caused by the deadly fogs and smogs which had been arriving every winter for almost 100 years.

1962 *Splendid Victorian arcade demolished*

Death of the Swan

I f Swan Arcade existed today and a plan was put forward to demolish it, there would probably be an uproar. At the end of the Millennium we greatly appreciate what is old, particularly if it has the quality and style of the shops-and-offices arcade which graced Bradford's Market Street until 1962.

80 years of shopping in arcade ends

A SALE notice on the window of a men's outfitters' shop in Swan Arcade, Bradford, today proclaimed: "The last day." For when the heavy iron gates of the 80-year-old arcade are next opened after tonight, the demolition men will move in. Swan Arcade, built at a cost of

But there were surprisingly few voices of protest raised when it was announced that the 1870s building was to be replaced by a splendid 1960s one. This was the post-war period of great architectural purges, when the decks were cleared for a brave new world of concrete and glass. Not only did Bradford lose Swan Arcade, but it also lost Kirkgate Market - to the subsequent regret of many of its citizens.

At the time, J B Priestley declared himself displeased at the plan, because it was in Swan Arcade that he used to work as a

Saturday, March 3, 1962

very young man. But Priestley had long since moved well away from Bradford by this time, and most of the citizens who had stayed here didn't really care much one way or the other.

When the demolition plan was announced in the autumn of 1960, the T&A recalled that the four-storey arcade had been built,

Continued on Page 105

VICTORIAN SPLENDOUR: *The ornate architecture inside and outside of Swan Arcade which fell out of favour in the late Fifties and early Sixties*

Continued from Page 104

at a cost of around £150,000, on the site of the old White Swan Inn.

"The man with the foresight to build it was Angus Holden, four times Mayor and a Bradford MP," the newspaper reported. "He named his arcade after the White Swan and incorporated graceful swans in stone and ironwork at the main Market Street entrance....Ground floor occupant included a cigar merchant, a cabinet maker and two tailors.

"At the start of the century mill owners established offices in the arcade but after many years it reverted to its original role as a shopping centre."

It was a stylish place. The T&A described it thus: "The names of the ground floor occupants were originally painted on the windows against a background which shut out the light. So hanging mirrors were placed in such a position that they reflected light from outside into offices and shops. More recently, there have been mirrors angled downwards from the sides of the avenues.

"The old lift, or chain of cages [driven by a gas engine], never stopped running in business hours but it went so slowly that it was easy to step in or out as it reached a floor level and no attendant

GONE: *The once proud old-fashioned shopping mall that had been 50 years ahead of its time gave way to the 'future' of Arndale House, above*

The old lift never stopped during business hours

How we reported the news

A sale notice on the window of a men's outfitters' shop in Swan Arcade today proclaimed 'The last day'. For when the heavy iron gates are next opened after tonight, the demolition men will move in.

Swan Arcade has been 'dying' for many months. Most of the 112 tenants in its shops and offices moved out weeks ago and there were only two doing business there on the last day. One was an outfitters' shop, still filled with racks of suits and coats which the staff will move over the weekend to Leeds, sometimes described as the 'city of arcades'.

Telegraph & Argus
From the T&A of March 3, 1962

The other was a confectioners', which was carrying less than its usual Saturday stock.

Former tenants and workmen removing fittings were the only other people at work in what was a dusty and melancholy scene. It is estimated it will take about four months to pull down the city's only arcade, which will be replaced by a more efficient building to marry with the new city centre.

was needed. It was replaced by an electric lift many years ago."

The arcade was acquired in 1955 by the Arndale Property Trust for a reported sun of between £225,000-£250,000 - although the exact figure was never dis-

closed. The year after it was demolished, Arndale House was built on the site. Just as Swan Arcade, when it was new, was described as being 50 years ahead of its time, so the T&A reported

that its replacement, according to one of the architects who designed it, was "structurally the most advanced building to be constructed in the United Kingdom".

T&A

1963 *The Beatles returned to Bradford as conquering heroes*

Now we love you!

MISS MARGARET ELSWORTH hands to the Beatles a donation for Oxfam given by members of the Bradford Gaumont staff.

HIS TIME BRADFORD GAVE HE BIG SCREAM
Beatles visit

By Peter Holdsworth

ERE were more than 6,000 sore throats in Bradford and district yesterday. There would have been a pair i-deaf ears, too, had not a kind Press colleague e some cotton wool plugs.

For the big scre went up on S would ha artillery h had nev li it

MAN DEAD IN BRADFORD FLAT FIRE

RUSSELL ROBINSON (39), who had a one-room fla. at 15 Marlborough Road, Manningham Lane, ford, was found dead in smoke-filled bedsitter

r had toppled over and merchandis e Slack.

What a difference a year makes. In 1962 President John Kennedy helped to avert the threat of nuclear war with the USSR. The following November he was shot dead in Dallas.
For The Beatles, over nine months in 1963 they rocketed from bill fillers to show-stoppers and chart-toppers. Their two sell-out shows at Bradford's Gaumont (now the Odeon) on the Saturday before Christmas, 1963, couldn't have been more different from their first appearance at the cinema back on February 2 of that year.
Then, the group was part of a package tour along with 16-year-old Helen Shapiro, Kenny Lynch, and Danny Williams. Britain was in

the grip of its worst winter since 1947. The Beatles were supporting Shapiro, whose star was fading: theirs was rising very fast. Please Please Me, their second single, hit No 2 in the UK chart.
The Beatles' presence in Bradford that winter went unremarked and unreported. The T&A has no record of how the show went. Nine months

Saturday, December 21, 1963

later it was a very different story. The Beatles left Bradford in February a promising group. They returned just before Christmas a phenomenon.
From Me To You, She Loves You, and I Wanna Hold Your Hand had each exploded at the top of the UK singles chart. Lennon and McCartney were pouring out instant classics, either for themselves or other artists, as fast as they could write them.
Britain had known nothing like it. The Teddy Boy seat-ripping frenzy which

Continued on Page 107

WITH THE BEATLES: *T&A showbiz reporter Peter Holdsworth chats to John and Ringo on one of their visits to Bradford. Below, first time around, they played second fiddle to Helen Shapiro*

Continued from Page 106

had greeted the advent of Rock and Roll in the mid-1950s was a mere shudder on the country's emotional Richter Scale compared to what was to come.

The artists associated with it, Bill Haley, Little Richard, Jerry Lee Lewis, and Elvis Presley, were Americans. Haley was fat and middle-aged, and the Presley phenomenon seemed a spent force.

By comparison, John, Paul, George and Ringo were a driving, rhythmic, melodic pop group; they had their own distinctive sound; their harmony singing was good enough to be a capella; they wrote most (and then all) of their own material; and they were funny, witty, and charming to meet.

Their young years, enthusiasm, and freshness represented the future as much as their hair styles and Cuban-heeled zip-up boots. They offered the young what Harold Wilson's Labour Party promised the country if elected to power: liberation from the past and its stuffiness, its lack of adventure, its fear of success.

Beatle-mania caused a sense of excitement and anticipation weeks in advance of the show. When the 8/6d and 15 shilling tickets (45p and 75p respectively) went on sale at The Gaumont on December 1, thousands were waiting to snap them up. Some youngsters had stood in line for 17 hours, defying the cold and the winter rain. Thirty-six years ago pop concerts were utterly different to the stadium events which were to follow. The Beatles performed a set of about 30 minutes duration.

They were preceded by a variety of other performers: Billy J Kramer and the Dakotas, Rolf Harris, The Fourmost, Cilla Black, Tommy Quickly, and the comedy group The Barron Knights.

There were two shows for a total of about 6,600 people. Thirty-two St John's Ambulance aides were on standby. Leave for two-thirds of the Bradford City police division had been cancelled.

The big day arrived. The Beatles were driven from London by their chauffeur, Big Bill. They rendezvoused with the police at

Fans waited for 17 hours to get a show ticket

Shibden Mill Inn, Halifax, and arrived at the venue at 3.40pm.

"A bit different to when we were last here," quipped Ringo. "We've even got a sofa in our dressing-room now."

On each of the occasions The Beatles took the stage they were greeted with a hail of jelly babies (Ringo had said he liked them), autograph books, and paper darts. Peter Holdsworth, the T&A's late show business reporter, was there and described the scene for the paper.

"The faces of many of the swaying, head-rocking girls had an expression of dervish ecstasy. In contrast one little old lady, who had obviously escorted her grand-daughter to the show, provided a study in perplexed astonishment.

"Yet wild as it all may sound, the feeling of merriment and pleasure was contagious. For the big scream was an infectious youthful endorsement of the joy of being alive.

"Although the young people made such a noise inside the theatre their behaviour outside was admirable."

After the two shows The Beatles didn't stay overnight, but were driven to Liverpool. The following year they toured America and took the country by storm. On Saturday, October 9, 1964, The Beatles returned to Bradford to begin their 27-date UK tour. John Lennon had just celebrated his 24th birthday.

Three days earlier the Duke of Edinburgh had sought to calm older generation nerves by declaring that The Beatles were "on the wane".

T&A

1964

Driver probably had heart attack at controls

Considering Bradford's location, it's a wonder that there have not been more serious rail accidents.

The long, steep drag out of the old Exchange Station, taking trains south or east, was always a potential killer if brakes failed. Luckily it didn't happen very often. But human frailty was another matter, and it was this that was ultimately blamed for crash on June 3, 1964, which claimed three lives.

A diesel train, its hooter blaring, raced for a quarter of a mile out of control before running into a stationary mail train in Exchange Station. Two men - one of them the driver - died. And an 80-year-old woman was fatally injured, dying a day later.

One survivor said: 'Coming through Low Moor I thought we were going faster than usual.

'About 400 hundred yards from the station

Wednesday, June 3, 1964

the driver started blowing the hooter continuously. I gripped the seat as hard as I could and waited for the crash'.

He was helped from the wreckage uninjured but shaken, and began to help others from the damaged first coach.

'There were people lying across the seats bleeding and moaning with pain and others were badly shocked' he said. Thirteen people in all were injured when the train, travelling at an estimated 50mph, crashed. Some of those on board, realising that something was badly wrong as the train rushed toward the terminus, started towards the back carriage to be further from the impact.

The cause was never fully settled, but at the public inquiry which followed five months later, there was evidence that driver Joe Hansell had been suffering from heart disease for some time.

It was suggested that he was startled by finding signals against him at Bowling Junction. 'The mental shock of this to such a particularly conscientious and responsible driver might well have induced the [heart] attack in the way sudden and severe physi-

cal exertion might have done', concluded the inspector, Col J R H Robertson.

Driver Smith, still conscious but in extreme pain, would have managed to do some of the correct things, such as sounding the hooter, while failing to release the safety device known as the 'dead man's handle', which would have stopped the train.

Col Robertson said nobody was to blame for Mr Smith not being taken off his duties.

His health problem had not been revealed in a medical examination only weeks before the crash.

His widow told the inquiry that a specialist had told her: 'There is nothing wrong with your husband's heart'. She said: 'My husband was so conscientious that if he had known he had some heart trouble he would have given up, and not risked his passengers'.

Two killed in Bradford station rail crash horror

TWO men were killed—one of them the driver and 13 people were injured, some seriously when the 4.25 p.m. Manchester Victoria diesel train crashed at speed into the stationary engine of the 5.47 p.m. Bradford to King's Cross parcels train on No. 4 platform at Bradford's Exchange Station at about 5.25 p.m. yesterday.

The driver, who was trapped for a short time in the crushed cab of the diesel unit as it was torn from the chassis, was John Arthur Smith (63), Clare Crescent, Green Lane, Wyke.

The dead passenger was Aubrey Mortimer (42), 8 Glenwood Avenue, Baildon, a railways permanent way inspector.

A British Railways spokesman said: "The diesel train came into the station out of control."

Injured detained at Bradford Royal Infirmary were:

Eric Lister, 201 Toller Lane.

The ambulance service

EIGHT ambulances were sent to the station, with Mr. James Clark, the Bradford ambulance officer, in charge of the operation. Within 20 minutes of the call's being received at the ambulance depot all casualties were either at or on their way to hospital.

Bradford (wrist and neck injuries)—condition "satisfactory".

Peter Ian Wallbank, Corner Lodge, 32 Bradford Road, Guiseley—"satisfactory".

Margaret Annie Rostron, 35 Pemberton Drive, Bradford (leg and head injuries)—fairly comfortable.

Florence Irene Simpson, 2 Oakwood Lane, Leeds 6 (feet and ankle injuries)—"fair."

Beryl Marsh, 133 Harehills Lane, Leeds (shock)—"satisfactory."

Bernard Field, 14 Strathmore Street, Harehills, Leeds (concussion).

These men died

Mr. J. A. Smith   Mr. A.

Douglas Brown, 103 Street, Bradford (rib injury).

George Frank Savage, Sydenham Place, Bradford injury).

John Neville Wharam, 32 ton Park Croft, Rawdon (shock).

Stephen Zulubak, 11 Hope Street, Bradford (shock).

Inquiry

Mr. Wilfred J. Ellaby, s master, said that an "on-th inquiry will be held tomorrow inquiry will be followed by a Minister Transport inquiry.

Mr. J. H. Goodyear, Chief

(Continued on Page

Woman injured as police car escorts

A DRAMATIC picture of last night's train smash in Bradford Exchange Station. One of the victims is released from the wreckage.

TWO FULL PAGES OF PICTURES OF THE SCENE ON PLATFORM 4 ARE ON PAGES 4 AND 5. A FURTHER PICTURE IS ON PAGE 11.

ACCIDENT: *How the T&A recounted the news of the Exchange Station tragedy*

Three killed by runaway train

1965 M62 opening led to Bradford's motorway connection

The missing link...

The balloon went up just after two in the afternoon. It was blue - the colour of a motorway sign - and rose accompanied by two blue Very lights. The switch had been pulled by Transport Minister Tom Fraser to mark a new bit of motorway, opened on January 29, 1965.

It linked the Preston and Lancaster bypasses, quite some way from Bradford, but it was significant because it was part of the new M62 which would, seven years later, finally give Bradford a motorway link with the outside world, via the M606 to Chain Bar at Cleckheaton. Bradford was always a victim of its location when it came to transport. The only

Friday
January 29, 1965

way out of town on the flat was north towards the Aire Valley. East, West and South meant a hill-climb.

But the M62 was different. Built to cross some of the least hospitable terrain in England, the new motorway used techniques suitable to the task in hand. Rock blasted from cuttings went to make the base for a six-lane road across the end of a high dam.

The test bed for the Scammonden experiment was reckoned to cost £200 a foot. But to those who regularly had to negotiate the Pennines along the winding, high roads through the villages, often impassable in winter, it would have been money well spent at twice the price.

If driving over the tops was bad, building the motorway was even worse. A windless day on the Pennines in summer is a rare thing. A winter's day without gales is about as common.

Tough men, well-paid, were the key to the M62. The revolutionary designs, the hi-tech approach to problems, the breathtaking engineering projects, would all have come to nothing but for sheer human determination to get the job done. 13-hour working days were not uncommon, and days off a luxury. Finally it was done.

In August, 1972, the M606 opened to traffic. It was only two and a half miles long, and didn't actually link up with the M62

HARD LABOUR: *Workers graft in often inhospitable conditions to construct the M62 trans-Pennine motorway*

directly - but Bradford was at last on the motorway network.

No longer would a trip to Manchester be an endurance test - and journeys to Hull would in future be functional, rather than scenic.

T&A

Motorway link was spur to Bradford revival

1966 Protestors marred PM's inauguration as varsity Chancellor

A splendid day out

That was the year that was. England defeated West Germany to win the World Cup at Wembley, and Harold Wilson's Labour Party increased its majority at the General Election from four to 96.
No wonder the Prime Minister was in a relaxed and affable frame of mind when he arrived in Bradford on Friday, November 4, to attend a civic reception by the Lord Mayor, Alderman Louis Cowgill, and to switch on the floodlighting of City Hall's clock tower.
Pointing straight up into the winter sky like a rocket fuelled up for flight, the illuminated tower seemed to symbolise the path of Bradford's progress. New roads, modern buildings in the city centre, and now, after 50 years of effort and argument, a university.
The following day's ceremonials began with a service of dedication at Bradford Cathedral.
From the Cathedral the dignitaries and guests walked in splendid autumn sunshine to St George's Hall where Mr Wilson was installed as the first Chancellor of Bradford University -

PROTEST:
Placards and boos greet Prime Minister Harold Wilson as he walks to his inauguration as Chancellor of Bradford University. Below fellow graduans, including Barbara Castle

Saturday, November 5, 1966

formerly the Bradford Institute of Technology - and made its first Doctor of Technology.
Anti-Vietnam War protesters among the cheering crowd booed and barracked, but the Prime Minister was not put out of humour by the demonstration. Until that summer's General Election he had kept his nerve and managed a boisterous House of Commons for nearly two years on a shoestring majority; a bit of booing was not likely to shake him.
The central theme of his seven-page address to the audience of about 2,000 focused on the need for Britain's excellence in technological research to flow into industry and manufacturing. The creation of more universities and

more graduates trained in the sciences was a step in this direction.
He said: "To this extent the Inauguration we are celebrating today is symbolic of four separate processes and trends in our national life…Bradford now becomes the 40th university to be established in Britain.
"Secondly, it is a symbol of the greater emphasis in our national life of applied science and technology…an emphasis itself symbolised by the creation of a great new Department of

State, the Ministry of Technology.
"Thirdly, this ceremony marks the identification of a new seat of learning, research and application, drawing its strength and vitality from the life and vitality of the region, and in turn making its own contribution to the future intellectual richness, industrial advance and social development of the region.
"Fourthly, it is a shining symbol of the partnership which is being forged between education, industry, and government," he said.
Honorary degrees were then bestowed on, among others Cabinet Minister Barbara Castle MP, and Bradford Grammar School-educated historian Dr Alan Bullock.
Mr Wilson and his wife Mary, accompanied by 900 guests, then repaired to the new University where they enjoyed a £5,300 buffet lunch of champagne, lamb cutlets, sandwiches and cakes. The Wilsons then returned to London, and Bradford got on with bonfire night.
Harold Wilson remained Chancellor until 1985.

T&A

1967

Fiery Yorkshire all-rounder loses England captaincy

In a spin over sacking of Brian Close

QUOTE from ex-skipper

'This last fortnight was the worst of my life...all that I am guilty of is playing cricket to the best of my ability for my employers'

ALE OF TWO EX-SKIPPERS — CLOSE AND MIKE
TH OUT TOGETHER AT MIDDLESBROUGH
BEFORE TODAY'S MATCH

COWDREY—NEW
OF ENGLA

CLOSE AXED: COWDREY GIVEN JOB

By DAVID SWALLOW

BRIAN CLOSE today talked of 'the worst fortnight of my life' as, 250 miles away, MCC announced the 16 players to tour the West Indies —omitting Close and naming Colin Cowdrey as captain.

3 0 AUG 1967

Close, England's captain for the last Test last year and r all this year, has won six out of the seven Tests in he has been captain, but it seems he has lost the job se of the " time-wasting " episode at Edgbaston, for h MCC's advisory committee censured him last week.

Close made a prepared statement at Middlesbrough today before going out to lead Yorkshire against Warwickshire. He said: "I am bitterly disappointed. Ever since I was appointed captain last year I have been looking forward to leading the country in the West Indies cause I believe they can be beaten.

Obviously MCC do not consider I am a suitable choice to lead England. That is privilege and I have no comment to make on that score. I know I am not indis-le. Nobody is in cricket. The only thing that matters is that English cricket s to the top.

"Now I can sleep easy. This last fortnight was the worst in my life, although I have not been bothered by a guilty conscience.

"All that I am guilty of is playing cricket to the best of my ability for my employers — Yorkshire.

CHOSEN ...

CC party for the West ill be: M. C. Cow-ent captain). I. J.

MCC selection body spurned — picked Close

The Telegraph & Argus says.....

IT'S LUNAC

So that's the end of Brian Close as England's cricket captain. His sacking is an act of sheer lunacy of cricket suicide. Gary Sobers, the West Indians, the Australians and probably even the Chinese will laugh up

There the matter should have rested.
But no, this was war, not a game; a war of North v. South, Yorkshire v. the Rest, professionalism versus the establishment. Some pompous commentators—Peter West on Sportsview last night among hem — even t only Close he might

Warwickshire mem themselves acted in ungentlemanly way t Brian Close at Edg Close has been successful as E captain, probably successful for his de — undefeated in matches. As a lead hard, shrewd

UPROAR:
The front page of the Telegraph & Argus with a forthright Page One comment attacking the sacking of Tyke hero Brian Close

Dennis Brian Close was one of the hardest men ever to pick up a cricket bat.

He was brave to the point of foolhardiness, fielding at suicidal short square leg, seemingly oblivious to the dangers.

Once, when

Wednesday, August 30, 1967

a ball had ricocheted off his head to be caught at gully, a horrified fielder asked him: "What if it had hit you on the temple?"

"He'd have been caught at cover" said Close.

As a captain he was adventurous, always trying to make things hap-

pen. "We'd try and take a wicket even when we'd no right to expect one" he recalled. He was also successful.

By 1967 he had captained Yorkshire to two successive County Championships and was - rightly in the view of cricket lovers everywhere - captain of England. Under him, they had won five out of six Test matches. And England

Continued on Page 112

SENSATIONALISM OVER CLOSE HAS BLINDED MCC AND EVERYONE

BRIAN CLOSE

LETTERS to the EDITOR

Sir—I have followed with great interest the many letters and articles in the "Telegraph" and other papers concerning the Close controversy, with all the bias, invective, partisanship, etc.

It seems to me that everyone, including the MCC and the Yorkshire Cricket Committee, has been blinded by all the sensationalism and quite failed to see the wood for the trees.

Surely there was only one course open to the MCC—after all the hullabaloo created by the Press—to summon the two umpires and receive their report. Then, and then only, should further action be taken, if it was established that Close had disobeyed or ignored their warnings.

In all walks of life— whether it be in industry or sport, there has to be someone in charge, and though duties may be delegated the responsibility still rests on the person in charge. I understand that the cricket rules state quite definitely that the umpires are responsible for ensuring fair play.

Even our Prime Minister may sack Ministers for incompetence but nevertheless the responsibility for the country's ills are still his, and his alone.
FRANK RAYMENT,
Bankfield Road,
Nab Wood,
Shipley.

Nonsense

Sir—It is reported in the London "Evening Standard" that you have published a front page comment on the Close affair.

I cannot understand how an editor can permit such incredible nonsense to be printed in [a] newspaper!

[...]land decided she must [...]orce do without Brian's [...]ilities for one reason or [...] reason only—because he [...]nted time wasting tactics [...] Warwick, [...]m of a y[...]

words he used unfair methods to avoid losing the match.

I am very sorry indeed for Close—and it is a thousand pities we shall be deprived of his sterling qualities — but regretfully I must say he only has himself to blame.
D. T. PHILLIPS,
Winterfield,
Oldlands Avenue,
Balcombe,
Sussex.

Only one man

Sir — I would like to say after having read your article on Brian Close published in the London "Evening News" tonight that I agree wholeheartedly with every word.

I myself am a supporter of Surrey, have been all my life,

but in my own opinion, there is only one man to lead England against the West Indies — Brian Close.
G. J. ROWE,
117 Tivoli Road,
West Norwood,
London SE 27.

Insult

Sir—What a disgusting and despicable way to treat a man! To be punished twice for one offence is bad enough, but when the punishment and its administration is a far greater insult to human decency and understanding than is the offence, then the strongest protest must be made.

One cannot have any f[...]in, or respect for, an organisation which adopts these [...]tics against a man who [...] the game, to the best of [...] ability, in the way that [...] same body has encourag[...] a fatuous system of awarding points in championship matches.
D. M. D. LAMBE[...],
Oaklands House,
25 Thornhill Road,
Steeton.

Cheshire man calls our comment irresponsible

Sir—This letter may refute at least some of the points raised in your extraordinary front page comment on August 30.

Your statement that there would have been no fuss had Close belonged to a county other than Yorkshire is, to my mind, both incorrect and irresponsible.

You claim the Warwickshire members acted in a "most ungentlemanly way" towards Brian Close at Edgbaston. Do you really consider Yorkshire spectators at any of their county grounds would have acted in a more gentlemanly manner towards Mike Smith if the positions [...] been rev[...]

have paid to see a match be tween two teams have ever right to express their feeling if they consider the match, fo[...] any reason whatever, fell short of their expectations. County members may not pay at th[...] gate but their subscription[...] contribute a great deal to th[...] game.

Peter West is a far from "pompous" commentator and [...] entirely agree with him whe[...] he suggested Close might still be captain if he had apologised for his time-wasting tactics. I have always b[...] Brian Close in the greate[...] esteem and that regard wou[...] have been higher still if [...] had been gracious enoug[...] make this [...]ology.

DEBATE: *Letters flooded in to the Telegraph & Argus voicing strong opinions, on both sides of the argument, from all over the country*

Continued from Page 111

fans were looking forward to seeing the redoubtable Close leading England in the West Indies.

The Windies were a formidable side with Charlie Griffith and Wes Hall probably the world's premier fast bowlers of the time, Lance Gibbs, an off-spinner who would walk into just about any Test side, and the incomparable Garfield Sobers, skipper, fast bowler, slow bowler, left-handed bat and a great fielder. There were Clive Lloyd and Rohan Kanhai, as well.

Then came August 18, 1967, at Edgbaston.

The Championship was at Yorkshire's mercy but Warwickshire had the upper hand in their match. Needing 142 in 102 minutes to win, Warwickshire found themselves batting on a wet pitch with a ball which needed frequent drying.

Yorkshire would get two points from a drawn game.

It was at this point that the cricket world divided into two camps. Did Yorkshire's drying of the ball, discussion of field-placings and general demeanour on the field constitute deliberate time-wasting, ensuring a draw? Or was Close doing

Continued on Page 113

OFF-BREAK: *Close in action for Yorkshire as a medium pace off-break bowler*

Continued from Page 112

his job, within the laws of the game, to do the best for his side?

Just under a fortnight later, the MCC made up its own mind. Brian Close was sacked as England captain and replaced for the West Indies tour by Colin Cowdrey.

The decision divided English cricket and the T&A, speaking its mind firmly, made headlines for the first time since its reporting had helped to precipitate the Abdication crisis 31 years before.

In a front page comment, headed in large white-on-black letters 'IT'S LUNACY', the T&A gave vent to feelings which were often hidden in the heart of northerners, but were never so far buried that they didn't sometimes pop vehemently out.

Defending Close's tactics at Birmingham it pointed out: 'Every team is guilty of this type of games-manship at some time or another and the present championship system, which awards two points for avoiding defeat, actively encourages it.

There would have been no fuss if Close belonged to another county

'At Edgbaston not even the umpires kept to the rules. They did not consult together, as the law requires them, to warn Close that his conduct might be illegal...'

Then the writer began to get into his stride, claiming 'there would have been no fuss had Close belonged to a county other than Yorkshire'.

But it was the conclusion which really started the letters flying: 'England has chosen to do without his qualities because he is not one of the "magic circle", does not have a double-barrelled name, went to the wrong school, speaks the wrong language. But above all he comes from Yorkshire and that is offence enough for some."

The T&A comment, having firmly nailed its colours to the mast by surrounding the story of the sacking and the comment with a thick black border, was quoted the length and breadth of the country.

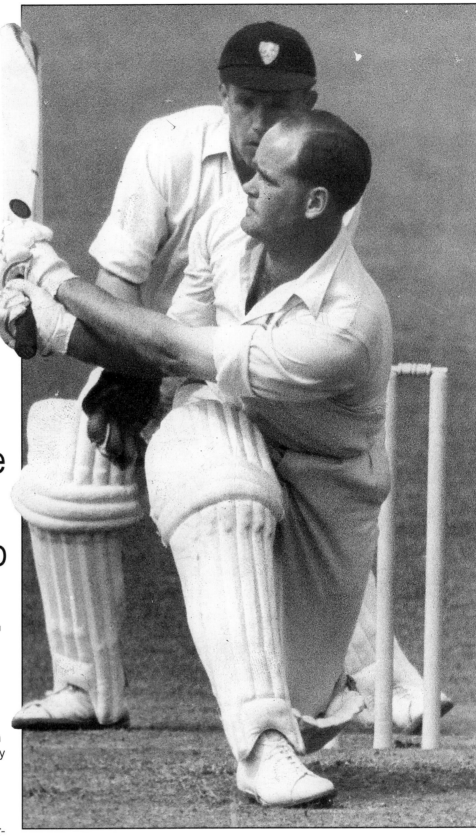

ACTION: *Close the batsman - an accomplished left-hander for county and country*

And it was from the length and breadth of the country that letters began arriving at the T&A. Some of them were surprising. Far from being a north-versus-south issue, the Close sacking seemed to divide on the lines of Gentlemen versus Players - though there were some odd opponents in either camp.

One letter decried the MCC's taking upon itself to act as a national cricketing authority without anybody granting it such authority. There should, said the writer, be a representative national body appointed by all the counties and con-sisting of professional cricketers as well as amateurs.

The letter was signed Rev W Cecil

Continued on Page 114

RUNS: *Close clips away another delivery for Yorkshire - but he never got the chance to show if he could beat the West Indies*

Continued from Page 113

Gibbins, Longthorpe Vicarage, Peterborough.

Another passed on 'the sympathy of myself and several of my workmates on the disgraceful way he (Close) has been treated by the MCC committee.

'Please believe me when I say Yorkshire cricketers and their tough approach to this wonderful game have many supporters in the south' wrote C H Burridge, from Fishbourne, Sussex.

Others from nearer home were less supportive of the sacked skipper. Keith Sagar, from Blakehill Terrace, overlooking Undercliffe Cricket Club, bastion of the Bradford League, wrote: 'Close's first responsibility is not to win cricket matches for his employers, but to maintain the standards of the game which gives him his employment.

'It is merely inverted snobbery to argue that because these standards derive from the days of the gentlemen they should be jettisoned now the players are in the ascendant. I want to see Yorkshire win the title. But even more I want to see cricke t remain a game proverbial for its fairness and sportsmanship'.

The war rumbled on in the letters page for weeks.

But Close remained sacked and Cowdrey took an England side to the West Indies. In the interests of fairness it has to be said

> Brian Close today talked of 'the worst fortnight of my life' as, 250 miles away, MCC announced the 16 players to tour the West Indies - ommitting Close and naming Colin Cowdrey as captain.
>
> Close, England's captain for the last Test last year and leader all this year, has won six out of the seven Tests in which he has been captain, but it seems he has lost the job because of the 'time-wasting' episode at Edgbaston, for which MCC's advisory committee censured him last week.
>
> Close made a prepared statement at Middlesbrough today before going out to lead Yorkshire against Warwickshire. He said: " I am bitterly disappointed. Ever since I was appointed captain last year I have been looking forward to leading the country in the West Indies because I believe they can be beaten.
>
> "Obviously MCC do not consider I am a suitable choice to lead England. That is their privilege and I have no comment to make on that score. I know I am not indispensible. No one is in cricket"

Telegraph & Argus
From the T&A of August 30, 1967

that Cowdrey, in the winter of 1967-68, was the last England captain to win a Test series in the Caribbean.

It also has to be said that he wouldn't, but for one of the most generous declarations in the history of the game (and his second of the match) by Garfield Sobers. He set England 214 to win in the last innings and, with Charlie Griffith out of the attack, England knocked the runs off for the loss of three wickets, Cowdrey hitting 71.

It's as well, because he would have come

back from the Windies vilified by Close supporters who would have been fervent in their beliefs as to What Might Have Been.

Of course there was consolation waiting in the wings in the shape of Raymond Illingworth, who left Yorkshire, went to Leicestershire and turned them into a formidable force before becoming England captain and getting his hands on cricket's Holy Grail - the Ashes, won in Australia...

T&A

1968 *Summer day the heavens opened in the city centre*

Flooded out by a monsoon

Telegraph & Argus masthead clipping:

BERKSHIRE

Telegraph & Argus **LATEST SPECIAL**

| Quote: 'It's flowing at five knots along Broadway' | Police frogman called out after subway alarm | Two injured when factory wall crashes at Idle | **INSIDE** |

BESIEGED — BY WATER

FOAMING TORRENT: *Workers stare in amazement as Canal Road became appropriately named for a few hours*

The storm which put out the summer sun and deluged Bradford on the morning of July 2, 1968, looks like an augury of disaster. The year was, in more than one sense, a watershed.

Martin Luther King was murdered, Senator Bobby Kennedy was assassinated, fiery and bloody rioting erupted throughout urban America, the Vietnam War reached an intensity with the Vietcong's Tet Offensive, Warsaw Pact countries invaded Czechoslovakia, and revolutionary-minded students in Germany, England and particularly Paris fought police in the streets.

Tuesday, July 2, 1968

The day that the rains came down was preceded by two days of stiflingly humid weather. On the Sunday, the last day of June, as Bradford sweltered a white-jacketed Paul McCartney did a spot of recording with the Black Dyke Mills Band in Saltaire, a tune called Thingumebob.

After tea at the Victoria Hotel Paul and his friends, together with his sheepdog Martha, left for London.

Monday seemed to mourn their absence. The afternoon sky went smoky black and a torrent of rain quickly cleared the streets and filled the Beck and the drainage system. Bradford was not put on flood alert, presumably because the authorities thought the worst was over. The following morning, however, the weather was even more humid.

Vast thunderclouds massed above the Aire and Wharfe Valleys. By 10am the day was going dark. By 10.15am day had turned into night. First came hailstones, the size of walnuts people told

Continued on Page 116

NICE WEATHER FOR DUCKS!: *Motorists in Petergate (above) and in Bridge Street (left) take the plunge as the flood waters deepen in the aftermath of the storm in July, 1968. On the right, Hall Ings and Forster Square station (inset) find themselves awash as worried pedestrians gaze down at the flooded Forster Square subway*

Continued from Page 115

the T&A. Killinghall Road was quickly covered with a white carpet of them. Then came the rain.

It was as though some malevolent power had scooped up part of the Atlantic Ocean and dropped it over Skipton, Bingley, Rawdon, Pudsey, Leeds, Rodley, Spenborough, Dewsbury, Huddersfield, and Bradford. Lister Park weather station reported that within 30 minutes 0.88 inches of rain fell on Bradford. In Pudsey 1.35 inches fell in 45 minutes. An ex-naval

man marooned in Bradford's city centre told a passing reporter that the current was flowing at about five knots along Broadway towards Forster Square. Water poured into the subway system, filling it like a bucket. Toilet attendants James Brown and Mrs Eva Brummitt had left their posts as soon as the water started to come in. Rumours of people trapped underwater sent PC Ronnie Hayward in a diving suit down among the depths. Fortunately all he saw were hundreds of chocolate bars and cigarette packets bobbing on the tide. Canal Road, the T&A side of Hall

Ings, and Thornton Road junction were all awash as the overflowing Beck gouted up surplus water. Bradford Library was flooded, some shop fronts caved in, vehicles caught in the thick of the flood were abandoned.

More than 600 emergency calls poured into the fire brigade. Two thousand telephone lines were put out of order including 800 into the Shipley Exchange.

The overall cost of the damage was

Continued on Page 117

Continued from Page 116

estimated to be £1m or more: a huge sum 31 years ago when the biggest transfer fee for a British footballer was the £110,000 Everton had paid Blackpool for Alan Ball in 1966.

Mercifully no one was killed or injured. Except for those trapped in doorways and those forced to abandon their cars, for most people the day when the rains came down in biblical proportions was rather exciting.

T&A

Beginning of the end

The last year of the Swinging Sixties, which was to culminate with British troops being sent to Northern Ireland to protect beleaguered Roman Catholics in Londonderry and Belfast from rampaging Protestants, began badly for Bradford.

Baird Television Ltd, which had factories at Lidget Green, Windhill, and Batley, announced the sacking of 610 women evening shift workers, with 125 full-time male workers to follow before the end of

Thursday, January 2, 1969

April. Two months before, 120 part-time workers on the evening shift had been sacked.

The company, which had recently been taken over by the Thorn Electrical Industries group, blamed the Labour Government's hire purchase restrictions and purchase tax increases for aggravating the normal seasonal decline in sales of television sets.

"There is no doubt at all about the future of the Bradford factory. It will go on," a spokesman for Thorns in London told the T&A reassuringly.

It did - for nine more years. In 1978 the entire factory was shut down and the remaining 2,200 workers were laid off. That was the start of three or four terrible years when the shake-out in textiles and engineering pushed unemployment in Bradford up to 30,000.

But in May, 1969, just under 13,000 men and women were claiming benefit in Bradford. In the UK the overall figure was 533,816 (compared with 1.28m now).

Why was the anonymous Thorn's spokesman so confident about the future of Baird's? Japan, which had revived its postwar economy by building gigantic oil tankers, was switching to motor-manufacture and domestic electrical goods.

"We are so far advanced technologically that we are even ahead of the Japs, who

OUT OF A JOB: *Workers at the Baird television factory in Lidget Green, Bradford, before the axe fell on 600 staff*

Pledge of no run-down — then notices go out to 23 workers
Now Baird men get their cards

TWENTY-THREE workers at the Baird television factory at Lidget Green, Bradford, are being sacked immediately. They

brought out their fully-transistorised colour set two months ago - 18 months after our own. Thorn's technology on colour is supreme…

"There is no question of Baird's being run down, of a major cutback there or even asking them to move to the South," he said.

The 610 sackings that took place the following day, a Friday, caused consternation for many families. The reaction of a 29-year-old mother of three is revealing for what it tells us about the cost of living 30 years ago.

"It's only three weeks since we moved into this new £3,500 house at Wibsey and we only took it on because of the five guineas a week I got at Baird's," she said.

A guinea was 21 shillings, or 105p. In today's currency the woman earned £5.25p

"The whole place is in a turmoil. Even the day staff are worried about their jobs. What I resent is the way this has all been handled. We've been treated like a flock of sheep…Our only chance seems to be in textiles," the woman added.

Her last remark is revealing too, for it shows that Bradford's staple industry was still perceived as having a future back in 1969, despite cut-backs and increased competition from parts of Europe and the Far East.

The reality was that in the 19 years between 1961 and 1980 some 53,000 textile jobs disappeared in West Yorkshire. When the Baird factory finally closed in 1978 textiles provided employment for little more than 20,000 people in the county.

T&A

1970

Bradford Park Avenue stunned by Cafe Royal vote

Kicked out of the League

Telegraph & Argus

No. 31,721   SIXPENCE   BRADFORD, SATURDAY, MAY 30, 1970

Cambridge United voted
in — big majority
against Bradford club

AVENUE GIVEN BOOT BY FOOTBALL LEAGU

From STANLEY PEARSON, CAFE ROYAL, LONDON

BRADFORD (Park Avenue) have been booted out of the Football League and
by non-League club Cambridge United.

Avenue won only 17 votes at the League annual meeting at the C
Regent Street, London, compared with 31 for Cambridge.

Member clubs re-elected were Darlington (47 votes), Hartlepool (42) and New
(31). Apart from Cambridge's 31 votes the only other non-League club to gain any sort of support was Wigan Athletic with 18.

The news came as a dreadful blow to the Bradford contingent in the packed meeting. The Park venue d...

Herbert Metcalfe — we will fight on-

Commen

On this sad day for the faithful who
Park Avenue through the last few fru
leading up to today's departure of the
Football League, our first thoughts a
Bradfordian who has fought so...
alive.

Many others have preceded Lan...
Metcalfe in the forefront of the battle
shown such enthusiasm in the face of su
personally committed himself to such a de...

The long years of arguing the pros...
possible Avenue - City merger are now
fortunate that it has had to be the Footba
and not the city itself, which has made the
Bradford is to be a one-club city.

It is, however, no good crying in
boots; that fund of enthusiasm at Park
has been given such a heavy shoulder
should not be allowed to die.

Whatever the future of Park Avenue
sphere, now is the time for the oft-dejec
in this area to get their shoulders behind
and begin the long uphill push into the...

PLEASE VOTE FOR CAMBRIDGE UNITED

Pink tights to save blushes

**DOWN
AND OUT:**
*Bradford
Park
Avenue's sta-
dium echoes
to the ghosts
of glories
past, includ-
ing the sharp
skills of for-
ward Kevin
Hector, inset.
Above, the
Football
League deci-
sion in the
Cafe Royal is
blazoned
across the
T&A front
page*

On February 10, 1968, Bradford (Park Avenue) had their last away win as members of the Football League. It was against Bradford City and gave great joy to Avenue's supporters.

Two years and three months later, their misery was profound.

The Football League had decided that it

Saturday, May 30, 1970

could do without Bradford, who had fin-ished bottom of the league for the third season on the trot and were applying for re-election for the fourth time.

In those days there was no automatic promotion and relegation in and out of the league - it was a matter for a vote by other clubs.

On Saturday, May 30, 1970, at the Café Royal in London, Football League pres-ident Len Shipman said: 'And now, gen-

Continued on Page 120

HOW HECTOR SALE MAY HIT AVENUE

-INS HAVE Facts
WELL IN behind
RECOVERY Shay
changes

Promotion bid —and "gates"— could suffer

Continued from Page 119

tlemen, the votes for associate membership of the League. Here they are:
'Darlington 47, Hartlepool 42, Newport County 31, Cambridge United 31, Wigan 18, Bradford (Park Avenue) 17.'
And that was that. Cambridge, who had had mini-skirted cheerleaders outside the Café Royal, were ecstatic.
Newport, who were convinced they were the ones for the chop, were mightily relieved.
And Avenue were out.
It was the end of a sometimes eccentric league story. Avenue had first tried to get to play among the big boys in 1907.
The Football League turned them down so Avenue, in a move which was strange as well as audacious, applied to play in the Southern League, from which Fulham had just been raised to higher status.
No matter that Bradford was emphatically not in the south - Avenue even offered to cover some of the expenses of teams having to travel from places like Reading and the London suburbs. At the same time there was the first of many suggestions that Avenue and their neighbours Bradford City should amalgamate.
The idea kept popping up - usually at lean times - in the years ahead.
Boldness paid off. Avenue started the season 1908-9 as new members of the Football League, which was then in two divisions.
It took them six seasons to get into the First Division and it was in 1915 that the club reached its zenith - finishing 9th in the season 1914-15.
The First World War then intervened and Avenue's star was never to shine so brightly again.
When the league resumed, Avenue lasted two more seasons in the top flight, were relegated into the Second in 1921 and went down to Division Three North the following year.
They were division champions in 1928 and managed to stay in the Second from 1929 to 1950 before dropping, but in 1958 had the dubious honour of being founder members of the new Division Four.
In the season 1960-61, Avenue had their last taste of glory, winning promotion to Division Three under a new manager, former Newcastle United and Scotland international hardman Jimmy Scoular.
They had two seasons in the Third before dropping in 1962-63, but at least that was a season when a rising star shone briefly at Park Avenue.

BACKER: *Eccentric businessman Herbert Metcalfe addressing a crisis meeting at the club in January, 1970, and, above, meeting the Press two days after the club was booted out of the Football League*

Kevin Hector was a quicksilver inside-forward who liked scoring goals.
He scored a century of goals for Bradford and when - amid controversy and something like mourning - he was transferred to Derby County in 1966 he repeated the feat for them.
The £34,000 transfer fee was a Fourth Division record, but it also signalled the start of the slide.
Avenue did not go gently into the outer darkness. In November, 1968, a Manchester businessman, Herbert Metcalfe, was co-opted on to the board. The following season he became chairman. He poured in money - at one stage £700 a week out of his own wallet (that's about £6,500 in 1999 terms) - to keep Avenue afloat. It was said that the players' wage packets arrived at the ground by van

straight from Metcalfe's Manchester home.
But Metcalfe's methods were at times eccentric and his appointments almost comic.
Manager Frank Tomlinson was plucked from a job running a sports club at the Hawker Siddeley works in Manchester.
And Metcalfe, stung by accounts of the club's goings on in the T&A, once rang football reporter Stanley Pearson and invited him to pick the side for the coming Saturday. Pearson wisely pointed out that the club had a manager, and picking the side was his job. That didn't stop Metcalfe sometimes picking the side himself.
But revolutionary ideas and bottomless pockets were not enough to save the club and in May of 1970 they were out of the league.
On August 15 they played their first game in the Northern Premier League. Herbert Metcalfe died suddenly in a Glasgow hotel while on a scouting mission. His counterpart at Bradford City, Stafford Heginbotham, said: "Bradford sport will not easily find so generous a man again" - praise indeed from a man who was never shy about putting his hand in his pocket at Valley Parade.
When the bell tolled for Herbert Metcalfe, it tolled for Park Avenue, too.
In 1974 the club was forced to resign from the Northern Premier League and from football itself.
A side of the same name now plays in the UniBond League Division One. Above that is the UniBond Premiership. And above that the Conference.
And above that is the Football League. Who knows..?

The T&A's reporter was once asked to pick the team...

1971 Protest greeted Ted Heath days after Commons Euro-victory

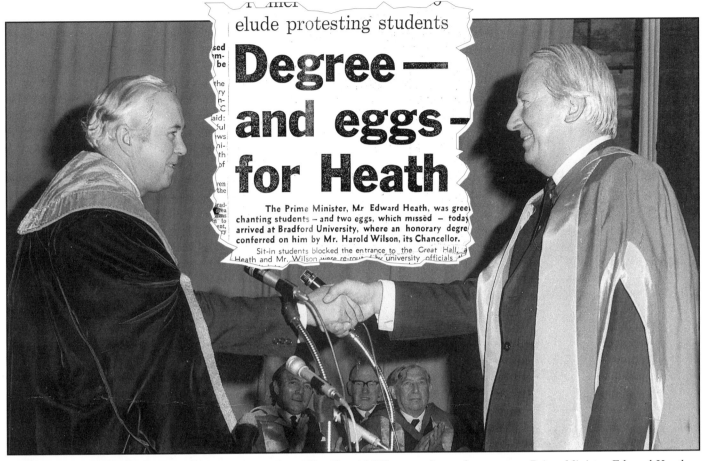

elude protesting students

Degree — and eggs — for Heath

The Prime Minister, Mr Edward Heath, was gree[t] chanting students — and two eggs, which missed — today arrived at Bradford University, where an honorary degre[e] conferred on him by Mr. Harold Wilson, its Chancellor.

Sit-in students blocked the entrance to the Great Hall, a[nd] Heath and Mr. Wilson were re-rout[ed] by university officials.

ACROSS THE DIVIDE: *Bradford University Chancellor Harold Wilson confers a doctorate on Prime Minister Edward Heath*

The yoke's on the PM

Five years after becoming Chancellor of Bradford University, Harold Wilson had the tricky job of conferring an honorary degree on the man who had displaced him as Prime Minister - Edward Heath.

Mr Wilson, however, was too much of a gentleman to allow political disagreements with his adversary in the House of Commons to mar a ceremonial occasion. He was aware of the demonstrators protest-

Saturday, October 30th, 1971

ing about unemployment and the Immigration Bill outside the University; but his responsibility was to make Mr Heath a Doctor of Technology and treat the degree ceremony as he would any other.

For his part Mr Heath was in high spirits. Only two days before, on Thursday, October 28, Parliament had voted to join the European Economic Community. Above all else the Prime Minister saw himself as a pioneer, dragging Britain kicking and screaming out of the past towards a prosperous European future, a future that included decimal currency which had only been legal tender since February 15 of that year.

"This marks the beginning of a period of change, of a time of challenge and of opportunity," he proudly declared after receiving his degree. He was addressing an audience at the inaugural opening of the University's latest acquisition, the Civil Engineering building.

On his way there he'd been hit on the leg by an egg hurled by a protester - one of two eggs counted by the T&A's reporter.

Inside the University about 50 students were sitting-in, registering their disapproval of both the degree and Mr Heath's presence. They were kept at bay by detectives, Special Branch men, and the University's

own security staff who locked all doors leading to the area where the Prime Minister would be.

A scuffle occurred in the vestibule of the Great Hall after one of the main doors had succumbed to the pressure from the protesters. A security guard was slightly injured, but the angry students were held back.

More barracking and optimistic shouts of "resign" followed Mr Heath's car as he was driven away from City Hall following a reception by the Lord Mayor and Lady Mayoress, Alderman and Mrs Herbert Moran.

T&A

1972 *Day they pulled the plug on Bradford's 'tracklesses'*

THANKS FOR THE MEMORY: *Bradford's last trolley bus leaves the city centre on March 26, 1972*

End of the road for trolley buses

When Bradford's last trolley bus left the city centre in 1972, heading for Thornton and laden with enthusiasts, it marked the end of the city's 61-year association with that particular form of transport. Bradford had been the first local authority in Britain to use trolley buses, and it was the last to get rid of them.

They had been a mixed blessing. They were clean and they were quiet, and their acceleration on Bradford's hills was most impressive. But they had their faults.

If there was a power cut, they all ground to a halt. They couldn't overtake, so at busy times often ran in convoys with the front buses packed and the ones at the rear almost empty. The trolleys, which carried the power from the overhead

Sunday, March 26, 1972

cables to the bus's motor, used occasionally to come off the wires on corners or roundabouts. When that happened, the conductor had to dismount and pull a long pole with a hook on it from beneath the rear of the bus and use it to put them back in position.

And there were few people who hadn't received a mild but disconcerting electric shock when they boarded the bus and earthed the built-up static.

The first trolley bus made its debut in the city on the Laisterdyke to Dudley Hill route on June 20, 1911. It was number 240 and closely resembled the tram

cars which operated on routes all around the city. For many years the trolleys were known as "rail-less trams" or, more popularly, as "tracklesses" - an expression used by some older Bradfordians right up to their disappearance in the early 1970s.

They were initially put to work on areas where the population was sparse, doing away with the cost of laying tracks (although, of course, the overhead cables had to be installed just the same).

Bradford Corporation didn't just run the buses. It also designed and built them. Despite the shortages of the First World War, it managed to build 18 single-deck trolley buses to operate on extended

Continued on Page 123

THE EARLY DAYS:

The Bradford trolley bus on the right (above) was built at Thornbury Works in 1914 and the other in 1923. Sixty years of trolley buses were celebrated in 1971 (inset picture) just a year before the city's last piece of trolley wire was cut in Carr Lane, Shipley (left)

Continued from Page 122

routes into the outer suburbs and villages around the city. And between 1920 and 1922 it built Britain's first covered top-deck trolley buses which, fitted with solid tyres, were put to work on the Bankfoot to Bolton route.

Four years later, the people of Idle turned down a chance to have trolleys running on their route instead of trams. They didn't fancy being shaken about on the solid tyres.

However, the introduction of pneumatic tyres made trolley-bus rides much more acceptable and gradually the trams were ousted from route after route. However, the two forms of transport continued in harmony right through the 1939-45 war, supplemented during the 1930s with motor buses which were thought to be more suitable for routes not requiring frequent services.

Despite the rising cost of electricity and overhead equipment in the 1950s, Bradford stuck with its trolley buses and even rebuilt more than 100 of them with new, modern bodies to lengthen their working lives. When the golden jubilee of Bradford's trolley-bus system was celebrated in 1971, enthusiasts from all over Britain flocked to the city to admire what had become a transport showpiece.

But the trolley buses' days were numbered. Barely a year after the jubilee the Council decided to switch to motor buses. The decision was not entirely a logical one. Because most towns in Britain were abandoning the trolley bus, it was decided that Bradford should follow suit - even though Bradford, with its hilly terrain, was well suited to that particular form of transport.

It was a mistake.

At least, that was the view of many of those who travelled on that last trolley bus on March 26, 1972, and expressed the hope that there might one day be a change of heart to bring their favourite form of transport back on to Bradford routes.

T&A

Hundreds say farewell to No. 844

End of the trolley bus era

1973 Yorkshire and England great given a CBE for Ashes triumph

Did Illy get just reward?

Much could be said about 1973 - the war in Vietnam, Watergate which was to bring down President Nixon, Britain's membership of the European Economic Community, the Yom Kippur War against Israel, the murder of Chile's President Salvador Allende in the military coup.

And twenty-two years after making his debut for Yorkshire against Hampshire at Headingley, Ray Illingworth was made a Commander of the British Empire in 1973's New Year's Honours.

Born in Pudsey in June, 1932, Illingworth was to become one of the shrewdest captains either Yorkshire or England ever had. His achievements

Monday, January 1, 1973

from that 1951 debut to his CBE award include seven County Championships and a Gillette Cup Final victory with Yorkshire.

He also captained Leicestershire to the County Championship and in 1970-71 led England to their first Test series victory against Australia. Taking the Ashes from the Aussies was no mean feat, especially in Australia.

In 1983, at the age of 51, Ray Illingworth captained Yorkshire to their first Sunday John Player League title.

His First Class career as a county and international all-rounder spanned more than 30 years during which he scored 24,134 runs, took 2,072 wickets, and held 446 catches.

He was for a spell a cricket columnist for the T&A, then went on to TV as a commentator - rivalling the brilliant Richie Benaud for assessing the balance of a match. In 1994 he was appointed chairman of England selectors - the one area where he can be said to have failed.

But Illingworth had to wait 18 years, until June, 1969, to lead England on the pitch for the first time. That was also the year his county career was resurrected with Leicestershire, after Yorkshire had bluntly rejected his request for a contract.

Illingworth's golden achievements showed there was indeed life after Headingley (oddly enough Yorkshire never won another Championship after he left), and in point of fact they probably merited a Knighthood, after all Leonard Hutton had received that accolade after winning back the Ashes.

Tough-minded but mild-mannered until roused and riled, Illingworth was pleased enough with his CBE, as he told the T&A at the time.

"I never dreamt that when I left Yorkshire so much would happen to me. This honour must be regarded as a tribute to the team which won the Ashes in Australia. I feel very proud today."

In 1979 he returned to Yorkshire as the county's first manager. Within months he removed the captaincy from Geoff Boycott. During the next four years cricket almost became a side issue as the Boycott Affair blew into a terrific storm.

Illingworth was essentially a player, a tactician with a gritty blend of experience, instinct and judgement - qualities which were of little use to him in the ferocious cut-and-thrust of the Boycott business.

The same could be said of Illingworth's term as chairman of England selectors, only in the latter case most of the cutting and thrusting was carried out in national tabloid newspapers.

TYKE HERO: *Ray Illingworth stepping out for Yorkshire, and above with his family outside Buckingham Palace when he received his CBE*

Telegraph & Argus

1974

Bradford became a dynamic large authority

A new beginning

Monday, April 1, 1974

Bradford warning over the danger of 'remote control'

Guard your freedom — Lord Mayor

By DENYS THORNTON, Our Municipal Reporter

The newly-installed Lord Mayor of the Bradford Metropolitan District, Coun. Tom Hall, told councillors today: "It for you to decide the shape of local government to come and guard zealously against further infringement of its freedom remain local."

Coun. Hall said at the Bradford City Hall ceremony: "This was promised to do, if elected. If you now fail to redeem that promise, my forecast is that local government will cease to exist."

Sign of the times

A day of changes at Bradford City Hall

Toughest Market

NEW ERA: *The new Lord Mayor of the new Bradford Metropolitan District Council, Councillor Tom Hall, is prepared for his inauguration in the mayoral robes*

On April Fool's Day 1974 a lot of people woke up not knowing where they were any more. Some, like the ones who had gone to bed in Ilkley and woke up in Bradford, were less than happy.

In places like Bingley and Shipley, leading citizens, who had gone to bed as councillors, rose as mere members of the public.

In the most far-reaching reform almost since time immemorial of the way Britain was run, the recommendations of the Maud Report had come into effect.

Bradford Corporation - a name redolent of paunches and watch chains - ceased to exist.

The city had become the Bradford Metropolitan District.

It was at the centre of a sprawling new local government area into which the likes of Keighley, Bingley, Shipley, Baildon and Ilkley had all disappeared. Communities who had once been uneasy neighbours had suddenly become bedfellows - a consummation that Shipley and Baildon had feared for years. Talk of bringing them into Bradford's embrace had been going on since the 1930s.

Ilkley, that staunch outpost of middle-class values, was unhappy about being brought into closer contact with the unashamedly proletarian Bradford, seeing itself as having more in common with Harrogate, which now found itself in North Yorkshire. Well, they each had

Continued on Page 126

Continued from Page 125

a Betty's Café. Harrogate didn't say much, though if an earlier plan, linking it administratively with Keighley, had gone ahead things may have been less placid…

Suddenly local government looked more professional. The evening meetings of small councils in places like Queensbury and Denholme, for so long a ritual of civic and journalistic life, passed into history - to the relief of many reporters but to the regret of many local people who saw being a councillor as a genuine public service.

True, there were a number of pompous, self-serving windbags on local councils. But in these days when government is largely by party caucus and the soundbite, it is not simply the glow of nostalgia that gives the impression that councillors of all parties genuinely had the interests of the community at heart as they gathered around mahogany tables, under portraits of their predecessors, to discuss seriously, and at great length, the siting of a new public convenience.

And it is interesting to note that, a quarter of a century after the great reform, more and more communities are trying harder, through the likes of parish councils, to

Now tourism for Bradford was a workable idea...

WIDE RANGE:
Bradford's City Hall now had under its wing the delights of Ilkley's Cow and Calf rocks, the Haworth Parsonage and Salts Mill

have their interests recognised once more.

But back on that epochal April Fool's Day, Bradford, suddenly nearly four times as big as it had been, reflected on its new identity. Whereas its parks and woods had been a source of civic pride, the city now found itself as custodian of the likes of Ilkley Moor and

Shipley Glen, the Bronte Country and Saltaire.

Tourism? It had been a sniggered joke when, in the 1960s, it was suggested that people might want to come here to enjoy themselves. Now a few visionaries began to look at the place again.

Perhaps it wasn't such a daft idea after all…

1975 Richard Dunn failed to take Ali's world heavyweight crown

On the last night of September, 1975, a fair-haired Bradford building scaffolder became British and Commonwealth heavyweight boxing champion.

Eight months later Richard Dunn, 31, climbed into a ring in Munich to fight for the heavyweight championship of the world. His opponent was the one-and-only Muhammad Ali, who took just five rounds to win on a technical knock-out.

Rugged Dunn remains Bradford's only world heavyweight boxing contender. How he came to earn his chance against Ali in America's bi-centennial year of 1976 is a story worth telling.

His first big professional pay day in 1969

Tuesday, September 30, 1975

earned him £220. Four years later Bunny Johnson beat him in the final eliminator for the British and Empire heavyweight championship. Then in 1974 he was knocked out by Jose Urtain in Spain.

"I came back as disappointed as hell. Janet (his wife) said I should have one more fight and if I lost I should pack it in," he told the T&A.

The 6ft 4inch Bradford man gave up-and-coming Londoner Tim Woods enough of a hiding to convince top-flight manager George Biddles to manage him.

Nothing remains all good or all bad for ever, and if 1973-74 represented Dunn's lowest point then 1975-76 was the pinnacle of his achievements.

In February he was matched against Commonwealth Gold medallist Neville Meade. Meade survived four rounds of hard-hitting but didn't come out for the fifth.

In September he was re-matched against Birmingham's Bunny Johnson, British and Commonwealth heavyweight champion with 21 consecutive victories to his name. The bout, at Wembley's Empire Pool, went the full 15 rounds. Referee Roland Dakin made Dunn the winner on points.

George Biddles had worked out the tactics; Dunn's hod-carrying physique and gutsy determination did the rest. Suddenly, he had acquired two titles.

He wasted no time in capitalising on his success. A breathtaking 35 days after the Johnson fight he fought Danny McAlinden. Dunn demolished his opponent with a second round knock-out, and became the first

KNOCKOUT BLOW: *Richard Dunn crumples beneath another heavyweight blow from Muhammad Ali in Munich*

Beaten by The Greatest

British heavyweight since Henry Cooper to successfully defend his title.

Three weeks later he was matched against the 26-year-old Texan Terry Krueger at the Royal Albert Hall. Krueger's 41 fights included 32 inside the distance wins.

Nevertheless he lasted one round more than McAlinden; Dunn knocked him out in the third.

To get the opportunity of fighting Ali, Dunn had first to defeat the German European Champion Bernd August, which he did in April, 1976.

This opened the way to his biggest fight, his biggest purse (£100,000), and his biggest

chance. He got in two or three good hits before Ali began to deck him at will, countering the Bradford man's gallant but clumsy forward surges with whiplash left jabs.

In October he lost his British, Empire and European titles to Joe Bugner in less than one round. At the age of 32 Dunn, who had 45 professional fights, retired.

In 1987 he was found working on oil rigs in the North Sea. After falling 40 feet from one and breaking both legs, he spent six years fighting to regain some semblance of fitness as well as compensation. In June, 1996, the 51-year-old Dunn, obliged to walk with a stick, was awarded £300,000. **T&A**

A touch too much sunshine

Mention long, hot summers and many people's eyes glaze over and they start reminiscing about 1976.

That was the year the sun came out in spring and stayed out until the end of autumn without a single cloud being seen in the sky - at least in our memories.

In fact, just for once, rose-tinted hindsight and truth have a lot in common. It got hot at the beginning of June. Within a couple of weeks there was talk of a serious drought in the offing, although a typical bank holiday weekend - it poured down - did a lot to replenish the falling reservoirs.

People in Bradford, of course, tapped their noses significantly and muttered about the fact that Bradford's water supplies - secured with great foresight and at great

The long hot summer of 1976

expense in the 1920s by the building of Scar House and Angram reservoirs - were now no longer our own.

The Bradford Corporation Water Department had gone, subsumed into something called the Yorkshire Water Authority when local government was reorganised in 1974.

But what the heck - a water shortage was a small price to pay for some of the best weather anybody could remember. And the sun shone on and it got hotter. In some parts of Bradford a good night's sleep had become an almost-forgotten luxury as the

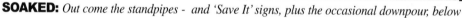

SOAKED: *Out come the standpipes - and 'Save It' signs, plus the occasional downpour, below*

thermometer hovered around the 80 degrees mark even in the early hours.

Manufacturers of soft drinks were ecstatic. So were landlords. The most energetic thing most people could manage in an evening was a walk to the pub.

As summer wore on, Britain's landscape started to change. The green and pleasant land started to turn yellow. Fields took on the colour of a manila envelope. Leaves wilted and farmers began to worry seriously not only about crops, but about whether they had enough water for livestock.

As July turned to autumn the clouds came, but they brought precious little water - only

relief from the relentless sun. Those who had once talked longingly of emigrating to somewhere with a hotter climate now discovered that there was something to be said for England's often perverse, but happily varied, weather.

In Bradford, Muslims knelt in Infirmary Fields at the bottom of Lumb Lane and prayed for rain. And the Government brought in its own patron saint of lost causes, Dennis Howell MP, as Minister responsible for the drought.

One or the other worked. The weather broke and the rain came and suddenly flushing the loo no longer involved a struggle with one's social conscience.

As the parched, cracked edges of the reservoirs disappeared beneath the rising water, Bradford looked back over a long, hot summer with mixed feelings.

Non-stop sunshine is something we often wish for. But, as the old saying has it, be careful what you wish for, because you might just get it. Perhaps the proper place for golden summers is in the memory.

T&A

1977 *'A year of fun, happiness and enjoyment'*

Such socks appeal!

BEST FOOT FORWARD: *Paul Hockney with a pair of the Union Jack socks he sported during his term of office as Lord Mayor, which coincided with the celebrations of the Queen's Silver Jubilee*

Bradford's new Lord Mayor wants to start camp for young folk

It would have been hard to have found a more suitable person than Paul Hockney to be Lord Mayor of Bradford during the Queen's Silver Jubilee year. Fun and fund-raising shared the top spot on his agenda.

Councillor Hockney, who represented Idle ward as a Liberal, set the tone for his year of office early on by revealing that in honour of Her Majesty's special anniversary, he intended to wear Union Jack socks for civic occasions.

However, barely a fortnight into his year of office, he was asking pupils at Bradford Girls' Grammar School if they could possibly knit him some more of these socks as he only had two pairs and had to keep washing them every night.

A month later Councillor Hockney took delivery of 70 pairs of Jubilee socks - not from the Girls' Grammar School knitters but from Ilkley businessman Mr Howard Scaife, who had responded to the Lord Mayor's challenge for someone to come up with a pair of socks for each of the members of Bradford Schools Band, who

Tuesday, May 24, 1977

were to play at a civic function at Keighley's Victoria Hall.

The T&A reported that Mr Scaife had scoured local department stores, determined to meet the challenge and present the socks as a gift in acknowledgement of the hard work and enthusiasm of young people during Jubilee Year.

During the year, the Union Jack wardrobe grew and expanded. The red, white and blue socks were joined by similarly-adorned wellington boots. Then came Jubilee ties, braces and pencils. Bow ties followed, made by a seamstress friend of Councillor Hockney and his wife Jean. A buttonhole came from another friend in London who heard him on national radio. Patriotic cufflinks were a gift from the eight girls on the switchboard at Bradford City Hall.

The Lord Mayor asked people to keep the Union Jack gifts rolling in. What he couldn't

use personally, he said, could be sold to boost the Silver Jubilee Appeal. That appeal caught the public's imagination.

An initial target of £50,000 was set to fund the Nell Bank Silver Jubilee outdoors activities centre on a 12-acre site near the river at Ilkley. When the final amount was totted up, it had reached £115,000 to establish a place where groups of children and teenagers could go to escape the pressures of inner-city life.

In among all the fund-raising Councillor Hockney - brother of artist David and himself a talented amateur water-colour painter - found time to put together an exhibition of his own painting and to shake countless hands.

By March of 1978, nine months into his year of office, he estimated that 50,000 hands had shaken his.

It was all part of what he described later as "a year of fun, happiness and enjoyment" - a year which also left a lasting legacy for the youngsters of Bradford.

T&A

1978 *Take over by combine spelled end for Brown, Muff's*

End in store

When Brown, Muff was taken over by Rackhams in 1978, it would have been a very hard job to find anybody in Bradford who approved of the change. Brown, Muff, after all, was one of Bradford's oldest established businesses - it was selling clothing at the time of the Battle of Waterloo. And Bradford liked to think that BMs epitomised the best of the place - thrifty, not given to showiness, conservative in the best way, polite and always willing to give value for money.

The store was born in 1814, the year before Napoleon's final defeat, when Mrs Elizabeth Brown, using a legacy from her late husband, set up a one-room shop in Market Street, selling 'underclothing, fustian goods and corduroy'. It prospered.

In 1834 her son Henry took over the running of the shop, and married Betsy Muff, daughter of a timber merchant. In 1845 he took her brother, Thomas Muff, into partnership.

In 1870, Bradford Corporation had one of its periodic street-improvement spasms and the store was demolished, to be replaced by the building which stands today and now includes

Monday, February 27, 1978

Dillons, the bookstore. The building is a year older than City Hall.

The name Muff was a 'modernised' version of the older Maufe, and in 1909 the family reverted to the older form.

What you got at BMs was value, friendliness and courtesy - and the knowledge that you were dealing with local people.

Hundreds of employees over the years would recall with genuine affection the family atmosphere of the store.

Not that there was any familiarity - customers were 'sir' or 'madam' no matter how little they

Brown, Muff's to be Rackhams

The name of Brown, Muff's stores in Bradford and Skipton is to be changed to Rackhams from February 27.

The news comes only days after the shock announcement

spent.

BM's wasn't cheap, but it valued its customers, from the richest woolman, surveying his empire over morning coffee in the restaurant, to the not-so-well-off mother, scraping enough together for a pair of shoes for school, knowing that they might cost thirty bob more than she could really afford, but they'd wear well or be replaced without question.

If you had a few bob, BM's food hall was a treat. For many years it was the only place to buy quality food in Bradford. In the days before supermarkets it introduced generations to the delights of such rarities as pate, French cheeses and fine wines.

It was a pioneer in industrial relations, too. In the 1960s it was quick to assure its staff that their wages would not go down just because their working week was to be cut to give them more leisure.

In these days of mobility and change, it might be hard to imagine a place where people not only spent their entire working lives, but were happy to do so; and, on retiring, were happy to stay in touch with old friends and colleagues. But Brown, Muff was such a place.

Not content with Bradford, the store spread its wings. In the 1960s it opened new premises in Skipton and Bingley. The Bingley shop did not live long, but the Skipton one remained until the Rackhams takeover.

House of Fraser, owners of Rackhams, bought their way to a majority shareholding and just before Christmas, 1977, the writing was quite literally on the wall for BMs - it was on the wall of the restaurant which, sweeping away years of tradition, became self-service.

The end came on February 27, 1978, when the store's name changed to Rackhams. BM's was no more - except in the affectionate memory of Bradfordians.

By a sad coincidence, only days before, it was announced that Debenham's, in Manningham Lane, was to close. The name had never really caught on. To those same Bradfordians who mourned BM's, Debenham's would always be known by its original - real - name, Busby's. The world of the big combines had finally crushed them both.

T&A

1979 *Severest winter for decades ushered in year of discontent*

Snow came to Snow(den) Street, Bradford, with a vengeance, making life difficult for motorists. Meanwhile, White Lane, Bankfoot, Bradford, on up to its name.

BLIZZARDS BRING WHITE BLOCKADE

BATTERED Bradford was today reeling under its heaviest fall since 1947 – and the forecasters warn there'll be no end let-up.

More than 24 hours of non-stop snow brought chaos to roads and scores of people in outlying districts stranded in their homes.

In Bradford, 10 inches of hard snow.

Throughout West Yorks as a tale of massive snowdrifts, blocked roads, abandoned cars.

The situation could soon be that supplies of grit were dwindling fast, but the national strike means the public sector there are no grit out in any

CLOSED

... road to Harrogat rescued by poli hours and mar night at Skipto Police ...

road to Harrogat rescued by poli hours and mar Skipto ...

Weather

Continuing very cold with further prolonged snow giving moderate or heavy falls turning into sleet or rain tomorrow and slowly dying out. Minimum temperature tonight minus 1 C (30 F) with slight or moderate frost, maximum tomorrow 2 C (36 F). Wind easterly fresh.

Outlook: Less cold with rain or sleet showers.

● Clockwise—Page 9.

with that. I have been here since December, 1966, and this tops the lot even though we have had some bad ones since then."

The village of NORLAND, near Halifax, has been completely cut off since 6 p.m. yesterday.

At DEWSBURY the town centre was virtually sealed off because cars were unable to climb the steep hills on the main roads out.

At KEIGHLEY gritters struggled to keep town centre roads passable. In nearby villages driving was almost impossible with drifts up to seven feet reported.

In BRADFORD and LEEDS buses were withdrawn last night as conditions grew worse. They were back on the roads today in time to help thousands into work—but on Monday services will be withdrawn completely as crews strike in support of public sector

scent and Queensbury and scores of minor roads.

Over the Pennines the M62 was open with speed limits of between 20 and 30 mph, but police were advising drivers to use an alternative the A646 Calder Valley road through on the road to Harrogate. They were rescued by police after five hours and many spent the night at Skipton Police Station shortly add scores of minor roads.

Over the Pennines the M62 was open with speed limits of between 20 and 30 mph, but police were advising drivers to use an alternative the A646 Calder Valley road through Hebden Bridge and Todmorden the road to Harrogate. They were rescued by police after five hours and many spent the night at Skipton Police Station ...

Over the Pennines the M62 was open with speed limits of ... road through Hebden Bridge and Todmorden the road to Harrogate. They were rescued by poli DRIF

... on people were marooned in huge snowdrifts on the road to Harrogate. They were rescued by police after five hours and many spent the night at Skipton Police Station sleeping on chairs in the parade room. One of the drivers, Mr. Ernie Leatherbarrow, of Durham, praised the two police officers who came to the aid

... on people were marooned in huge snowdrifts on the road to Harrogate. They were rescued by police after five hours and many spent the night at Skipton Police Station sleeping on chairs in the parade room. One of the drivers, Mr. Ernie Leatherbarrow, of Durham, praised the two police officers who came to the aid

Over the Pennines the M62 was open with speed limits of ... marooned in huge snowdrifts on the road to Harrogate. They were rescued by police after five hours and many spent the night at Skipton Police Station sleeping on chairs in the parade room. One of the drivers, Mr. Ernie Leatherbarrow, of Durham, praised the two police officers who came to the aid of all ... on people were marooned in huge snowdrifts

... on the road They were res after five hou spent the nig Police Statio on the road They were res after five ho spent the nig Police Statio on the road They were re after five ho spent the nig Police Statio on the road They were after five spent the Police Sta on the r They were on th after five h spent the Police Stati on the road They were after five ho spent the Police Stat on the ro They were after five h Police Sta

BIG FREEZE: *The winter of 1979 was the prelude to a year of huge problems for the general public*

In the deep political midwinter

I t became known as the Winter of Discontent, the season of strikes and trades union unreasonableness which ousted Jim Callaghan's Labour Government from power and began the 11-and-a-half year domination of British politics by the iron maiden Margaret Thatcher.

The worst spell of bitterly cold and icy weather since 1963, which lasted from January to March, seemed to herald even

Saturday, January 20, 1979

greater change to come in the country's social and political climate.

Oddly enough it all started with a pay freeze. Public sector wage increases, which had been frozen at ten per cent, were halved to five per cent; Prime Minister Callaghan believed that Labour's accord with the Trades Union

Congress would hold the line; he was wrong. Lorry drivers went on strike for a month, and the phenomenon known as secondary picketing brought allied industries to a standstill. Three thousand textile workers were laid off. Hospital workers belonging to NUPE went on strike, as did ambulance crews and dustmen. Broadcasting was affected too. ITV went off the air for three months, and The Times

Continued on Page 132

SNOW ART: *Making the most of the heavy snowfall with some saucy ice sculpture*

The British public was getting it in the neck from every quarter

Continued from Page 131

newspaper remained unpublished for nearly a year.

Both the value of the pound and inflation rose - the latter to 16 per cent by the end of this watershed year which, among other historic events, saw Israel and Egypt sign a peace treaty, and the establishment of an Islamic state under the Ayatollah Khomeini in Iran. It was also the year when the USSR invaded Afghanistan.

The year started coldly with heavy snowfalls. Nearly three weeks into January the weather got even worse. Twenty-four hours of non-stop snow blew down on Bradford in a blizzard. On January 20 the T&A reported that there were ten inches of undrifted snow. The consequent chaos for commuters and traffic may be imagined.

No let-up for the coming weekend was forecast, and on the Monday the nation faced a national strike by public sector workers. Council gritting machines would be off the road, heating in schools would be kept turned off, domestic refuse would not be collected, and people requiring emergency hospital attention would be transported by green Army ambulances.

The switching off of heating in more than 100 Bradford schools as well as public swimming pools was symptomatic of the larger fuel crisis which Britain had been experiencing since 1973 when the members of OPEC (Oil Producing and Exporting Countries) had drastically increased the price of crude oil. The revolution in Iran six years later made matters worse.

As the cost of Britain's oil imports went through the roof, the price of petrol rose too. North Sea oil and gas were not yet being pumped inshore - at least not in sufficient quantities to make a difference to the country's balance of payments.

SNARL UP: *Manchester Road, above, and the city centre, left, are choked with traffic crawling through the snow*

Continued on Page 133

COLD COMFORT: *Drivers struggle up the hills outside Bradford city centre, only to be greeted by big drifts on the tops, below*

Continued from Page 132

The weather remained terrible. On March 17, officially the last day of winter, ten inches of snow fell. By March 20, every ambulance station in West Yorkshire bar two was in the grip of industrial action. Five thousand ambulance staff were on strike nation-wide, 700 of them in West Yorkshire.

Civil servants in social security offices, in dispute with their employers, came out in a series of one-day strikes which affected welfare payments. The general public was getting it in the neck from every quarter.

The afternoon that Bradford Council announced spending cuts of £3m torrential rain lashed the Metropolitan District; flooding in the north, particularly in and around Skipton, was especially severe. Perhaps it was the sheer quantity of water about which attracted homeless Vietnamese boat people to Ilkley. With a double-election looming in June - for the House of Commons and the European Parliament - the grand old man of British politics, Harold Macmillan, came to Bradford on June 5 to address a Conservative Party rally at St George's Hall.

The 85-year-old former Prime Minister, without the use of notes, delivered a wonderful performance which touched even those non-Conservatives present.

"It's a popular thing to say that Britain has declined. Some say it is in decline - even ambassadors appear to hold that view - but it is only a phase. It is a dangerous thing to say the British people is declining. They have their phases, they have their moods. But once they have made up their minds they don't give in easily. We only need the leadership, we only need the spark.

"The next decade, the next ten years, will see England not reproached for her decline, but proud and strong as a lion awakened," he said like a father whose faith in his erring children was unshaken.

Later that month Mrs Thatcher's Tories swept all before them. But there was no snow on the ground in June, just the memory of bags of uncollected garbage and, reportedly at least, unburied bodies.

Barry Seal, former leader of Bradford Council's

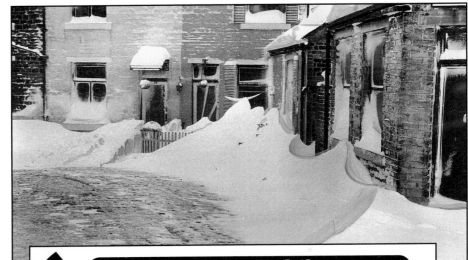

How we reported the news

> Battered Bradford was today reeling under its heaviest snowfall since 1947 - and the forecasters warn there'll be no weekend let-up. More than 24 hours of non-stop snow brought chaos to roads and left hundreds of people in outlying districts stranded in their homes. Lister Park, Bradford, reported ten inches of undrifted snow. Throughout West Yorkshire it was a tale of massive snowdrifts, blocked roads, and abandoned cars. The situation could soon be desperate as supplies of gritting salt are dwindling fast, and Monday's national strike by workers in the public sector could mean there are no gritting machines out in any case.

Telegraph & Argus

From the T&A of January 20, 1974

Labour Group, was elected to serve as West Yorkshire's first Euro MP - a job he kept for 20 years by winning more elections than Mrs Thatcher.

Just as the winter had ended with a blizzard, summer burnt itself out with a fantastic blaze in Manningham Lane on the evening of August 29. Debenham's store, which had closed in April the previous year, inexplicably went up in flames. The three-storied turreted building, which had opened in 1908, was utterly destroyed despite the presence of nearly 100 fire-fighters from all over West Yorkshire.

1980 *Newspaper production leapt into the modern age*

MAKING THE NEWS: *A magnificent glass-fronted Bradford & District Newspapers Press Hall building grew from the foundations, right*

Let the new press roll...

All jobs produce their own small languages - esoteric words and phrases, meaningless to the outsider and a source of delight to those in the know.

For 112 years the Telegraph & Argus had been put before its public thanks to such devices as flongs, chases, elrods, and a stone which was actually made of steel.

By 1979 it was time for a change.

The electronic revolution had been changing newspaper production for some years and it was time for the T&A to get modern.

Its two presses had collectively put in almost a century of service and were getting weary. But we'd been on the streets practically every day through two world wars, one great depression and every County Cricket Championship in Yorkshire's history - so a gap while a new press was installed was unthinkable. Instead, it was decided to build a new hall alongside the T&A buildings in Hall Ings, and to install what would be Europe's most modern printing press.

Eighteen years later, the T&A presses underwent another £3m refurbishment creating a super-press capable of printing even bigger papers with much more colour.

In 1980, the excavation work for the foundations,

NEW START: *The site next to the T&A building earmarked for the new presses*

Saturday, June 7, 1980

on the site of what had once been the old County Courthouse, began in 1979. The work of building began soon afterwards, and the roof went on on June 7, 1980.

In parallel with this was a change inside the older part of the building, from hot metal printing, involving a noisy and stuffy series of processes involving a molten alloy of lead, bismuth, to what was then known as 'cold type' - computer-aided photo-typesetting.

It was cool, clean, quiet and, in its early days, often riotously unreliable. Older hands were heard to mutter darkly that, in the old days, if anything went wrong you could normally fix it with a screwdriver or, in extremis, a hammer. Electrons were less easy to handle.

But it was smoothed out with a lot of hard work and even more patience.

The clattering Linotypes, one by one, fell silent. The transitional stage was over. In 1981 the T&A and its associated publications went from rotary press to web-offset lithography - the result being a cleaner product.

And Bradford had gained a striking new piece of architecture.

T&A

1981 — *Five years of fruitless police work ended with a chance arrest*

Ripper's reign of terror is ended

CAUGHT: *Peter Sutcliffe, the Bradford lorry driver who turned out to be the Yorkshire Ripper, who had terrified women in the area for more than five years*

They had crowded into the town hall to see a monster. But when they saw him, he wasn't at all what they'd expected.

He had the beginnings of a bald patch in the middle of his strikingly black, curly hair. His black beard was neatly trimmed. His skin looked sallow in the yellow lights of the court. He was slightly built and spoke not at all.

Later, when the 'trial of the century' began, his voice would surprise his audience. It was high-pitched, almost piping, reminding those who knew him of one of his most marked characteristics - the snorting giggle with which he greeted much in life.

But on a winter afternoon in Dewsbury Magistrates'Court, where he was charged with stealing two number plates from a car in a scrap-

Monday, January 5, 1981

yard, there was nothing, absolutely nothing, to suggest that the smallish man in the dock had kept the north of England in fear for more than five years.

Peter William Sutcliffe, a lorry driver

Continued on Page 136

BUTTERFIELD ILLUMINATED SIGNS Sunbridge Rd BRADFORD 22244

Telegraph & Argus

No. 34,834   12p

BRADFORD, MONDAY, JANUARY 5, 1981

centaur. Fine British Clothes for Men

Bradford man to appear in court after swoop on car

JOY OF THE RIPPER HUNTERS

By Sue Butterfield

BRADFORD lorry driver Peter Sutcliffe was due to appear in court today charged with "a serious offence" after being quizzed by Ripper Squad detectives for more than 48 hours.

And jubilant West Yorkshire Police said they were now scaling down the hunt for the Ripper.

Sutcliffe, 35 and married, lives at 6 Garden Lane, Heaton, a peble-dashed detached house which was besieged by pressmen last night after the sensational news of his arrest was released.

Police on anti-vice patrol in Sheffield city centre made the arrest which, it is claimed, will end five years of Ripper terror throughout Yorkshire and Lancashire.

They spotted a parked Rover V8 bearing number plates stolen from a car in West Yorkshire Checking it out the two uniformed men found Sutcliffe in the car with a woman thought to be a prostitute. He was helping police with their inquiries yesterday.

West Yorkshire Chief Constable Ronald Gregory told a packed press conference late last night "You can take it from me we are absolutely delighted with inquiries at this stage."

He said his heartfelt thanks went out to the Sheffield policemen—Sgt. Robert Ring and PC Robert Hydes—who made the arrest at about 11 p.m. last Friday.

Secret

Mr Gregory told the press conference that man was brought to West Yorkshire as a result of discussions between the south Yorkshire Police and the West Riding Police, further inquiries were made and this man is now detained here in West Yorkshire and he is being questioned in relation to the Yorkshire Ripper murders.

Mr Gregory would not say where Sutcliffe was being held.

Second remand on sex charge

A SHIPLEY teenager made his second appearance at Bingley Court today, charged with unlawful sexual intercourse with a female against her will at Shipley in February last year.

He was also charged with going equipped for burglary on New Year's Eve with a wood, wire cutters and a knife in his possession.

blanked his two police officers, he was remanded in custody until January 12 after a three minute appearance.

Reporting restrictions were not lifted. The defendant is representing Mr Desmond Jones who made no application for bail today.

The defendant previously appeared in court on Saturday.

Has George had the last laugh?

The smile on the face of George Oldfield tells the whole story. Assistant Chief Constable Oldfield, head of West Yorkshire CID, led the hunt for the Ripper until last month when his deputy Jim Hobson took over.

Mr. Oldfield's health had suffered — he had two heart attacks 18 months ago — but it was with obvious satisfaction that he announced last night the news that a man had been detained in Sheffield.

Police had always said they wanted a bit of luck to

George Oldfield in the thick of the hunt.

back up the intense work of sifting and checking which had taken up thousands of hours.

Picture of the suspect

WILMA McCANN, 28
LEEDS, OCTOBER 1975

EMILY JACKSON, 42
LEEDS, JANUARY 1976

IRENE RICHARDSON, 28
LEEDS, FEBRUARY 1977

PATRICIA ATKINSON, 32
BRADFORD, APRIL 1977

Continued from Page 135

from Bingley, was the Yorkshire Ripper. He never denied it; never once said he had not killed his 13 victims. What he was to say was that God, speaking to him from a headstone in Bingley Cemetery, where Sutcliffe was a gravedigger, had told him to do it - to go out and kill prostitutes, who were the causes of all the evil in the world. That many of his victims were not prostitutes was, in effect, God's fault, he was to tell the Old Bailey jury when he stood trial.

They did not believe him - nor did they take much notice of the psychiatrists who had sworn that Sutcliffe was a paranoid schizophrenic.

Peter Sutcliffe, the jury decided, was bad, not mad. He was jailed for life, with a recommendation that he should serve at least 30 years in prison; and thus ended the career of the man who blighted the lives of millions for over five years.

While he was at large, no woman felt safe; and no man felt at ease if the woman or women in his life had to be out after dark.

His 'campaign' began in July, 1975, with an attack on Anna Rogulskyj in Keighley. The attack was interrupted and a 12-hour operation saved the life of his victim.

He was disturbed again when he attacked office cleaner Olive Smelt five weeks later in Halifax. She, too, survived although beaten around the head with a hammer.

On the morning of October 30, 1975, a milkman found the body of Wilma McCann on playing fields in Leeds. She had been battered on the head with a hammer and stabbed 14 times in the stomach and chest. She was the first victim to die.

The second was Emily Jackson, killed in January, 1976, in a similar way, but stabbed 52 times. Then came Irene Richardson, battered and stabbed to death in February 1977. There was such a gap between the first two killings and the third that police were reluctant to make a connection; but the means of her death - battered senseless with hammer blows, then stabbed and slashed in the neck, throat and stomach - suggested she was the third victim of the man newspapers and the public were beginning to call the Yorkshire Ripper.

RED LIGHT DISTRICT: *Bradford's Lumb Lane, former haunt of Bradford's prostitutes where Sutcliffe stalked his prey. Inset: Sutcliffe at the wheel of a lorry*

The three victims who died were all prostitutes. So was Patricia 'Tina' Atkinson, whose battered and mutilated body was found in her flat in Oak Avenue, Manningham, on April 24, 1977. Two months later the pattern changed. Sutcliffe stalked and killed teenager Jayne MacDonald, in Chapeltown, Leeds on June 26. She was not a prostitute. The outcry against the Ripper grew stronger after this murder.

Those less inclined to moralise pointed out that none of the women deserved to die, no matter how they chose to make their living. It was to bring the whole subject of violence against women into clearer focus.

Women picketed the showing of films like

Dressed to Kill and Violation of the Bitch. And others organised their lives with more caution. University students organised safe travel to and from evening events while many women took to arming themselves with sharpened combs, blinding hairspray aerosols and knives.

A fortnight after killing Jayne MacDonald, Sutcliffe struck again, this time battering and stabbing Maureen Long on waste ground at Laisterdyke. She survived. But the ferocity of the attack left her memory impaired and her description of her assailant - six feet tall, collar-length wiry blond hair, large hands - was wide of the mark.

Continued on Page 137

JAYNE McDONALD, 16
LEEDS, JUNE 1977

JEAN JORDAN, 21
MANCHESTER, OCTOBER 1977

YVONNE PEARSON, 22
BRADFORD, JANUARY 1978

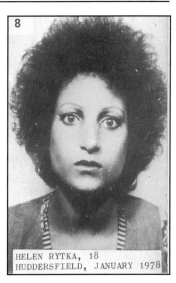

HELEN RYTKA, 18
HUDDERSFIELD, JANUARY 1978

BARBARA LEACH, 20

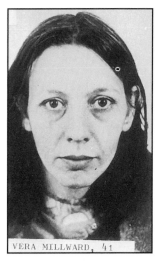

VERA MILLWARD, 41

JACQUELINE HILL, 20
LEEDS, NOVEMBER 1980

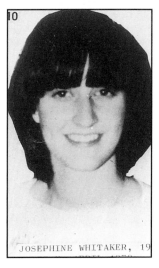

JOSEPHINE WHITAKER, 19

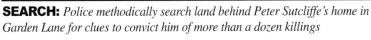

SEARCH: *Police methodically search land behind Peter Sutcliffe's home in Garden Lane for clues to convict him of more than a dozen killings*

Continued from Page 136

When the body of Jean Jordan was found in October, 1977, on an allotment at Chorlton, Manchester, her injuries suggested a Ripper attack, but the place didn't. It was to be early the following year before the police making up the Ripper Squad confirmed that Jean Jordan was a victim. By this time they had a rare clue. A five pound note found in Jean Jordan's handbag (in search of which Sutcliffe had returned feverishly to Manchester) was one of a batch from the Midland Bank at Shipley paid out in wage packets from local factories. Find the man to whom the fiver was paid and you had a prime suspect, argued the police.

Detectives working through the possibles arrived at Sutcliffe's new home in Garden Lane, Heaton, on November 2. Questioned about the night on which Jean Jordan had died, he said he was at his own housewarming party.

It was the first of a number if times Sutcliffe would be seen by the police - a series of interviews which was to show the weakness of the whole investigation. As the hunt for the killer went on, paperwork - still, despite the advance of computer technology, the mainstay of police investigations - proliferated to such an extent that it became an unwieldy

mass of cards and reports in boxes. Sutcliffe was seen by police on more than half a dozen occasions when suspicion fell on him. But each time he was left in the clear because there was no knowledge among the visiting officers that he had been seen before. The shoebox system let them down. A simple computer programme would have put Sutcliffe more firmly in the frame much earlier.

Meanwhile the body of Yvonne Pearson, who had been missing for some weeks, was found on waste land off Arthington Street, Bradford, on January 21, 1978.

Continued on Page 138

Continued from Page 137

Ten days later teenage prostitute Helen Rytka was killed while plying her trade in Huddersfield.

On May 17, Sutcliffe returned to Manchester and killed Vera Millward in the grounds of Manchester Royal Infirmary.

Then there was a lull. The police were in two minds - they hadn't a clue about the killer (although they had several clues all of which, had there been the means to put them together, would have pointed at Sutcliffe) and one unspoken thought was that he would have to strike again to give them a chance of catching him.

Another was that, sickened with self-disgust, their quarry had killed himself.

Then, almost a year after his last strike, Sutcliffe killed teenage building society clerk Josephine Whitaker on playing fields in Savile Park, Halifax. She was the second victim to die who was not a prostitute.

The outcry was loud, and it got louder when Bradford University student Barbara Leach was murdered in Ash Grove, a few yards from the Mannville Arms.

Next came civil servant Marguerite Walls,

PROTESTS: *The Ripper's reign of terror brought into sharp focus the issue of violence against women, and led to street protests outside cinemas*

Sutcliffe was interviewed by police nine times

battered and stabbed in the grounds of a house at Farsley.

Then another student, Jacqueline Hill, was killed behind the Arndale Centre in the middle of Leeds.

By now the outcry was deafening. Was the Ripper a ghost? Superhuman? Able to vanish into thin air? And what were the police doing?

The answer was that they were doing their best; but their best was not good enough. They were using 19th century methods to track a man who was using a 20th century motorway network. On the night of Jean Jordan's death, Sutcliffe had indeed been at his housewarming party - but between taking his family home to Bingley and returning to Heaton, he had driven fast to Manchester, chosen his victim and dispatched her.

A breakdown, a flat tyre, a stop for a drink with friends - all would account reasonably for an hour or so delay in returning home. Manchester, in the early hours of the morning, with nothing on the road, is no distance.

The police who finally arrested Sutcliffe were not in the Ripper Squad. They were beat bobbies in Sheffield who found Sutcliffe sitting in his Rover in Sheffield with a prostitute he had just picked up. They had no reason to suspect anything until a radio check confirmed that the number plates, held on with sticky tape, didn't match the car. He was arrested.

How we reported the news

Bradford lorry driver Peter Sutcliffe was due to appear in court today charged with "a serious offence" after being quizzed by Ripper Squad detectives for more than 48 hours. And jubilant West Yorkshire Police said they were now scaling down the hunt for the Ripper. Sutcliffe, 35, and married, lives at 6 Garden Lane, Heaton, a pebble-dashed detached house which was besieged by press men last night after the sensational news of his arrest was released.

Telegraph & Argus
From the T&A of January 3, 1981

Police on anti-vice patrol in Sheffield city centre made the arrest which, it is claimed, will end five years of Ripper terror throughout Yorkshire and Lancashire

He asked to be allowed to go behind a wall to relieve himself. The policemen agreed. It was only a hunch - brought on by the news that Sutcliffe was being questioned by the Ripper Squad - that made one of them, PC Bob Ring, return later to examine the spot. There, on a pile of leaves behind a small oil storage tank, he found a ball-pein hammer and a knife.

It was still many hours before Sutcliffe was to confess. Then, polite and unemotional throughout, he dictated a statement which took him more than 15 hours, detailing the killings and the attacks.

He was to remain unemotional throughout preliminary hearings and throughout the trial, which ended on Friday, May 22, 1981, with a majority verdict from the jury of murder on all 13 counts.

As he went to prison, Chief Constable Ronald Gregory - whose seeming insistence that a tape later shown to be a hoax contained the actual voice of the Ripper, with a heavy Wearside accent, had probably allowed Sutcliffe a year more at large than he might reasonably have expected - listed the mistakes his force had made.

Central to them was the lack of expertise in computers. Sutcliffe was interviewed nine times, mainly after being seen in red light areas, but no connection was made.

But at the end, said Gregory, Sutcliffe had got away with it for so long because 'he was clever enough not to leave any clues'.

And that is the key: there is no easy way to catch a random killer let loose on a motorway network.

1982

Twins made it another first for family

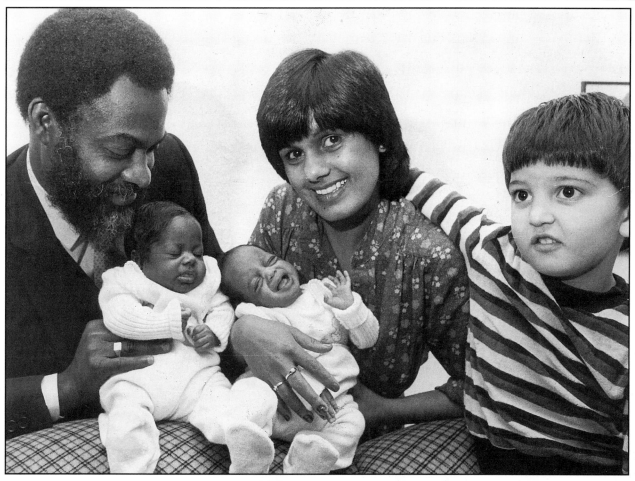

IN THE NEWS AGAIN: *Carlton and Satwinder Duncan and adopted son Jamie admire the new born twins Nathan and Natasha*

Double joy for Duncans

The Duncan family had a habit of making the news. Carlton Duncan was Bradford's first black headmaster, taking over Wyke Manor School in 1982.

When his wife Satwinder gave birth to twins, on August 16, 1982, they made the news, too, because they were not only Bradford's first test tube babies, but the first black ones in Britain.

Patrick Steptoe, who had pioneered in vitro fertilisation - leading to the first

Monday, August 16, 1982

such birth, that of Louise Brown in 1978 - helped the Duncans, who had been trying to have children for five years. Mrs Duncan was told she could not have children - because of blocked fallopian tubes - just two days after Louise Brown was born.

She had already had two unsuccessful courses of treatment with Mr Steptoe at his Cambridgeshire clinic when she conceived the twins.

Nathan and Natasha were born by caesarian section at Bradford Royal Infirmary. Nathan, the smaller of the two, was in the special baby care unit at the infirmary for seven weeks before

going home to his family, including his adopted brother Jamie.

On a sadder note, Satwinder's parents did not share her joy.

'My family is Asian and they wanted me to have an arranged marriage,' she said.

'They disowned me when I married and I've never heard from them since. I wrote to my mother about my babies but I have heard nothing and do not really expect to.

'Although I wish I had some family back-up, especially when the children are so young, it has meant that I have learned to cope very quickly'.

T&A

1983

Doom and gloom at Valley Parade

City's great escape

The news was what everyone interested in professional football in Bradford had been expecting. Sitting in the High Court in London Mr Justice Harman formally ended the life of debt-ridden Bradford City FC (1908). Thirteen years after Bradford Park Avenue FC had failed to gain re-election to Division Four, the city had lost its FA Cup-winning company, and was within ten days of losing the football club completely.

The Football League had set a target date, August 8, for interested parties to come up with a salvage package which included a minimum share capital of £150,000 and a promise to repay creditors.

The 1908 Company, which had gone into receivership at the end of June, owed 99 organisations, individuals and the Inland Revenue a total of £374,000. Supporters were furious, and mystified.

Friday, July 29, 1983

Only a year earlier, manager Roy McFarland had taken City into Division Three, and the club lottery was said to be bringing in an annual six-figure sum. But in 1982 the club was £155,000 in debt. From 1982-83 a trading loss of £123,000 was reported by chairman Bob Martin.

Allegations of financial mismanagement and worse were rife among supporters and percolated into the council chamber of City Hall, the scene of several long and agonising debates. The Council wanted to help, but how?

The day before the High Court order,

Tordoff pulls out of 1908 company deal

CITY'S FINAL SEVEN DAYS

29 JUL 1983

A £200,000 lifeline has been thrown to Bradford's sinking soccer club by the council's management committee — but it is unlikely to prevent the 1908 Company

Three pledge

the then Management Committee voted to buy the ground and make a loan of up to £100,000. The chairman, Councillor Ronnie Farley, voiced the hope that businessmen Jack Tordoff and former City chairman Stafford Heginbotham would settle their differences and form a new company to save the club.

In the weeks leading up to the High Court decision, City players such as Joe Cooke, Ces Podd, and big Bobby Campbell went down to Pennine Radio to appeal for support, and a public meeting was held inside Valley Parade. A petition was started, calling on the council to save Bradford City. An appeal was started too, which finally raised £43,000.

Perhaps it was this which persuaded Jack Tordoff and Stafford Heginbotham to join forces. From a business point of

LONG FACES:
Bradford City players appeal for support on Pennine Radio (left) while (above) City chairman Stafford Heginbotham (left) chairs a Press conference announcing the club's plight to the world

view, the 1908 company's shares could be bought comparatively cheaply from the Receiver Peter Flesher. In the event of a new company being successful, the value of these shares would increase. To meet the minimum share capital requirement of the Football League, the 1908 company's assets, including the ground, were re-valued at the necessary £150,000. Those assets were then transferred to a new company, Bradford City 1983, in exchange for 150,000 £1 shares.

The Receiver sold these shares to Jack Tordoff and Stafford Heginbotham for £40,000 - 26.6p a share - because that was as much as he could get. This cash was used to pay some of the 1908 company's creditors. The £43,000 raised by the public was used to run the new 1983 club and pay players' wages. Peter Flesher also sold Valley Parade to the 1983 company for about £100,000. The deal was financed by a mortgage from Bradford Council, to be repaid over five years.

Bradford City Football Club was saved as a result of private business acumen, supporters' passion, and public money.

T&A

1984

City gripped by The Honeyford Affair

Race saga of head Ray

BATTLE: *Ray Honeyford, head teacher at Bradford's Drummond Middle School, who sparked angry protest scenes, below, outside City Hall, and who eventually resigned for £71,000 in December, 1985, below left*

There was standing room only in Committee Room One at City Hall for the meeting of Bradford Council's schools education sub-committee.

On trial was 50-year-old Bradford headmaster Ray Honeyford. For the best part of the preceding eight months The Honeyford Affair had polarised opinion throughout the Metropolitan District and was to do so well beyond Yorkshire. It was debated in the House of Commons and within No 10 Downing Street.

Tension had been growing between the council and head teachers over compulsory race awareness courses for which the heads claimed they didn't have the time. Some Labour Group politicians dismissed this as an excuse.

Honeyford, headmaster of Drummond

Monday, October 22, 1984

Middle School, became worried about what he said was the harmful effect of race relations decrees on the education of Asian children. His particular target was mother tongue teaching. To become proper citizens of a Western democracy, he said, Asian children should be able to think, speak and reason in English.

He argued his case in The Salisbury Review, a subscription-only magazine of Conservative thought edited by the intellectual Roger Scruton.

At first there was no public reaction. Then, an officer working in the chief executive's office at Bradford Council tipped off a Yorkshire newspaper about the article, suggesting that it might make a good row.

There was a demonstration outside Honeyford's school in Green Lane, Manningham, and 238 parents, mainly Asian, applied to have their children withdrawn. Honeyford's enemies expressed outrage that he had been allowed to write what they considered racist remarks. They called for his dismissal.

Honeyford believed the school's Parents Action Group had more to do with politics. He wanted it scrapped.

And so it went on for nearly two years. What began as a little local difficulty became a national talking-point on programmes such as Question Time and Any Questions.

But in October, 1984, The Honeyford Affair reached crisis-point. The schools education sub-committee voted 7-1 to impose a six-point package of measures on him; he was given six months to carry them out, with up to eight different council officers carrying out checks on his progress. Also, he had to implement 40 recommendations by ten education advisers.

Subsequently, the acrimony intensified. Honeyford was suspended in April, 1985,

after a Labour motion of no confidence at a meeting of the schools education sub-committee was passed 8-7 with Liberal support.

In June, Drummond Middle's governing body held a two-day meeting at Ilkley after which they recommended his re-instatement, a decision supported by the High Court that September.

Honeyford's return to work was greeted with demonstrations and a lot of angry language.

Eventually, worn down by it all, Honeyford offered to resign.

On Saturday, December 14, 1985, the T&A announced that he had accepted a £71,000 package including a single lump-sum payment of £42,500 in settlement of all outstanding claims against the council.

T&A

1985 56 people died after four terrifying minutes at Valley Parade

Bradford City's day of disaster

You could see it from a mile away. Early that Sunday morning, May 12, the eerie glow of a single floodlight shone like a halo in the smoky blue air above Valley Parade.

It marked the place where 12 hours previously triumph had turned into a terrible tragedy.

The light marked a place of grieving and unutterable sorrow. It was to mark a place of flowers too, thousands and thousands of them which were to bank the entire length of what had been the main stand at the home of Bradford City Football Club.

Saturday, May 11, 1985

Fifty-six people died, scores more were injured or traumatised. These facts are scarred forever across the collective consciousness of Bradford, and indeed many other towns and cities; people had come from all over the North to watch City's young team parade the Third Division Championship trophy before the last match of the season.

Eleven thousand filled Valley Parade. The game against Lincoln City was proving to be a scrappy goal-less affair when, shortly before half-time, a

Continued on Page 143

DISASTER: *Flames begin to lick through the tinder dry boarding of the main stand at Valley Parade, right, and police start to clear the terraces. Within seconds, the small fire has engulfed the whole stand, below, and 56 people will have lost their lives, and scores of others been scarred physically and mentally for life*

Continued from Page 142

puff of smoke rose from the seating at the far end of the main stand.

Spectators standing on the unsheltered Kop and in the cow-shed of the Midland Road directly opposite watched in bemusement as the smoke became a puff of flame, no bigger than a bush.

Within seconds the flame was taller than a tree. A gust of wind fanned it up to the tar-covered roof.

On top of the Midland Road stand the camera crew from YTV swung their camera from the game, which was still going on, to the main stand. People were scattering. Flames licked the edge of the roof and then, like a trail of gunpowder, flared along the length of it. A thick cloud of oily black smoke piled into the sky, reminiscent of Dunkirk during the war.

City's then-captain was Peter Jackson. "I was standing near the corner flag, by the tunnel, when the ref stopped the game and said we would have to see what happened.

"I saw my wife Alison and daughter Charlotte on the players' balcony. I went out and got them. Most of the players went outside into the road and after three-quarters-of-an-hour we went up to the Belle Vue pub for a roll call.

"When I got home all I did was sit on the settee in

Continued on Page 144

Continued from Page 143

my kit with my daughter on my knees, I don't know for how long. I just sat there and couldn't believe what was happening; it was just unreal," he said.

Such was the intensity of the heat, which could be felt across the other side of the ground, the stand was destroyed in just four minutes.

Bradford's deputy Lord Mayor Bill Nunn and his wife Betty, the Lady Mayoress, had been in it, playing host to the civic heads from the city's twin towns in West Germany, Belgium, and France, who had come over for the Championship day.

"The match hadn't been that interesting. I was thinking ahead about plans for the evening. Most of the party had left the stand to get a cup of tea just before half-time. I hung on because it looked as though City might score."

"I looked to the left and saw smoke. I thought a smoke bomb had gone off. Then we saw fire. I made sure my wife and the burgomeister of Hamm got out. Fortunately someone had opened one of the rear doors and we walked out of the the ground.

"We went to the Norfolk Gardens Hotel (now the Stakis), where our guests were staying, and had a conference about whether we should go ahead with the evening's events. We didn't know, we didn't realise, we were told that everybody had got out of the ground," he said.

Most people thought that, including T&A journalists who had been watching the game from the Midland Road area. Within a couple of hours of going back to the paper's old newsroom the number of fatalities was put at between nine and 20.

Calls came in from all over the country, and then all over the world.

Detective Superintendent Roger Wiseman was within a week of retiring from West Yorkshire Police. That Saturday afternoon he was on duty at Leeds Road, Huddersfield Town's former stadium. Then he heard a police message for personnel carriers to go to Valley Parade to assist the ambulance service. He immediately got into a patrol car and rushed to Bradford.

"I have never seen as much shock on police officers' faces. There was a dull sense of cold shock. They were standing there in dirty and burnt uniforms, some were trembling, there was a feeling of unreality.

"I stayed all night and supervised the removal of the bodies. It was the worst job of my career. We arranged for a policeman to be responsible for the bodies right through to the inquest. We were picking up jewellery and wristwatches. It was a long cold night.

REPORT: *Mr Justice Popplewell gazes at a floral tribute at the ground as he gathers evidence for his report which would change forever Britain's ancient sports grounds*

Convoys of casualties were taken to BRI

BEFORE THE TRAGEDY: *City players parade the championship trophy to the crowd before the game*

"One thing I'll never forget was the Salvation Army. They stood on the terraces all night handing out food and coffee to the officers. By 6am we had got all the bodies out. I went home at about 7am."

Convoys of casualties were driven to Bradford Royal Infirmary, which had a burns clinic. Doctors set up a production line, allocating victims to wards depending on the nature of their injuries. In three hours BRI staff had checked 190 people. By 8am all the patients were in the wards. Consultant plastic surgeon David Sharpe said it was like a wartime situation. He brought in a team of 13 surgeons from hospitals throughout the North - a tenth of the country's burns experts. In three days

they operated on 57 patients; in 90 per cent of cases skin grafts to the hands were successful first time round.

"If we had not done that there would have been all sorts of problems. The patients would have been on the wards for weeks and weeks…It was very humbling to see how they coped with this horrific ordeal.

"It was a unique incident and I learnt a lot about human nature. I learnt that there is an awful lot of good in people," he said.

Bradford Council, led by its dynamic chief executive the late Gordon Moore, reacted to the disaster with great speed, tact, and determination. Social Services set aside four to five staff to operate a helpline.

Continued on Page 145

AFTERMATH: *Prime Minister Margaret Thatcher was one of many public figures to visit the site of the disaster, left.*
Above, a memorial service held amid the ruins of the Valley Parade ground, and right, the permanent memorial to the victims of the fire erected outside City Hall in Centenary Square

Continued from Page 144

Within 48 hours an officer was put in charge co-ordinating money-raising appeals for the fire disaster fund. A senior personnel officer joined by Bradford lawyer Roger Suddards met organisers of the Penlee and Aberfan appeals to learn about the best way of running the disaster fund.

The church quickly organised special services at Bradford Cathedral and later at Valley Parade. The then-Bishop, the Right Reverend Robert Williamson, visited casualties at BRI, St Luke's, and Pinderfields at Wakefield.

Interviewed by the T&A two days after the fire the Bishop dared to ask the most difficult of questions. "Was there not evidence at the ground of something stronger than death itself, in all those people risking their lives to save others? Perhaps it was a reflex to do so, but what caused that? I have always found on the other side of disaster there is courage and self-lessness."

Pity Poor Bradford, a 17th Century ghost is said to have wailed. The

The people of Bradford rallied together superbly

world did; but Bradford collectively rallied superbly in the face of such tragedy. The £4m raised for the disaster appeal was duly distributed through a trust fund without the slightest controversy or complaint.

On July 24 Mr Justice Popplewell, who had held a seven-day fire inquiry at City Hall, published his interim report recommending radical changes which has led to greater safety improvements at sports grounds holding more than 5,000 people.

On Sunday, December 14, 1986, a re-built Valley Parade opened with a game against an England XI who included Peter Shilton and Kevin Keegan.

City won 2-1.

T&A

1986
Bradford lad who potted his way into snooker history

Cue Joe, king of the world

Monday, May 5, 1986

He was, said the TV pundits, the world champion from nowhere. But Joe Johnson was adamant - he wasn't from nowhere, he said. He was from Bradford and very proud of it.

And Bradford was proud of him when, on the night of Monday, May 5, 1986, he raised the world professional snooker championship trophy at the Crucible Theatre, Sheffield, after beating Steve Davis 18-12 in the final.

At a time when snooker was suffering from a rash of sex-and-drugs scandals, there was nothing flash about Johnson. He was as solid and homely as a plate of Yorkshire pudding, a devoted family man, a father of six who had had to battle his way to the top armed with natural talent, two-tone shoes and a pair of eyebrows which became nationally famous as they writhed above his cue.

He'd gone into the finals as a 150-1 outsider who had not held a cue until he was 14 when he challenged his dad Ken at a Butlin's holiday camp. He turned professional 11 years later, in 1978, after years of steady progress in the amateur ranks. His

Continued on Page 147

IT'S ALL MINE: *Joe Johnson holds the world championship trophy aloft (left) after beating champion Steve Davis (right) 18-12*

Continued from Page 146

professional career was also steady rather than spectacular, and he did not play on TV until 1983 when he met former world champion Terry Griffiths in the Coral UK Championship. Shortly before, he had reached the final of the Professional Players' Tournament.

But there was nothing to hint that he might upset all the odds at Sheffield in 1986. Unfancied was not the word. Even when he got into the final itself, you could get 5-1 on Johnson, while Davis was quoted at 8-1 on.

But the bookies had misread the former gas fitter from Bradford Moor. He got past Terry Griffiths 13 frames to 12 in a gripping quarter-final and met Tony Knowles in the semi.

He started that match in some pain with an abscess at the base of his spine, but by the last session the pain had eased. More importantly the crowd had, as it tends to in snooker, got behind the underdog.

There was more than Bradford behind him when he stepped out against the

' I felt sorry for Steve. Everyone shouted for me'

formidable Davis. The frames went like this (Johnson's scores first): 24-85, 60-49, 0-108, 14-111, 70-0, 68-36, 74-14, 13-66, 4-108, 1-76, 27-64, 72-20, 95-22, 63-37, 76-8, 0-137, 85-26, 57-44, 66-11, 86-36, 25-84, 31-73, 70-40, 7-100, 69-9, 60-63, 49-32, 64-38, 83-40, 86-27.

Johnson's long potting finally broke Davis and got the crowd on his side - audiences love the adventurous. But Johnson was - typically - apologetic about the support he got: "I felt for Steve because everybody was shouting for me and he has done nothing wrong.

He is a perfect gentleman."

Davis had, indeed, done nothing wrong. But what Joe Johnson, modest, likeable, workmanlike, plain, ordinary Joe Johnson, hadn't got his head round was this: the public liked him.

They liked him because he was like one of them, and because he'd deserved to win and he'd won, at the end, by doing his absolute damndest and giving the game his all.

And just to prove it was no fluke, he got to the final the next year as well. This time he lost to Davis and was, typically again, generous in defeat. In the post-match TV interview he said: 'Steve Davis, number one in the world and world champion - it's about right'.

And that night he got another great reception at his Morley snooker club where, the year before, he had celebrated by singing with his band Made in Japan.

But it was the wrong name. Joe Johnson was undoubtedly Made in Bradford.

1987   *First steps taken to transform a Victorian ruin*

Miracle at the mill

WORKS OF ART: *Jonathan Silver with some of the Hockney paintings he helped bring to Salts Mill*

Mrs Hockney at champa...

That's my boy..mum is wowed by display

by John Hewitt

DAVID HOCKNEY's 87-year-old mother Laura walked into an art exhibition yesterday and was astonished to find works by Bradford's top international artist hanging from overhead heating pipes.

But she was bowled over by the show — Hockneys — one of the ...old — in th...

Monday, November 2, 1987

Salts Mill was closed in February, 1986, after 133 years as a textile factory. For months the 17-acre site lay neglected. The state of Sir Titus Salt's pride and joy was reflected in the worsening condition of his surrounding model village.

On June 10, 1987, the mill was purchased for under £500,000 from the Illingworth Morris company by Bradford-born entrepreneur and art lover Jonathan Silver. He took possession of it a month later and immediately set to work improving both the exterior and the interior.

Although various activities took place at the mill, the enterprise which first put it and the village of Saltaire on the map did not open until Monday, November 2, 1987. Within two years, the 1853 Hockney Gallery was attracting public interest and international publicity from Melbourne to Los Angeles.

With typical panache, the 37-year-old Silver celebrated the opening of the world's first gallery dedicated to the works of his friend David Hockney with a champagne reception for hundreds of guests including the artist's 87-year-old mother Laura and other members of the family.

The 10,000 sqft, rectangular former spinning room contained 56 paintings, prints and drawings, mostly hung from former steam pipes. The scent of fresh flowers arrayed in an assortment of exotic vases and the sound of classical music filled the air. Silver was in his ele-

ment. Nearly ten years later, on September 25, 1997, Jonathan Silver died from cancer after a two-year battle. His wife Maggie, daughters Zöe and Davina, and brother Robin spoke at a commemorative celebration of his life before an invited audience of 500 at the mill on Sunday, December 14. David Hockney, the poet Tony Harrison, Sir Ernest Hall, Jonathan's former business partner at Dean Clough, Halifax, and concert pianist, also made contributions. The guests could take stock of the mill's development in the decade of Jonathan's ownership, and how the success of his particular kind of economic regeneration, a mixture of culture and commerce, had benefited Saltaire.

The celebration took place in the third Hockney Gallery, for more pictures by the Bradford-born artist had been acquired over the ten years. Dinner was served in Jonathan's American-style Diner, the walls of which were covered

Continued on Page 149

Continued from Page 148

with Hockney's laser-printed colour photographs of North Yorkshire.

A second Hockney Gallery was adjacent to the Diner. Next door was The Home, a store run by Robin Silver and his wife Pat.

Through the Diner's North-facing windows, the serrated roof of a high-tec electronics factory belonging to Pace Micro Technology was visible. The decision by Pace to relocate to Salts in 1990 was the key to everything else in the next seven years.

Booming demand for Pace's products meant rapid expansion and increasing income for Jonathan which he re-invested, either in more art for the mill or improving the infrastructure of the place.

Before his death he helped conclude the sale of Salts Mill land for £1.1m to Filtronic plc, Prof David Rhodes' burgeoning high-tec electronics company. Rhodes chose Salts for his new HQ because he admired Jonathan and liked the environment.

In November, 1987, Salts was virtually empty. Ten years later 2,000 people had jobs in the various enterprises located at the mill. More lived in private flats or worked in Bradford Health Authority offices in the New Mill opposite which had been restored and renovated as a result of what Silver had done at Salts. Jonathan brought 22 shows and exhibitions to the mill including a specially-

RISING FROM THE ASHES:
Jonathan Silver and David Hockney (left) helped the ruined Salts Mill (above) recapture the pride it had in the last century (below)

The first gallery dedicated to Hockney's works

commissioned verse play by Tony Harrison, at least three Hockney world premieres, and two charity cabaret evenings by Alan Bennett and Victoria Wood which raised more than £60,000 for a children's hospital and Bradford's Cancer Support Centre.

In 1996 awards rained down on Salts Mill and the village. The Civic Trust's prestigious Centre Vision Award was followed by Europe's highest accolade for conservation-led regeneration, the Europa Nostra Award.

Three years later the Government nominated the whole of Saltaire for World Heritage status.

On April 26, 1999, at a Regeneration Through Heritage meeting in the restored Great Western Railway shed in Swindon, Prince Charles - who had visited the mill in October, 1996 - showed slides of Salts Mill and paid glowing tribute to Jonathan Silver's patience and vision.

His vision is kept alive by Maggie Silver, the owner of the Salts Estates company which runs the mill. Since Jonathan's death she has gradually introduced new ideas and improvements, including a coffee bar above The Diner. Exhibitions of Hockney's latest work continue to come.

T&A

1988

Bingley's star swimmer clinched Olympic title

Heart and Seoul for Gold…

Monday, September 19, 1988

Telegraph & Argus

GOLDEN TOUCH

Adrian grabs Seoul glory by a fingertip

Imagine going to bed at 9.30pm and getting up at 5am every day for ten years, not to earn a living, but in the hope that one day you will swim the 100 metres breaststroke fast enough to win an Olympic gold medal.

Daunting, to say the least.

But that's the regimen which Bradford Grammar schoolboy Adrian Moorhouse, from Bingley, accepted from the age of 14. Being the best requires unwavering dedication and determination, and the young Moorhouse wanted to be the best.

With constant support from his mum and dad, Kathleen and Clifford, he gave his whole life to swimming.

His dad would drive him 16 miles to Leeds where Adrian swam for two hours. Then he was driven home for breakfast before setting off for school.

"After morning training I'd get to school late and often fall asleep in class," he told the T&A 18 months before the 1988 Olympic Games in Seoul, capital of South Korea. "I could only think about swimming. I HAD to think swimming."

Another two-and-a-half hours of swimming practice was scheduled for the evening or afternoon - depending on whether it was term time. Although there must have been occasional temptations to

Continued on Page 151

			A FINAL
1.	MOORHOUSE, A.	GBR	1:02.04
2.	GUTTLER, K.	HUN	1:02.05
3.	VOLKOV, D.	URS	1:02.20
4.	DAVIS, V.	CAN	1:02.38
5.	DEBNAR, T.	HUN	1:02.50
6.	SCHROEDER, R.	USA	1:02.55
7.	MINERVINI, G.	ITA	1:02.93
8.	POSWIAT, C.	GDR	1:03.43

MEN'S SWIMMING — 100m BREASTSTROKE

CLOSE TO GLORY:

Adrian Moorhouse surges into the lead barely a couple of strokes from the final touch. Inset, the TV confirmation of his gold success

Continued from Page 150

break the routine, do something different just for a change, Adrian Moorhouse appears to have shown amazing self-discipline; he stuck to his 'early to bed and early to rise' programme.

One incentive may have been the money which wool merchant Clifford Moorhouse was investing in his son's career.

From 1978, when Adrian was 14, right up until Seoul where Olympic gold was finally won, Mr Moorhouse told one national newspaper: "It's cost me at least £10,000 a year."

About £100,000 in all, spent on food, equipment, staying in hotels, and attending swimming tournaments all over the world to support his son.

At least he and his wife had the comfort of knowing that their son had bags of talent and ability.

Between 1981 and 1987, for example, he was Great Britain 100m champion on six occasions and 200m champion on five. Before retiring he won three more 100m championships. In the same period he won two Commonwealth Games gold medals and three European Championship golds.

So on September 19, 1988, the 24-year-old Moorhouse must have felt confident as he prepared to take the plunge and go two lengths of the pool against the world's best.

Whatever plan he had in mind before hitting the water soon vanished as he

All the years of dedication now began to pay off

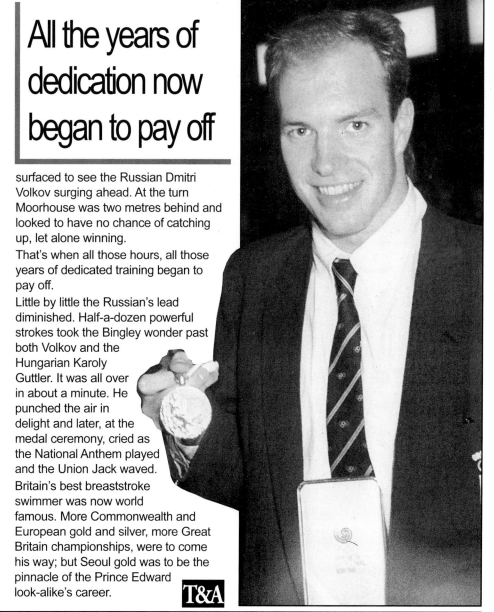

surfaced to see the Russian Dmitri Volkov surging ahead. At the turn Moorhouse was two metres behind and looked to have no chance of catching up, let alone winning.

That's when all those hours, all those years of dedicated training began to pay off.

Little by little the Russian's lead diminished. Half-a-dozen powerful strokes took the Bingley wonder past both Volkov and the Hungarian Karoly Guttler. It was all over in about a minute. He punched the air in delight and later, at the medal ceremony, cried as the National Anthem played and the Union Jack waved.

Britain's best breaststroke swimmer was now world famous. More Commonwealth and European gold and silver, more Great Britain championships, were to come his way; but Seoul gold was to be the pinnacle of the Prince Edward look-alike's career.

T&A

Verse and worse

Seen on its own, the burning of Salman Rushdie's The Satanic Verses in Bradford's city centre on a gloomy January afternoon in 1989 doesn't explain much.

The demonstration accompanying the ritual

Saturday, January 14, 1989

immolation did not comprise angry readers, outraged by what they had found in the 547-page novel; but although those who had not read it outnumbered those who had, everybody present had either read about it or had been told about it.

The book-burning, which actually took place 20 minutes earlier than scheduled because the T&A photographer present was due at another job somewhere else in the city, was not even the first

Continued on Page 153

Rushdie's crime was to question the authenticity of holy writ

BURNED: *The Satanic Verses is ritually burned in Bradford, sparking an international crisis*

Continued from Page 152

time this had been done. A previous burning in Bolton had largely been ignored.

Non-Muslims were not aware that in other parts of the world Rushdie's 1988 Whitbread Award-winning book had been banned and excoriated as a blasphemous attack on things Islamic, as the following extract of a letter to the T&A demonstrates.

"The book contains distorted, unfounded, imaginary and despicable material about the Prophet of Islam, and the Islamic history. The Muslim concept of God, the character and personality of the Prophet of Islam, the lifestyle of the Companions of the Prophet of Islam, the sanctity of Muslim institutions of prayers and pilgrimage, and many other areas of Muslim religion, culture and history have been ridiculed with the sinister motive of portraying millions of Muslims all over the world as barbarians."

Rushdie's crime had been to question, in a work of fiction, the authenticity of what is taken for holy scripture, in this case the Koran.

The Satanic Verses implicitly asked a number of questions. How could Muslims be so certain that the Koran was the undiluted word of Allah transmitted, over a period of time, to the prophet Mohammed? Supposing that Satan, ever prepared to create mischief, had somehow intervened in Mohammed's dream-thought process to slip in a few wicked verses? If the Devil was a reality wouldn't he have tried to lead Mohammed astray - just has he had tempted Christ three times in the wilderness?

Such suppositions are standard in Western reasoning, and have been so since the 18th Century Enlightenment. Questioning the basis of any claim is the accepted standard practice of police work, investigative journalism, virtually all science, history, and prose fiction.

Rushdie wasn't the only writer to challenge the orthodoxies of Islam, so what was all the fuss about?

That question cannot be answered without explaining events preceding and following the book-burning.

Ever since the ayatollahs of Iran had tried to create an Islamic theocracy in place of the Western-style constitutional democracy of the former Shah, Muslims all over the world had been thrown into turmoil. How truly devout were they? What had they done to defend Islam in the same way that the revolutionaries had in Iran, or the Mujahideen had in Afghanistan against the invading communists of the Soviet Union?

Mikhail Gorbachev had removed the Red Army from Afghanistan, and now seemed determined to dismantle the USSR's Eastern European empire - an idea reinforced by the fall of the Berlin Wall on November 10, and the subsequent collapse of totalitarian regimes in East Germany, Czechoslovakia, Bulgaria, and Rumania.

With communism on the way out, the world had a vacancy for another kind of political force - not modern capitalism, but historic Islam. All that was required to unite Muslims everywhere was a common goal, a common enemy.

Continued on Page 154

Continued from Page 153

Salman Rushdie and his novel seemed to fit the bill. However, the fiercest protests were confined largely to Muslims in Pakistan. The book-burning in Muslim-populated Bradford went some way to rectifying that; but the really decisive blow was delivered on February 14.

It was made by an ageing Ayatollah Khomeini, Iran's leader. Exhausted by the eight-year war with Iraq, the people of Iran were restive. Khomeini learned about the protests against Rushdie's book and, ever the politician, saw that he could make great political capital out of the situation.

So on Valentine's Day he issued his fatwa, his ruling. Muslims the world over had a duty to pursue the blasphemous author and bring about his death in punishment for what he had written.

This did the trick. British Muslims who had expressed no interest in Khomeini throughout the Iran-Iraq war suddenly hailed the Ayatollah (as they were later

The burning of Rushdie's book polarised opinion across Bradford

to hail Saddam Hussein during the Gulf War). Overnight, Khomeini's authority as Islam's world leader was reinforced.

National identity became secondary to religious identity. Even young children were heard to declare that they were not Pakistani, they were Muslim. A worried Norman Tebbit, a Tory party grandee, wanted to know where their true loyalties lay; would they cheer for Pakistan or for their native England in a Test Match, he wondered.

A new phrase was the subject of much argument throughout all branches of the media: Islamic Fundamentalism.

With its emphasis on the priority of religion over politics, and the primacy of Islamic Sharia or religious laws over secular laws of non-Muslim countries, Islamic Fundamentalism was a worrying phenomenon. For some reason it was to flourish for several years in the Manningham part of Bradford.

Rushdie, now threatened with murder by a foreign State, was placed under 24-hour Special Branch protection. He

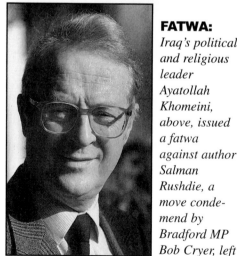

FATWA: *Iraq's political and religious leader Ayatollah Khomeini, above, issued a fatwa against author Salman Rushdie, a move condemned by Bradford MP Bob Cryer, left*

Fears that burn in the hearts of Muslims

was to remain hidden or shadowed until 1998, when Iran's more liberal-minded leadership reportedly said that the fatwa against Rushdie should not be pursued.

The book-burning issue polarised opinion and feeling in Bradford as much as the Honeyford Affair had done, and the 1991 Gulf War was to do. But by the time of Operation Desert Storm, Britain's Islamic Fundamentalists had created a new institution for themselves: the Muslim Parliament of Great

Britain. It was founded in Bradford.

Official political opinion in Bradford was largely muted. Only Labour MP for Bradford South, the late Bob Cryer, publicly and unequivocally condemned the fatwa and the book-burning.

Historically, the irony of the Rushdie book-burning is that it blazed forth in the year that it did - the 200th anniversary of the French Revolution, with its clarion call of Liberty, Equality, and Fraternity.

T&A

End of the line for pie shop

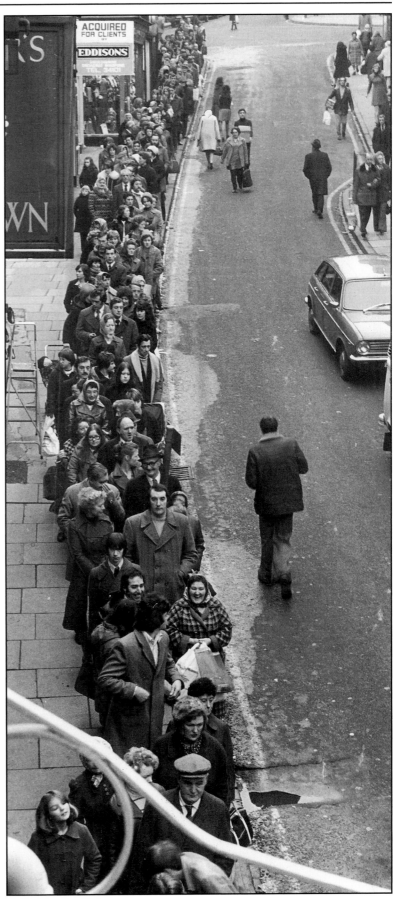

It was an odd time of year to lose this particular landmark - odd and a bit sad. When Philip Smith & Co, Yorkshire's oldest pork shop, closed in Ivegate in 1990, it was December and Christmas was coming.

Christmas - that was when Philip Smith's came into its own.

All year it was busy, dispensing fast food two centuries before anybody had heard of a burger. But in the run-up to Christmas it was at its best - its windows glowing like a ship dressed overall for a naval regatta, its unfailingly friendly staff smiling as they served arguably the finest pork stand pies there

Saturday, December 1, 1990

were. You had to get your order in early for a stand pie, traditional centrepiece of the festive table on Boxing Day. And even when it was ordered you had to queue - boy, did you have to queue!

Up to the top of Ivegate, round the side of the old Grosvenor Hotel down towards Sunbridge Road and into the twilight the people stood. For many it was as much a part of the ritual of the season as the Alhambra pantomime or going to see Father

Continued on Page 156

RITUAL: *The queue for a Philip Smith's pork pie snaked for yards up Ivegate as shoppers waited for the best pie in the land to grace their Boxing Day dinner table - until closure in December, 1990*

END OF THE LINE: *Owner Peter Brambani outside his shop along with queuing customers, and below, shutting up for the last time in December, 1990*

Continued from Page 155

Christmas at Busby's. Smith's pies were a local legend. The small pork ones, hot from the oven and dripping gravy, were the stuff of hungry dreams, while the pork sandwich, made with 'mucky dripping' was the sort of thing for which you would walk miles.

Every bit of the pig went into Smith's and came out deliciously transformed - faggots, savouries, roast belly pork, sausages, chops and spare ribs had a devoted public following. And no matter how many people worked behind

FINAL CURTAIN ... The blind comes down for the last time for Peter, left, and staff

THE END: For city's Peter the Pieman

THE PIE has finally gone to the sky.

by ROD HOPKINSON

Devotees got one last pie to savour for evermore

the counter (usually half a dozen) sometimes there weren't enough. Then, suddenly, it was all over. Principal partner Peter Brambani decided to retire on health

grounds and a buyer could not be found for the asking price. The staff could not raise the money to keep their beloved business going and eventually the place was sold for £275,000 to become a sweet shop.

The last day was a sad one for the city. Old customers dropped in to say their farewells and devotees of the Smith's pie made sure they had one last one to savour.

One regular said later: 'I bought four pies that day, and ate one there and then.

'I put the others in the freezer and made them last for three months.

'When I ate the last one I cried - I would never taste another...'

T&A

Attack changed dog law

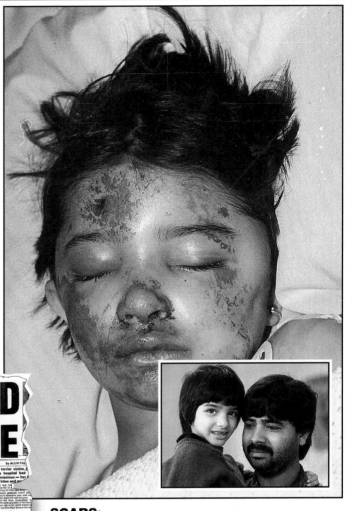

Dog bites man, the old newspaper saying goes, is not much of a story. But when a 65lb pit bull terrier savaged six-year-old Rucksana Khan the story helped to change the law.

The dog's unprovoked attack on the little Bradford girl happened on the afternoon of the Spurs-Nottingham Forest FA Cup Final - the game in which Tottenham's Paul Gascoigne twice hurled himself into pit bull-style tackles and wrecked a knee ligament.

Rucksana was playing out with her skipping rope in the company of an aunt and other relatives, near the gates of Green Lane First School, just off Manningham's Lumb Lane. On a nearby field, where lads usually play scratch games of football and cricket, a 21-

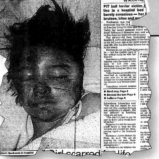

Saturday, May 18, 1991

year-old woman was exercising her pit bull terrier. Spotting the group near the school gates, the dog broke free from its owner.

"The dog came out of playing fields and started sniffing at some children," the aunt, Nashin Bi, told the T&A. "Then it showed its teeth and began snarling and grabbed Rucksana. She just said 'Auntie' and the next thing she went unconscious."

At more than half-a-hundredweight, the pit bull was heavier than Rucksana and had no trouble shaking her about in its jaws for an estimated 15 minutes while four men bravely tried to force the dog to let go of Rucksana. The dog's owner reportedly ran away.

SCARS:
Rucksana in hospital after the attack, and inset back home with her father

Tariq Hussain, Rucksana's neighbour, gave a graphic description of the struggle to the T&A. "Three guys were already tackling the dog, but it still wouldn't let go. I thought it had a piece of cloth in its mouth but it was the girl. They managed to free her and one of the guys was holding the dog by its collar. Another was punching it. One hit the dog with a piece of paving stone but it never felt a thing. This was no ordinary dog."

Eventually the dog ran home. Police cornered it in the kitchen of the owner's flat and a vet administered a lethal injection.

Meanwhile, Rucksana was unconscious in hospital with 23 bites to her back, five to her chest, three deep bites to her left-hand side, and numerous scratches and bruises to her face. One of her lungs was slightly perforated. Surgeons spent two-and-a-half hours repairing her fractured ribs and treating the bites.

The attack made national news. Home secretary Kenneth Baker described it as "appalling" and said the Government would crack down on the owners of dangerous dogs, with fines of up to £1,000. He did consider the destruction of breeds deemed to be dangerous.

Some dog owners resented the backlash, and the British Veterinary Association opposed the mass killing of dogs. But generally the public wanted action of some kind to curb the irresponsible ownership of potentially killer dogs.

This was demonstrated in a poll carried out by the T&A four days after the attack. More than 1,000 people responded, the vast majority of whom wanted pit bulls, rottweilers, alsatians, dobermanns, and their crossbreeds to be muzzled in public.

The Government did rule that in public dogs should be muzzled and on a leash.

Rucksana and her family were inundated with letters and messages of sympathy and support, as well as presents of toys. After 11 days in hospital, Rucksana returned home, her face showing only a slight scar. "I am so happy now," she said.

T&A

1992

Alhambra Theatre plunged into financial crisis

A £2m stage fright

SHINING STAR: *Bradford's Alhambra Theatre, which endured a financial crisis only six years after its re-opening, and despite attracting some of the top names in the country to perform in its magnificent setting*

Less than six years after Jacques Delors, then Commission president of the European Economic Community (EEC), officially opened the newly-refurbished Alhambra, the theatre was hurtling towards financial ruin.

Rumours had been circulating in and around City Hall for weeks that all was far from well with the theatre, but it took a T&A investigation to find the facts and disclose them to the public. The theatre's top management had over-spent by up to £2m, partly on prestigious

Friday, October 16, 1992

but unsuccessful shows such as Alan Rickman's Hamlet, staged at Robin Mills, Greengates. In addition, in a three-month period since that August, more than 5,000 tickets for shows had been given away free.

Some City Hall politicians reacted with surprise, saying that financial reports had given no indication that anything was

Continued on Page 159

PROBE: *Anamaria Wills, left, the Alhambra's general manager, who was suspended on full pay during the probe into the theatre's finances six years after the official opening of the renovated building in October 1986 by EEC president Jacques Delors, above. Right, Peter Tod, the theatre manager whose shrewd stewardship had brought the Alhambra to national prominence*

Continued from Page 158

wrong. Others reacted differently, demanding an inquiry into just how the over-spend had been allowed to accrue. Five days after the T&A's exclusive story the Alhambra's general manager Anamaria Wills, who had occupied the post since May, 1989, and the theatre's finance officer Tony Long were both suspended on full pay pending the outcome of an internal investigation.

The public was bemused: for six years little else other than the most fulsome praise had been heaped on the theatre. The Royal Shakespeare Company, the National Theatre, London's Royal Ballet had all brought shows to the theatre.

The inimitable Rudolf Nureyev had danced there. Prima ballerina Natalia Makarova had staged her innovative world premiere production of Swan Lake there in 1988.

A few in the arts establishment criticised the T&A for seemingly attacking a cherished cultural icon, despite the tremendous backing the paper had given to the theatre during an earlier crisis in 1983.

At that time the Alhambra was a 69-year-old building badly in need of an internal overhaul and an external face-lift.

Built in 1914 by Francis Laidler, it was bought by the council for £78,000 in

1964 after Mr Laidler's death and the voluntary liquidation of his Bradford Alhambra Theatre Company.

Television and the cinema between them reduced the theatre's audiences. The building itself was antiquated, its bar area was far too small for the size of the auditorium. Through the 1970s annual losses became common and doubt grew about whether the theatre was financially sustainable.

The building badly needed modernising. Bradford Council couldn't make up its mind for the very good reason that a whopping 30 per cent rate rise had been imposed by the Tories.

Continued on Page 160

Continued from Page 159

Economically and socially Bradford had spiralled into a depressing state; many politicians felt unable to justify devoting millions of pounds to doing up a crumbling theatre when houses and schools were falling apart.

On October 26, 1983, the Liberals supported a Labour amendment and the council voted 44-40, effectively killing a Tory proposal that £7.2m should be spent refurbishing the theatre. Tories like the late Tom Hall, and Ronnie Farley viewed the Alhambra as a future asset which would assist Bradford's regeneration.

News that the theatre was in imminent danger of exiting left, forever, excited a huge public response. More than 25,000 people signed a petition to save the theatre.

The likes of the late Sir Laurence Olivier, Billie Whitelaw, John Hanson, and Leslie Sands, added their protests and support.

Bradford's three political leaders, Councillors Phil Beeley (Labour), Paul Hockney (Liberal), and Ronnie Farley (Tory), the chief executive, the late Gordon Moore, and two other officers, went to Brussels to seek EEC aid. West Yorkshire's then-Euro MP, Barry Seal, played a key role by setting up meetings with the right people. The result of their efforts was the promise of £2m from the regional development fund.

On an unusual date, February 29, 1984,

How we reported the news

Bradford's award-winning Alhambra Theatre is in financial crisis, it was claimed today.

A team of finance experts is investigating the alleged overspend, which senior councillors say could be as much as £2 million by next April, the end of the financial year.

And the T&A can reveal that at the same time more than 5,000 tickets for shows at Yorkshire's premier theatre have been given away since August to help fill the house, a practice known in showbusiness as 'wall-papering'.

Today angry Tories accused chief officers of a cover-up after they refused to hand over vital information about the public-owned theatre's finances.

Coun Margaret Eaton, Tory community and environment committee spokesman, said: "We are concerned that the overspend could be related to the number of free tickets being given away to fill the theatre"

Coun Eaton was also concerned about the type of expensive productions being put on in the city.

She said: "We should be looking at the programming and the ticket sales and working out how the programming can be made more commercial"

Telegraph & Argus

From the T&A of Friday, October 16, 1992

the T&A reported that the Alhambra had been saved. It had been included in a £25m capital programme package.

In all, about £8.2m was to be spent transforming a jaded family heirloom into the sparkling jewel in Bradford's crown, which is exactly what it looked like when it re-opened in 1986.

For three years the Alhambra went from strength-to-strength under the eccentric but shrewd eye of theatre manager Peter Tod, who brought great shows, paying shows, into the main auditorium. This legacy of success made the Alhambra's financial decline in the three

Continued on Page 161

A jaded family heirloom turned into a jewel in the city's crown

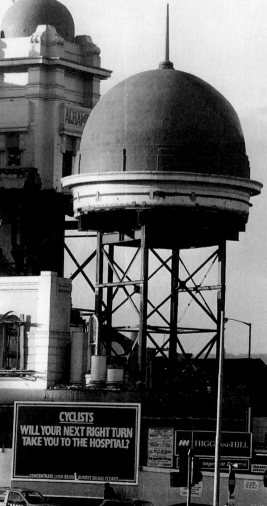

RESCUED: *Bradford's Alhambra Theatre grew from a derelict site in 1914, far left, under the guidance of Francis Laidler, then teetered on the brink of being demolished in 1983, above. The council eventually decided to spend millions on a total refurbishment and extension costing £8.2m, preserving its Edwardian splendour, but bringing its facilities bang up to date, left and below*

Continued from Page 160

Continued from Page 160

years until 1992 all the harder to understand.

Subsequently Tony Long, the theatre's finance officer, left the council's employ. After a protracted internal inquiry Mrs Wills was eventually fired in March, 1993, but successfully challenged the way the decision had been carried out at an industrial tribunal. In June, 1994, she was awarded about £11,000 in compensation.

That November the council secretly agreed an even larger pay-off figure for its former education director Sari Conway in a case that went to the High Court.

T&A

1993 *Amanda won the hearts of the nation and a princess*

Diana's little heroine

In October, 1998, 18-year-old Amanda Thompson of West Lane, Keighley, announced her engagement to Curt Barker.

The T&A photograph showed a smiling Amanda with shoulder-length fair hair. The Huddersfield University student had more than one reason to be happy; earlier in the year she had been told by doctors that she was clear of leukaemia.

Five years earlier Amanda had virtually no hair - the result of four gruelling chemotherapy sessions to combat the blood disease which was diagnosed in January, 1993.

But her cheerful, never-say-die attitude and, above all, her selfless charity-raising efforts on behalf of other leukaemia victims won

Monday, October 18, 1993

her the affection of the public and the admiration of public figures such as Esther Rantzen, Princess Diana and opera star Lesley Garrett.

In fact Amanda had been raising money for charity since the age of three by dancing and playing the piano. About £6,500 resulted from her efforts over ten years or so. Another £3,500 was raised remarkably quickly after her leukaemia diagnosis.

Rather than feel sorry for herself, Amanda redoubled her charity efforts and, in due course, these efforts led to her nomination for a Hearts of Gold award on Esther Rantzen's BBC TV show which highlighted unsung heroes.

STAR GIRL: *Amanda is met by Diana, Princess of Wales, during her brave fight against leukaemia*

The nomination - each year some 5,000 nominations were received - led to an appearance on the show on October 19, 1993. She had no idea she was on the show until she walked on stage at a top London recording studio and saw, to her surprise, a cheering audience. Amanda thought she was going to make another record with Lesley Garrett.

"It was absolutely fantastic. I couldn't believe my eyes when I saw my family and friends and all the doctors and nurses. A few minutes later Esther Rantzen appeared and gave me my Hearts of Gold badge," Amanda said.

While she was in front of the cameras she was handed a letter of congratulation from Princess Diana.

The late Princess was patron of the Malcolm Sargent Cancer Fund for Children to which Amanda had donated the proceeds of a recording of Ave Maria with soprano Lesley Garrett.

In her letter, Princess Diana said: "Very special greetings to Amanda and your family for all your courage and achievements."

The following year Amanda and her mum Sylvia were on a Bank Holiday caravan trip when they heard an SOS on their campsite radio, calling for Amanda to get in touch with Esther Rantzen's That's Life TV show.

She immediately rushed to London and was filmed playing the piano. On June 10 she returned to the capital to complete the recording and hand over a cheque for £157,000 to the Malcolm Sargent Fund - royalties from her recording with Lesley Garrett.

Amanda eventually played the piano for Princess Diana in 1996, the year before the Princess died from her injuries in that car crash in Paris.

When Amanda announced her engagement last year she received a bouquet of flowers from the ever-thoughtful Esther Rantzen.

T&A

1994 Water was scarce as long hot summers created a drought

DRIED UP: *Yorkshire Water area district manager Mike Twiggs surveys the cracked bottom of Angram Reservoir during the drought of 1994*

Left high and dry

The privatisation of public water authorities by the Conservatives in 1989/90 was always a controversial issue, but never more so than in the mid-1990s.

A combination of long dry spells, wastage through leaks in pipelines, the removal of water from rivers such as the Wharfe and the Nidd, and water executives getting huge amounts of extra cash through share options, brought the public mood to boiling point - especially in 1995.

But that long hot summer was preceded in 1994 by hot and sometimes uncomfortably humid weather throughout most of June, July

Thursday, August 25, 1994

and August, culminating in the imposition of a hose-pipe ban by Yorkshire Water which started on August 25.

Some people enjoyed the heat, including Warwickshire's West Indian batsman Brian Lara. On June 6 he scored a record 501 not out against Durham, racing to 1,100 first class runs in just seven county matches.

Occasional downpours were insufficient to compensate for a depleted average rainfall. Yorkshire Water was six weeks away from seeking approval from the Department of Environment for a drought order.

Thirst for quality puts drain on resources

The thirsty populations of Bradford and Leeds are coming close to drinking two Yorkshire rivers dry.

The River Wharfe and River Nidd contain such good quality water that exceptionally high amounts are being abstracted to feed public supplies, the National Rivers Authority has revealed.

Stretches of the Wharfe at Otley and Pool-in-Wharfedale have suffered some of the worst "low flow" problems in the country, while reservoir levels in the Nidd's catchment area are falling.

The hosepipe ban affected all of Bradford, Kirklees, Calderdale, Craven, and parts of Leeds. The urban areas of Guiseley, Drighlington, Farsley, Gildersome, Calverley, Hawksworth, Morley, Rawdon, Woodhall and Yeadon also came under the ban's umbrella.

To make up for the deficiency, Yorkshire Water drew more water from the Wharfe at Addingham - 27 million gallons a day in fact. Some conservation groups objected that if this measure continued or were to be increased, fish and wildlife dependent on the river would be put in jeopardy.

British Summer Time officially ended on October 23 without more drastic measures. The stage was set, however, for more turbu-

Continued on Page 164

DROUGHT: *Standpipes were put on standby, above, but never actually used in either drought year. Instead, Yorkshire Water tankered in millions of gallons of water, right, to stop the taps running dry. Left, YW chairman Gordon Jones faces another grilling from the Press over the handling of the crisis*

Continued from Page 163

lent scenes in 1995 which are worth recollecting.

In February melting snow and torrential rain caused widespread flooding, especially in and around Ilkley. The public supposed that water-levels in reservoirs would surely shoot up as a result; but what they did not bargain for was a seven per cent increase in their water bills.

Ominously, the spring was dry. At the end of June Yorkshire Water advised customers to cut back on demand, and followed that up in what was a very hot July by imposing a hosepipe ban.

Unfortunately, this happened a week after YW had said that water stocks were plentiful.

On August 15, YW set up 240 stand-pipes in the Wrose area of Bradford. This was to prove so ineffective that YW talked seriously of introducing rationing. Some

The public were incredulous of the PR machine

among the public were incredulous. Relations with customers were not improved when Yorkshire Water's £127,000-a-year managing director Trevor Newton explained how he had economised with water - by not bathing for four months. Half a bowl of water was good enough for a thorough wash, he said.

Later he had to admit that he really economised by taking baths and showers at the home of his wife's parents - outside the Yorkshire area.

Perhaps it was this bizarre episode, as well as revelations about water-losses through leaks, which induced YW to employ a spokeswoman at a reported salary of £80,000.

The threat of rationing brought on a wave of panic-buying of bottled mineral water which went on into September, despite torrential rain on the seventh. Yorkshire Water still talked about applying for a drought order as weathermen compared annual rainfalls and told a disbelieving public that more rain was needed.

Two months later Yorkshire Water declared record half-yearly profits of nearly £100m.

In March,1996, in the week before an inquiry was due to begin into the crisis-hit company, both Trevor Newton and Yorkshire Water's chairman Gordon Jones (salary £189,000 a year) announced their departure.

T&A

1995

Bradford rocked by rioting of hundreds of youths

STAND-OFF: *A police dog handler in riot gear stands in front of smouldering debris in Oak Lane, Manningham, Bradford as a group of youths congregate during the 1995 riots that scarred the city's image*

Eruption of discontent

A Saturday morning in the early summer of 1995 is a day that many Bradford people will remember for a long time.

It is the morning they turned on their radios and televisions and learned that during the previous balmy night their city had been torn by rioting and lit up by arson.

The T&A that day reported an appeal for calm by the then MP for Bradford West, Max Madden.

Saturday, June 10, 1995

But it was to no avail.

So were the day-long efforts by police and community workers to calm the situation. That night even more ferocious rioting broke out in Manningham and the trail of destruction reached down towards the city centre.

The Sunday night seemed set, at one stage, for a third bout of riots. However, although 300 people gathered outside the Lawcroft House police station, peace was maintained and the crowd dispersed.

The following day was a very blue Monday for Bradford.

"We must heal these wounds" declared the T&A's headline as the people of Bradford set about repairing the physi-

Continued on Page 166

WRECKAGE: *Burned out cars litter the forecourt of the Citroen garage at Whetley Hill after rampaging youths laid waste businesses all the way into the city centre. Far left, how the T&A reported the weekend of violence and rioting in several pages of special coverage*

Continued from Page 165

cal damage to the city. But the worst harm was to the morale and reputation of the place, and to the fragile harmony between its different communities.

The inquest began immediately as conflicting theories were put forward as to why it happened. It was to be 17 months later that the full facts emerged - months in which the Bradford Commission set up by Bradford Congress had gathered and sifted evidence from about 200 people to not only clarify what happened on that alarming weekend, but try to find out why.

The Commission noted that tension had been building throughout the previous summer in the Manningham

area, where community activists had taken to the streets to rid the area of its prostitution problems. The police initially were highly sceptical of this "vigilante" action, fearing it would spark violence towards the vice girls.

And indeed, although the organisers of the campaign banned any verbal and physical hostility, there were several instances of prostitutes being attacked and on one occasion a pimp threatened a group of activists with a handgun.

Tension mounted when the television series Band of Gold focused nationwide attention on prostitution in Manningham, bringing in coach loads of sightseers on their way to Haworth and Emmerdale country.

Continued on Page 167

RUINED: *More evidence of the devastation wrought on Bradford during the summer nights when racial tensions exploded into violent action*

Continued from Page 166

The action worked, though. Gradually the prostitutes left Manningham and moved down to Thornton Road and the police were grudgingly forced to accept that the community's efforts were proving effective.

Then two weeks before the riots a café frequented by prostitutes in Lumb Lane was firebombed. It was a portent of what was to come on the night of June 9 - a warm summer's evening on which a group of youths were playing football in Garfield Avenue, Manningham. They were making a noise, so a local resident rang the police to complain.

The two officers sent to the scene asked the youths to move on.

When they refused, two of the youths were arrested and put in the back of a

Youths went on the rampage, destroying everything...

police car.

The T&A, summarising the Commission's account of events, reported: "One youth was chased into a nearby house. The family later claimed that

in the house an officer hit a baby being held in his mother's arms. This claim was always denied by the police and was never fully substantiated.

Problems started to get out of hand and the officers drew their batons and arrested two more youths. A crowd of around 60 people then gathered outside nearby Lawcroft House police station, in Lilycroft Road, demanding the four prisoners' release."

Scuffles broke out, there were more arrests, and soon 300 people were gathered in Oak Lane where wooden pallets were dragged into the road and set alight. Cars on the forecourt of the BMW garage were torched. It was 4am before order was restored.

As dusk fell the following day, even

Continued on Page 168

Continued from Page 167

more ferocious violence erupted. It started when a group of youths demolished a wall outside the police station and began hurling bricks.

The T&A reported: "By 8pm Oak Lane was sealed off but a pack of youths went on the rampage, destroying everything in their paths. Drinkers in pubs along White Abbey Road cowered in fear as everyone was attacked and motorists were singled out and beaten. The Citroen garage in White Abbey Road was gutted and hundreds of windows were smashed at businesses. By midnight a pall of smoke hung over the city from the several fires and the garage in scenes reminiscent of the blitz.

"The next day the city awoke to find its reputation as a multi-racial community in the same tatters as the Manningham area. On every street there were smashed windows, gutted cars and rubble strewn across the

T&A

T&A comment as the Commission reported

'

In a front-page Comment on November 21, 1996, the day the Bradford Commission report was published, the T&A said:

"A lack of vision. A lack of direction. A lack of strategy. A lack of focus. The conclusions of the Bradford Commission's report into last year's Manningham riots could hardly be more stark in its indictment of the city's inability to cope with the huge challenges imposed by the changes in its cultural and ethnic mix over more than 30 years.

Worst of all, perhaps, is the apparent mutual lack of understanding between the police and ethnic minority communities. The report says the police showed their 'ignorance of the local population and its concerns...and the local population showed their ignorance of necessary and proper police procedures.'

There have already been many people on both sides who have attacked such criticisms and many who complain that the report fails to offer a tick-list of actions to put the city back on the tracks. But as the report itself points out, 'there are no quick-fix solutions'.

The problems facing Bradford are too diverse, the tensions and misunderstandings too deeply entrenched to be solved by the introduction of a few headline-grabbing schemes.

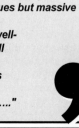

At best such actions could only paper thinly over the cracks; at worst they could provide political stepping stones for those more interested in furthering their careers than tackling the real issues afflicting Bradford.

The Commission's report is, in fact, far more subtle and - potentially - far more valuable than it could ever have been had its authors chosen to meet those easy-answer expectations. It brilliantly throws the ball back into Bradford's court.

Work out the answers for yourselves, it says. With the unwritten rider that, by doing so, the citizens of Bradford will

Telegraph & Argus

From the T&A of November 21, 1996

achieve more lasting and more effective schemes. Start communicating, start sharing, start working together, it says.

But it doesn't simply leave the city and its people to solve their own problems: the report leaves behind not just huge clues but massive signposts to the way ahead.

Bradford, it says, has a lot of well-intentioned people pulling in all sorts of different directions or operating in a vacuum. What is needed, it says, is a concerted effort to pull them all together....."

'

1996 *Prince of Wales gave business initiatives a royal boost*

WARM WELCOME: *Prince Charles shares a laugh with crowds lining the streets around the Carlisle Business Centre in Manningham when he arrived to perform the opening ceremony*

Charles was our darling

L illian Moorhouse got the surprise of her life when she nipped out in the rain to do a bit of shopping in Saltaire's Victoria Road.

Walking up from the station, holding an umbrella and surrounded by officials and guests, was the future King of England, smiling away and chatting amiably.

Thursday, October 24, 1996

"I only came out for some bread," Lillian told a T&A reporter. An equally surprised Renee Norton, who

Continued on Page 170

Continued from Page 169

just happened to be passing by, reacted quickly by giving Prince Charles a kiss on the cheek.

Folk simply don't expect to see the Prince of Wales on a wet Thursday morning in October in Saltaire. He hadn't been to Bradford since 1989. What was the purpose of this visit?

He had come to Salts Mill and the Carlisle Business Centre in Manningham; but these visits were not merely ceremonial or goodwill trips - his chance to shake hands and boost his popularity.

He came to talk about matters close to his heart - economic regeneration, the preservation of old buildings, and employment initiatives connected with Business in the Community, of which he is president, and his three trusts.

The Prince's Action Trust, the Prince's Youth Business Trust, and the Prince's Trust Volunteers, schemes which to date have been going for 23

years, 13 years and nine years respectively. The first alone has provided grants for more than 500,000 people.

He spent the morning at Salts Mill, touring the mill's art galleries and businesses accompanied by Jonathan Silver. Then he chaired a meeting of about 20 people in the old Salts boardroom. These people comprised the steering committee of yet another of the Prince's public interests, his Regeneration Through Heritage initiative.

The Prince's argument is that it is far better to regenerate old buildings like Salts Mill and put them back to work in the community than it is to take up more green-field sites for invariably less attractive new buildings.

After that he held a private meeting in Titus Salt's former coach-house, on which the late Jonathan Silver spent many thousands of pounds restoring and converting into a house for

Continued on Page 171

GREETINGS: *Crowds reach out to greet the Prince in Carlisle Road, above, and in Saltaire, right during his visit to the city*

ALL SMILES: *The Prince enjoys animated chat at lunch, above, and views the David Hockney exhibition at Salts Mill with the late Jonathan Silver, left*

Continued from Page 170

his family. Mr Silver presented the Prince with a small David Hockney painting as a memento of his visit.

The public got more of a chance to see the Prince during his afternoon visit to the Carlisle Business Centre where he was to address 100 people representing Bradford businesses about the work of the Prince's Action Trust.

Upon arrival, a smiling Prince was happy to greet people waiting to catch a sight of him before touring the building. He was delighted by the fact that the centre, like Salts Mill, was the living proof of the validity of his case for restoration rather than demolition. In another age Carlisle Business Centre was Carlisle Mills.

Public money and European grants totalling £4m transformed what was a derelict building into a splendidly designed and equipped complex consisting of a conference centre, meeting rooms, offices, workshops, and a training area stocked with computers and visual display units.

Gurdev Dahele, the centre's chief executive, told the T&A that the young people of Manningham had told him they wanted computers - not snooker tables; they were conscious of where the future lay and did not wish to be left behind.

The Prince's visit came only months after the Manningham riots. The Prince's Action Trust stepped in with funds to take a racial mix of 15 youths on residential trips to North Yorkshire, Scotland and France, with groups of young people from other areas. The courses involved active participation in role-playing and how to write a curriculum vitae for prospective employers.

Everybody felt that the Prince's visit was a demonstration of confidence in the people of troubled Manningham, and appreciated his good humour and concern for their future.

T&A

1997   *Queen's visit was the highlight of a year of Centenary joy*

Crowning glory for city's centenary

This was the year when Bradford officially marked its centenary as a city, and the Queen and the Duke of Edinburgh added their royal presence to the proceedings.

In fact the Queen and Duke's arrival on March 27 was the highlight of the whole 12 months.

Bradford's big year was also marked by a seven-part series of historical supplements produced by the T&A which reflected the city's growth and development since 1897.

Thursday, March 27, 1997

But before recalling that royal Thursday, some other events of 1997 need to be remembered.

Bradford Bulls rampaged away with the Super League Championship, but missed out on the double by succumbing to counter-attacking St Helens in the Silk Cut Challenge Cup Final at Wembley.

On the last day of August, Diana,

Princess of Wales, died from injuries received in a car crash in Paris, along with Dodi Fayed. For a week the nation was convulsed. Royal palaces were surrounded with candles and flowers. Press and public criticism obliged the Queen to make a special broadcast on

the eve of Diana's funeral service at Westminster Abbey.

The service took place on Saturday, September 6, and was watched by about 2 billion people across the world. That night another memorial event of a sort took place at St George's Hall. It was a charity concert in honour of Roger Suddards CBE - lawyer, theatre-lover, author, and English Heritage Commissioner - who did so much for his beloved Bradford at the time of the fire disaster. He had died suddenly at the age of 65 at the end of 1995.

It was also the year Tony Blair's New Labour, swept along by a national swing

Continued on Page 173

The Queen's visit was the highlight of the celebrations by a very long way

MAUNDY: *The Queen hands out the small bags of coins, above, which were guarded by Beefeaters, left*

Continued from Page 172

of more than 13 per cent, routed the Conservatives at the General Election on May 1. Labour took 419 seats and the Liberal-Democrats had their best result for decades with 46 seats.

All five seats in the Bradford District were either retained or captured by Labour. Ann Cryer, wife of former Bradford South MP Bob Cryer who died in a car crash in 1994, ousted Gary Waller from Keighley. And Chris Leslie, just 24, caused the biggest upset of all by turning Sir Marcus Fox's 12,000 majority at Shipley into a 2,996 majority for Labour. Sir Marcus had

held the seat for 27 of his 69 years.

Prime Minister John Major accepted defeat before all the results were in. He had paid a flying visit to Bradford the day before the Queen's arrival, touring the National Photographic Museum before going on to Halifax and Huddersfield. If Mr Major momentarily assumed all the bunting had been put out for him he was sadly mistaken.

Indeed, the Prime Minister's visit caused barely a ripple in the city because the police, the civic authorities, Bradford Cathedral ministers and administrators, and an awful lot of other people were preparing for the Queen.

Continued on Page 174

SERVICE: *The Queen and the Duke of Edinburgh chat with the Bishop of Bradford, the Right Rev David Smith, and the Provost, the Very Rev John Richardson, after the service*

Continued from Page 173

WALKA-BOUT:
Crowds gather in Centenary Square as the royal motorcade arrives, left, and the Queen chats with onlookers, above, before laying a wreath at the fire disaster memorial, below

Her Majesty's visit was a triple-whammy. She had long ago agreed to the annual distribution of Maundy Money at the Cathedral. Advance warning enabled both Bradford Council and Bradford City Football Club to ask the Queen to make a day of it.

The royal train arrived at Forster Square station at 10.40am. A thousand people in the Cathedral awaited the arrival of the Queen and the Duke. They were preceded by the Yeoman of the Guard, the monarch's ceremonial bodyguards. After the service the Queen handed over the small red and white bags of money - worth just over £6 - to people selected for their service to the community and the Church of England.

From the Cathedral the royal party, accompanied by civic dignitaries were driven to the junction of Market Street and Bridge Street, where they got out of their cars and walked the short distance to Centenary Square. Along the way the Queen and the Duke stopped to greet flag-waving well-wishers.

Bradford Youth Orchestra and a choir of schoolchildren sang A Whole New World, from the show Aladdin.

The Queen, dressed in a tangerine coat and hat, with black accessories, unveiled a stone outside City Hall, and then walked across to the Bradford City fire disaster memorial where she carefully placed a wreath, watched by relatives of the 56 disaster victims and Mrs Liz Suddards, wife of Roger

Continued on Page 175

TOUR: *After leaving the square, below, Her Majesty travelled to Valley Parade to open a new stand, guided by City chairman Geoffrey Richmond. Inset, T&A sports reporter David Markham introduced her to celebrities including Sir Bobby Charlton and Stuart McCall, below right*

Continued from Page 174

Suddards who master-minded the creation of the disaster appeal trust which raised £4.25m.

Then it was time for lunch. The Queen and the Duke were escorted into City Hall for a reception by the Lord Mayor Councillor Gordon Mitchell and the Lady Mayoress Mrs Peggy Mitchell.

The Queen completed her hat-trick of engagements at Valley Parade where she was introduced to guests including Sir Bobby Charlton, ex-Bradford City hero Bobby Campbell, and Stuart McCall - then still at Glasgow Rangers. Then, accompanied by club chairman Geoffrey Richmond, Her Majesty officially opened the £1.5m Ciba stand along Midland Road.

That wasn't the end of the occasion, however. Gerry Marsden sang You'll Never Walk Alone, and youngsters from Bradford's performing arts group Stage 84 staged a pageant celebrating Bradford's centenary. There was a multi-cultural dance too which featured a specially-written anthem, Spirit of Hope.

It was a day of colour and pageantry which the city's centen-ary fully deserved. The Queen's visit was the highlight of the ceremonials that year by a very long way.

T&A

1998

The people of Bradford rose to challenge of MRI appeal

T&A launches its biggest-ever appeal, for...

£1 MILLION!

by MIKE WAITES
T&A Reporter

Help us buy a healthier future - AND save lives

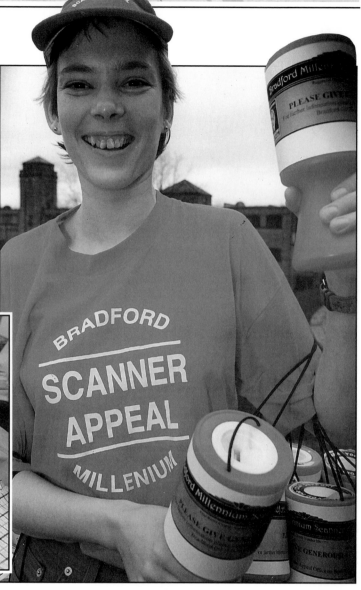

£1m TARGET: *A host of crazy fund-raising stunts by the people of Bradford ranged from the humble collecting tins, right, to head shaves, below, parachute jumps, abseiling, gift sales, gala events, donations...you name it, the people of Bradford did it to buy their 'own' MRI scanner, far right*

£1 million?

One of the things Bradford people have excelled at over the years is rising to a fund-raising challenge. Give them a worthy cause and they go for it with boundless energy, enthusiasm and ingenuity. This was the year when they proved yet again that when it comes to digging deep in their own pockets and persuading other people to do the same, they are unbeatable.

The challenge had begun the previous summer when the T&A, in partnership with Bradford Hospitals NHS Trust and other bodies in the city (including Sovereign Health Care), launched an appeal to raise £1 million to buy a Magnetic Resonance Imaging (MRI) scanner and equip a special suite for it at the BRI.

Acquisition of this important diagnostic tool was seen as a huge step forward in pinpointing a host of illnesses and conditions without the need for Bradford

people to travel to Leeds or Halifax to be scanned. With this state-of-the-art scanner in the heart of the district, problems could be identified much more speedily and relevant treatment begun.

Dr Roger Lowe, head of radiology at the BRI and the leading consultant behind the appeal, said the scanner would be of huge value in all branches of medicine, especially in assessing brain and nervous disorders, cancer, diseases of the heart and blood vessels as well as joint and bone problems.

He described it as "a quantum leap in technology, like moving from silent movies to talkies".

The people of Bradford didn't need

much persuading of the potential merits of the scanner. They threw themselves wholeheartedly into fund-raising. The ball started rolling during the rest of 1997, but it was in 1998 that the pace really accelerated, spurred on by the news that by the first month of that year the total had already reached £275,000.

In January alone, City of Bradford Band members blew their bagpipes for the scanner, a dozen regulars of a Great Horton pub had their heads shaved, Micklethwaite villagers held a home-baked and gifts sale, members of Buttershaw St Paul's AODS sang their hearts out in Showboat, T&A cricketers trounced a team from Sunwin House, a

Continued on Page 177

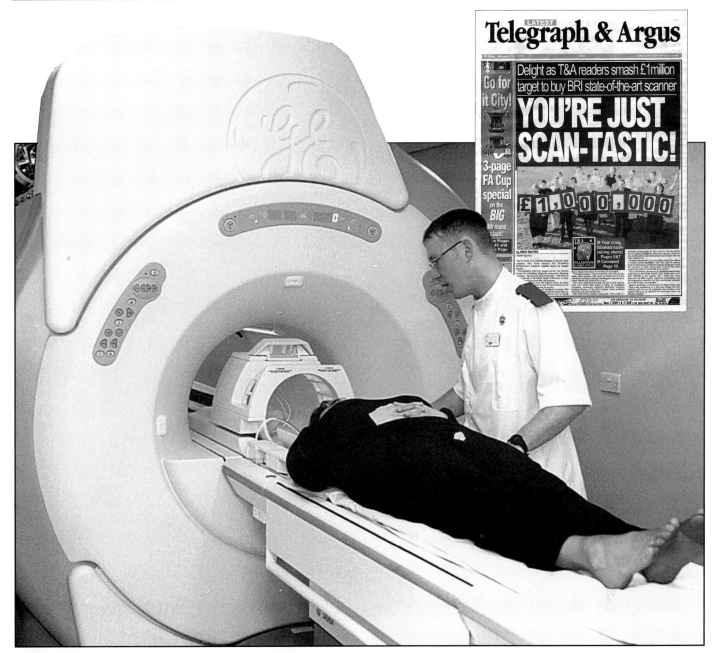

No problem at all!

Continued from Page 176

Bradford office furniture firm donated £5 for every desk and work station sold, and much, much more happened.

And so it went on, for month after month, as Bradford people - individuals, families, groups, businesses - organised events of every kind to add their ten, hundreds and sometimes thousands of pounds to the fast-growing fund.

More heads were shaved, beds were pushed, long and short sponsored walks were undertaken. People leaped from planes and floated to earth below parachutes. They abseiled down tall buildings. They trundled each other along in wheelbarrows. Postmen did a Full Monty.

By the beginning of April the fund had reached £415,000 and the push was on to get it up to the halfway mark by the end of April. In fact the £500,000 was late in coming - but only by a week, and only 40 weeks into the appeal.

That total had been boosted by pound-for-pound match-funding from Sovereign Health Care for the first £250,000. It had been given a good shove upwards in 1998, too, by £10,000 raised by a ball organised by Omar Khan of the Shah Jehan restaurant.

Other big events pushed the total ever higher: £25,000 in May from a glittering ball at the Cedar Court Hotel; £28,000 in October from a fashion show by London-

based designer Roland Klein. In December Bradford supermarket chain Morrisons added £25,000. By the end of the year the total was barely a whisker away.

And on January 22, 1999, the T&A was able to announce to the wonderful people of the district: "YOU'RE JUST SCAN-TAS-TIC!" The £1 million target had been reached in just 18 months.

The scanner was bought and began work the following June, rapidly proving its worth by slicing its way through the waiting list for diagnostic scans. It was the People's Project, and thousands of Bradfordians had every right to be proud of their role in making it possi-ble.

T&A

1999 *Bradford went wild as City gained promotion to Premiership*

CELEBRATION: *Stuart McCall acclaims the victory, left, and Peter Beagrie does a headstand as the team gathers after the Wolves game to begin a long week of celebrations as City climb into the Premier division for the first time in seven decades*

At about 3.16pm on Sunday, May 9, 1999, Bradford City Football Club beat Wolverhampton Wanderers 3-2 away from home, and made history.

People living within a couple of miles of Valley Parade didn't need to have the radio or TV on to hear the news; 15 minutes after the final whistle had sounded in Wolverhampton, the car-horns started in Bradford.

Along Manningham Lane and Keighley Road they came, blaring

Sunday, May 9, 1999

cars with claret and amber flags and ecstatic young men and women hanging out of the windows going bonkers. Passers-by cheerfully waved back. The few who looked bemused by the outburst of high spirits that sunny spring afternoon soon learned from others... BCFC had just gone into the Premier League.

By 4.15pm several hundred people were already outside the stadium, waiting for the team to arrive home. More were arriving by the minute. Honking cars and pick-up trucks did occasional circuits of the area. Some Asian lads

parked their cars and turned up the thumping disco sounds to add to the party atmosphere. Anxious families came out of their houses wondering what all the noise meant, but were soon chatting and smiling at the boisterous antics in the street.

Premier way to end the Millennium!

The young danced, sprayed beer over one another, and booted a small plastic football high up into the air. Dads and mums, sons and daughters, hundreds wearing claret and amber striped shirts, laughed and sang, and one or two cried.

Continued on Page 180

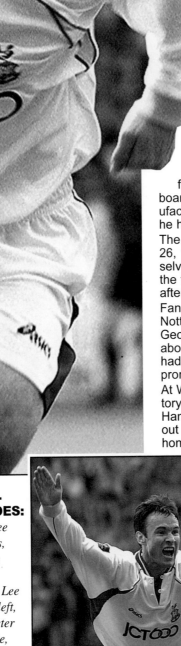

Continued from Page 179

At about 6.30pm the first Wallace Arnold coaches started arriving back from Wolverhampton. Supporters who had been to watch the most important league game City had played in 70 years stumbled out of the buses to a hero's welcome. "I can't believe it, I can't believe it," was said over and over again, as groups of friends re-lived what had happened.

Wolves had taken an early lead, as had Ipswich - City's East Anglian rival for the second automatic promotion spot in Division One. Then City's Beagrie, Mills and Blake scored three cracking goals to take their combined league total to 52. Beagrie missed a penalty, and Wolves thwacked the post with a free-kick.

Then the final whistle blew, Wolves fans sportingly applauded, and the car-horns started. Next season Bradford City FC would be playing Manchester United, Arsenal and Liverpool. Instead of Gresty Road, Vale Park and Bramall Lane, City's supporters could look forward to visiting Old Trafford, Highbury and Anfield.

This was their finest hour, and the club had enjoyed several good ones since Geoffrey Richmond became chairman in January, 1994. He had built the Midland Road stand and Campbell's, the supporters club bar next door to Valley Parade: he had made the club financially sound and brought new blood on to the board in the shape of multi-millionaire electronics manufacturer Prof David Rhodes and his son Julian: and he had twice helped the club gain promotion.

The first time was also on a Sunday afternoon - May 26, 1996. Against the odds City had hauled themselves into the Division Two play-offs and had reached the final by defeating Blackpool 3-0 away from home, after losing the first game 2-0.

Fans queuing for tickets for the deciding match against Notts County at Wembley made a point of thanking Geoffrey Richmond for giving them so much to cheer about. They could hardly believe that at long last City had a chairman who delivered exactly what he promised.

At Wembley, City were helped to a comfortable 2-0 victory by a wonderful solo effort from youngster Des Hamilton. Thirty-thousand City fans sang their hearts out on that overcast afternoon. The 200-mile journey home along the M1 was a fluttering trail of triumphant claret and amber scarves.

If many City fans were in a state of disbelief after the Wolves game it was for this reason. The older ones especially had become accustomed to failure, disappointment, as well as tragedy. In the past the club's good times had been obliterated by the bad ones - the fire disaster in 1985, the failure to win promotion in 1987-88, the subsequent transfer

GOAL HEROES: *All three strikers, Robbie Blake, above, Lee Mills, left, and Peter Beagrie, right, grabbed a goal apiece to send City fans into seventh heaven*

Continued on Page 181

Fans could hardly believe that City had a chairman who delivered exactly what he promised

Continued from Page 180

of John Hendrie and Stuart McCall, relegation to Division Three (which became Division Two after the Premier League started in 1992).

Now in less than five years two major successes had taken them out of the jog-along clubs and put them among the elite. No wonder some of them could not believe it.

City's amazing success may be ascribed to a formula: RMMBBJ. The component parts of this elixir are Richmond, McCall, Mills, Blake, Beagrie, and Jewell.

Stuart McCall's free transfer from Glasgow Rangers ten years after he had left Valley Parade was the catalyst which helped City's young manager Paul Jewell effect a transformation in the team both on and off the pitch.

McCall, who hates to be on the losing side even in a practice match, had been a professional since 1982 and had played in all the world's top competitions. He played in 43 of the 46 league matches; his inspirational qualities and consistency earned him the Player of the Year title from the supporters.

He started the Premiership season 35 years old but with 719 English and Scottish league, cup,

Continued on Page 182

NERVES:
Fans back home in Bradford watching the game on TV can hardly bear the agony as the game is balanced on a knife edge. Left, for manager Paul Jewell the agony is over as the final whistle blows and he can hug his team of heroes

TOP MAN:
City chairman Geoffrey Richmond, above, takes the salute of the crowds gathered in Centenary Square to welcome the conquering heroes after their open top bus ride through the district, right

Continued from Page 181

European and International matches and 77 goals to his credit.

Lee Mills, Robbie Blake and Peter Beagrie scored two-thirds of the 82 league goals which earned City 87 promotion points; Beagrie probably had his best-ever season as a goal-scorer, knocking in 12. Robbie Blake, who was almost sold on after a drink-drive offence, looked fitter and hungrier for success. His solo skills and ability to make and score sensational goals (he got 16 in the league) was a key factor, as was his partnership with Lee Mills. The latter looked every inch a 20-goals-a-season striker. Strong in the air, fast and difficult on the ground, Mills gave the forward line the power it had lacked since Bobby Campbell's departure. He finished the campaign with 24.

All fans wanted to do was fill their hearts with pride

Other players such as Jacobs, Moore, Lawrence and goal-keeper Gary Walsh had played their part but when the team arrived back from Wolverhampton at about 8pm the crowd, which had grown to several thousand, was in no doubt about their hero of heroes. Every time Stuart McCall showed his face the cheering increased in intensity.

With his flame-hair and never-say-die spirit,

Continued on Page 183

Continued from Page 182

Stuart symbolised all that they hoped for, all that they valued.

The crowd knew little or nothing about the four-figure win bonuses, nor the six-figure lump sum which Geoffrey Richmond shared among the first team squad as a reward; all they wanted to do was cheer and fill their hearts with pride.

This they did the following evening when the team made a triumphant tour of the Metropolitan District, from Keighley to City Hall where they were greeted by thousands.

On the Thursday night a celebration fixture was arranged against a John Hendrie XI at Valley Parade. The party atmosphere of Sunday prevailed. But the night's outstanding moment was when Geoffrey Richmond was given a standing ovation as he walked to the centre of the pitch. Even after he reached it the applause continued. The night ended with Rock music, communal singing, tears in the eyes, fireworks, and a lap of honour by tired but happy players.

No one got hurt, no one was abused. For five days the diverse communities of Bradford were united by City's fantastic success.

Manchester United made history by being the first English club to win the FA Cup, the Premiership, and the European Champions Cup. Kevin Keegan took over from Glenn Hoddle as manager of England's national side.

But the last year of the 20th Century belonged to the players, staff and supporters of a club which had had more than its share of tragedy. The triumph was hard-earned and well-earned; and the joy of it shined all over the world. From Australia to Canada scores of jubilant faxes and congratulatory e-mails poured into the T&A.

The Bantams' fantastic success was the epitome of a venture launched by the Telegraph & Argus to find the very best that Bradford could produce in a host of areas.

In February the T&A had announced its

How we reported the news

It was a welcome fit for heroes - and the City players were HEROES.

Thousands of jubilant supporters who had cried and cheered through 90 minutes of agony turned up at Valley Parade with one mission - to give the men who had given their all a homecoming to end all home-comings.

Those who couldn't get to the Wolves match headed for the ground after they heard the final whistle on the television or radio.

Valley Parade was the place to be - to celebrate with fellow fans.

They came on foot, in cars, by taxi and they waited - a sea of claret and amber singing, chanting and revelling in the glory of a historic afternoon.

As the minutes turned to hours - they didn't care how long it took - they shared a common purpose. And when, finally, just after 8pm, the players' coach arrived via a back way because of the massive throng, there was a surge of anticipation.

The waiting was over.

A police officer stood on top of a portable building to tell the crowds where the players would appear.

At first there were faces at a window, then they appeared - all of them heroes.

Telegraph & Argus

From the T&A of Monday, May 10, 1999

grand ambition: to seek out, with the backing of some of Bradford's most dynamic businesses and organisations, the district's outstanding community heroes.

These were to be the individuals who, week in and week out, do all they can to help others, and the organisations which have made a real difference to the quality of life at the grassroots.

As this book went to press, plans were well advanced for a glittering pre-Christmas Millennium gala awards night to honour the people and groups chosen to be named as Bradford's Best. This was also to be an occasion on which to celebrate some of the things this large and varied district has to be proud of - a chance to raise a toast to its achievements and its achievers as the century draws to a close.

In fact, Bradford approached the Millennium with lots of reasons to be well satisfied. Shrinking traditional industries

were being successfully replaced by dynamic hi-tech companies. Improvements to the city centre, including Centenary Square, meant that it was looking more attractive than it had done in years. The Bantams had blasted their way into the Premiership. The Bulls were riding high.

And through their efforts for the MRI scanner the people of Bradford had demonstrated to the world, and to themselves, that when it comes to raising funds they are in a Premier League of their own - the very best.

Dedications

Mr I G Mullinder
Mrs A Hudson
Peter & Winifred Dolby
Mr Philip Rushworth
Clare & Benjamin Watson
Mr Arthur Whitehead
Mrs Vera Knapton
Brian & Florence Appleyard
Graham D Epton
James Derek Willis
Alice A Chapman
Walter Johnson
John Brian Webster
Jim & Pat Watson
Mr T Wright
John & Joyce Burns
Mr Kenneth Halmshaw (Teacher)
    20.12.49 - 03.03.98
Matthew J Hornby
Charlotte Hunter
Derrick Baron
David Bould
Mr S J Cole
Desmond A Walsh
Janice Maloney
George & Mary Bastow
Peter Timothy Aykroyd
Michael John Gill
Mr F Maden
David Brian Baines
Anthony Joseph Crosdale
Charles Mudd
Doris Taylor
Simon N Callaghan
Mr & Mrs Gordon Ramsey & Joan
Ackroyd
Malcolm Robertshaw
Mr F T K Jagger
Mr Frank Garrod
Brian Rafferty
David Fenton
Thomas N Walls
Malcolm Yearsley
Eric Wilson
Mrs Ethel Craighan
Joan Clark
Mrs C Butler
Shirley Harrison
Mr Neil Johnson
Ray Moore
Marc Lawrence
Philip Hall
Alan Anthony Jenkins, 04/08/39
David Shackleton

Shirley Gaunt
Hetty Phillips
Joyce Havers
Mrs C M White
Mrs Betty Wood
Mrs Margaret Bradford
Audrey May Thorne
Mrs Kathleen Paine
Mr Brian Paine
Mr Brian Smith
Mr Frank Pickard Lupton
John, Linda, Anthony & Matthew
Cook
Steve Abbott
Mr J C Hartley
Mr J G Prentice
Shirley Potter
J P Brady
Robin A Pepper
Mr David Pearson
Mr J A Rae
Mrs Sheila Graham
Miss Moira Priestley
Margaret Elizabeth Shimbles
N D Hudson
Mrs T M Fitton
Mr D Thompson
Mr Denis C Hill
Mr A Marshall
Emma Bendrien 18 years of Age on
01.01.00
Mrs E Gardner
Dr A D Pratt
Geoff Kelly
Philip Bartle
Douglas Bartle
Mrs Sheila A Carr
Thomas Andrew Milnes
Alexander Stephen Milnes
Rebecca Alice Nash
Dennis Wood
Jack Womersley
Mr Philip Standeven
Trevor Hodgson
Audrey Worley
Arthur Worley
Thomas Walker
Audrey Baren
Craig Money
Joan Forrest
Sandra Mary Clayton
Constance Nash
Wilfrid Starkey
Mr P Laycock

Nicola Goode
Jack Fortune
Brian Hudson
Mr Albert & Mrs Eileen Murgatroyd
Donald Smith
Andrea Drage
Peter J Dickinson
Gordon Ernest Craven
Bessie Daphne Moorhouse
Edward Jagger
Mrs Mary Towler
Mrs Nina Brighouse Thomson
Malcolm Couzens
Willie Robinson
George Allsopp
George Rishworth
David Constantine
Anthony L West
Peter & Valerie Hall
Joan & Ernie Armitage
Harry Baker
David Pickard
Joshua Leslie Jameson Harding
The Gilmour family of Oakworth
Margaret & Ken Taylor
Harry H Shaw
Mr E Turnbull
Mrs C Shepherd
J Lewis Nicholl, I. Eng., M.I.I.E.
(Mech.)
Eric Dean
K Elaine Hepworth
Brian Pickford
Harold Harrison
Mr Richard & Mrs Karen Ackroyd
and family
Kenneth & Gillian Robinson
Mr S M & Mrs J Cashman
Phyllis Mary Jarrett
Mrs A H McDermott
Mr R A Rhodes
Mr L Watson
Joseph Mortimer
Betty Clague
Moira Ramsden
Mr Harry Senior
Mr Douglas H Tordoff
Jonathan C Raby
Mr A G Maclauchlin
David Burnet
Gary Firth
Bob Watson